PAUL AND THE RELIGIOUS EXPERIENCE OF RECONCILIATION

PAUL AND THE RELIGIOUS EXPERIENCE OF RECONCILIATION

Diasporic Community and Creole Consciousness

Gilbert I. Bond

WESTMINSTER
JOHN KNOX PRESS
LOUISVILLE · KENTUCKY

Scripture quotations from the Revised Standard Version of the Bible are copyright © 1946, 1952, 1971, and 1973 by the Division of Christian Education of the National Council of the Churches of Christ in the U.S.A. and are used by permission.

Book design by Sharon Adams
Cover design by Jennifer K. Cox

First edition
Published by Westminster John Knox Press
Louisville, Kentucky

This book is printed on acid-free paper that meets the American National Standards Institute Z39.48 standard. ♾

PRINTED IN THE UNITED STATES OF AMERICA

05 06 07 08 09 10 11 12 13 14 — 10 9 8 7 6 5 4 3 2 1

Library of Congress Cataloging-in-Publication Data is on file at the Library of Congress, Washington, D.C.

ISBN 0-664-22271-4

Contents

Preface

Paul is a creole. This work attempts to demonstrate how I reached this conclusion. Paul's mystical encounter with the Spirit of the risen Christ results in the birth of creolian consciousness. The most startling result of this radical transformation of Paul's consciousness is the reconfiguration of his identity from the exclusive otherness of the Pharisee to the inclusive otherness of the Apostle of Jesus Christ. Paul's divinely altered relationship with the social and holy other results in the creation of creolian sacred communities that we retrospectively identify as the *ekklesia* of Corinth, Galatia, Rome, Philippi, and Thessalonica. Creolian consciousness is, in the words of Gerard Manley Hopkins, chromatic, exhibiting broadscale latitude and range across the spectrum of differences, "which are sliding or unmarked by clear borders."[1]

Paul's passionate labor as an Apostle struggles heroically to give birth to creolian communities heterogeneously composed of Gentiles and Jews in the context of a holy *Mitwelt* which mediates and embodies Paul's transformed self and new experience of the sacred as manifest most abundantly in the experience of being "in Christ." Creolian consciousness is one of the enduring characteristics of diasporas wherein identities are mixed and the power to control cultural boundaries and police purity are highly threatened. Paul's experience of "in Christ" and the communities he created and nurtured enabled him to embrace the chromatic spectrum of his diasporic identity and to integrate the acceptable dimensions of his self—intentionally enacted through his membership in the community of Pharisees—with the unacceptable dimensions of his self, those aspects unintentionally immersed in Greek Gentile culture.[2]

One result of this boundary-breaking experience of transgressive identity is the release of creative spiritual energy. This legacy of Paul continues to inspire and inform communities of Christ two millennia later. There are, however, tragic consequences to this development. One is the substitution of the chromatic latitude of creolian consciousness which gives birth to identities of inclusive otherness within sacred communities, for the diatonic parochialism that often made Christianity function as a tribal religion which displaced its Jewish antecedents and incorporated anti-Semitism as an integral part of Christian identity and theology.[3]

Paul's legacy is also a source of theological creativity, most notably represented by Augustine and Luther. While the contributions of these two theological giants are of undeniable importance to the development and understanding of Western conceptions of the self, their diatonic diminishment of creolian Christology has left the dominant Western church traditions bereft of the empowering practice of reconciliation as enacted by Paul in the face of the social and cultural other. The stream of consciousness in Western Christianity, with the exception of powerful minority tributaries, is a history of the recreation of identities of exclusive otherness, a commonplace characteristic of the fallen condition of this world Christ so loved.[4]

The other side of this tragic legacy belongs to Paul. While he lived a life of exemplary faithfulness and dependency upon Christ, he never fully inculcated creolian consciousness into the center of Christian self-understanding which could embody and embrace chromatic Christology as passionately as the apostle. Paul is willing to compromise across several areas of relationships within the sacred cultus of the *ekklesia*, but he will not suffer the creation of yet another mono-ethnic tribal community of believers. With the eventual decline of Jewish membership in the church and the restructuring of post–second temple Judaism, creolian Christianity in the tradition of that which Paul attempted to live as the practice of reconciliation in bonded fellowship with unlike followers of Jesus Christ eventually became marginal to the consciousness, identity, and practice of being Christian. The passion and power of being "in Christ" as a new creation capable of recognizing the Holy otherness of God in one's social and ethnic other, and entering into communion and covenant with one's nontribal brother and sister in Christ, became displaced by various and competing soteriologies which still define and dominate Christianity today.

In the process of examining Paul's experience, this project also examines and questions some of the foundational structures of phenomenology, one of which is phenomenology's reliance upon subjectivity as the fundamental principle of consciousness that also determines one's mode of being. Within the course of applying phenomenological insights to the issues of Paul's experience I examine the relationship between the construction of subjectivity and the creation of the self.

The self, in this project, is understood as an internalized, interpersonal, emergent interpretive structure whose existence is both socially dependent upon and somatically situated within the mediating structures of the *Mitwelt* and the comprehensive order of the *Lebenswelt*. The methodology employs a phenomenological interpretation of authentic texts of Paul in order to disclose those dimensions of his experience that are defined and transformed by his participation in the sacred. As a project in hermeneutic phenomenology, the method proceeds from a phenomenological interpretation of texts to experience, and from experience to questions of being as defined by Paul's relationship to the structures of the sacred.

Chapter 1 proposes a reinterpretation of phenomenology in its classic formulation by Edmund Husserl and its adaptation by scholars of *Religionswissenschaft* as a phenomenology of religion, and outlines the working method of a phenomenology of religious experience as an approach to the reinterpretation of Paul.

Chapter 2 provides the theoretical outlines for a phenomenology of consciousness constructed upon the mediation of the self, rather than the immediacy of subjectivity. This altered phenomenology will provide the structure for a phenomenology of religious interpretation of Paul's transformative mystical experiences. The materials for this reconstruction are drawn from William James's investigations into the self (which is composed of many selves), object-relations theory, and the multiple theories of shame. A correlation is established between the emergence of the self and the emergence of the symbol as in interrelational creation of community into which the self is thrown, and upon which the self is etiologically dependent. The interrelationship of self, community, and the formative and deformative effects of the affect shame become the basis of my thesis that Paul's struggle to create interethnic communities of reconciliation is inseparable from his transformative experience of the sacred and the resulting transformations of self, both heterogeneous phenomena.

Chapter 3 builds upon the work of James and attempts to create a phenomenology based upon the mediation of experience through the self and its modes of consciousness. The role of shame as a phenomenon associated with the self is examined from the perspectives of affect theory, object-relations theory, and the anthropology of shame/honor culture. The first two sections of this chapter attempt to disentangle Paul from the two principal personalities responsible for shaping the Western portrait of him: Augustine and Luther. The approach of Augustine focused upon his struggle with two opposing wills; with Luther, the problematic is the seemingly interminable afflictions of conscience. Each theological figure interprets his own spiritual struggle through the language of Paul's experience. The third and final sections shifts the fundamental interpretive question from issues of religious experience to conceptual problems in the analysis of diasporic culture and religion.

Chapters 4 and 5 examine Paul's mystical experience and the creation of communities of reconciliation as a diasporic phenomenon in general, and interethnic reconciliation as a process of creolization: the attempt to cultivate creolian consciousness capable of participating in a new heterogeneous realm of the sacred; communities composed of alien *ethnoi*; identities based on inclusive otherness that struggle to become a community and embrace their unlike members. These chapters apply the reconstructed phenomenology based upon the experiential consciousness of the self to the mystical experiences of Paul, and his efforts to create interethnic communities. Paul is presented as the embodiment of Diaspora cultural convergence, Greek and Hebraic, both prior to and after his mystical transformation. His resulting dislocation from the community of Pharisees and relocation into communities of Jews and Gentiles marks the emergence of creolian consciousness in Paul and the acceptance of the fundamentally heterogeneous composition of his authentic self, which is inseparable from the integration of vulnerability into his affective core. Reconciliation, as the creation of interethnic community, is actually a process of creolization, an attempt to cultivate and impart a heterogeneous sacrality among Jews and Gentiles, and to inver the cultural code of honor and shame by Paul's personal embrace of both sacred impurity and sacred vulnerability as embodiment of the creolian Messiah, Yeshuah.

Chapter 1

William James and Phenomenology of Religion

William James, one of the philosophical founders of the method that would come to be known in Europe as phenomenology, provides resources in his writing for a rethinking of the philosophy's foundations. James was a protean American thinker from a generation that produced Charles Peirce, W. E. B. DuBois, and other New England Olympians, whose philosophical interest embraced both systematic inquiry into ideas *and* experience. His writings helped establish the basis for the uniquely American philosophical tradition, pragmatism, which allowed others such as Josiah Royce, George Herbert Mead, and John Dewey to flower in its light. With both intellectual mettle and a spirit of New World wonder, James and his intellectual offspring resisted the Kantian closure of experience that exiled religion to the system of ethics and the realm of the irrational. James's thinking moved in the direction of both what could be termed phenomenological psychology and phenomenology of religion, and still stands at the intersection of unexplored creative possibilities.

Among his vast corpus, James produced at least two classic works, each representative of a proto-phenomenological method: *The Principles of Psychology* and *The Varieties of Religious Experience*.[1] *The Varieties of Religious Experience* continues to inform contemporary academic investigations and is the subject of analysis

1

and reinterpretation.[2] The definition James provides as the basis of his inquiry, although challenged and contested, remains a referential starting point: "Religion, therefore, as I now ask you arbitrarily to take it, shall mean for us the feeling, acts, and experiences of individual men in their solitude, so far as they apprehend themselves to stand in relation to whatever they may consider the divine."[3] Within this oft-quoted passage, James presents not only a working methodological definition of the subject, religion, but a definition of the religious subject. While James was careful to disentangle the phenomena of religious experience from systematic doctrinal formulations, liturgically prescribed actions, and the matter of theology,[4] the description of his religious subject is presented in pristine Protestant solitude.

The individual who encounters the Divine, alone, is a distinctly different character than the person James presents in *Principles*. He presents not a solitary individual but a self: "*In its widest possible sense, however, a man's Self is the sum total of* all that he CAN call his, not only his body and his psychic powers, but his clothes and his house, his wife and children, his ancestors and friends, his reputation and works, his lands and horses, and yacht and bank-account."[5] Unlike the religious subject, the self exists and is suspended in a relational matrix of other selves and material objects and derives its existence from its relatedness, which includes the psychic, the communal, and the cosmic.[6]

Although James opposed Kant's a priori categorical presuppositions and Descartes's rejection of experience and the world as sources of knowledge, this isolated individual who stands at the anthropological center of Calvinism ghostly resembles the isolated subject who sits at the philosophical center of Cartesianism. European phenomenology can in one sense be understood as a philosophical protest against a totalization of the epistemological subjectivity of hegemonic Cartesianism and a concomitant struggle to reform rather than abandon the basic structures of the cogito.

Descartes created an epistemology and ontology based exclusively upon the power of the subjects on positing and representation, which emerges after the negation of the world and his body.[7] The Cartesian cogito comes into existence as *creatio ex nihilo*. Descartes displaces God, becomes the creator of a new order, and substitutes the cogito for the divine Logos. Dahlia Judovitz describes the results: "Man as the subject of knowledge is the creator of a new order that imitates and challenges God's creative capacities. The subject of knowledge thus emerges in a dominant position, for the world can now be conceived only in relation to it and as its extension, its product. The creative will of the Cartesian subject thus rivals God's will, since his newly created order challenges the preordained order."[8]

The theocentric cosmology that had provided order, including the location of ideas (*eidoi*) within the creation, imploded and collapsed into the cogito. Augustine, in contrast, perceived that all of creation emanated from the divine Logos, and derived its being from the forms (*eidoi*) that ultimately resided in the mind of God.[9] In Descartes's system, not only do ideas reside in the mind, but being becomes synonymous with subjectivity, which is derived from objectification of the world, including the subject's body. "For Descartes himself the *cogito* is only a moment of thought; it concludes an operation and opens a new series; it is contemporaneous with a vision of the world in which the whole of objectivity is spread out like a spectacle on which the *cogito* casts its sovereign gaze."[10] The supremacy of the cogito expresses itself as the principal agent of order and meaning, but its exclusive privilege of determination is the issue of an act of violent disruption that amputates the organic relationship between knowledge and experience.

The convulsive consequences of Descartes's philosophy can be seen in the redefinition of the person from that of an inseparable member of an interpersonal and corporate matrix to that of an autonomous subject. Francis Barker notes that the body, under the gaze of the Cartesian subject, becomes silent: "The Cartesian body is *outside* language; it is given to discourse as an object (when it is not, in its absent moment, exiled altogether) but it is never *of* language in its essence."[11]

The body is no longer the mediation of meaning or the site of divine or human inscription. Rather it becomes the object of representation and knowledge due to the passing of the self into Cartesian subjectivity. Even though, according to Descartes, the body possesses "the capacity for speech," it no longer "speaks." "Man's definition as a corporeal schema becomes the pretext for the reaffirmation of reason, here described through man's capacity to use speech. However, by reducing man's body to a machine, which is merely the passive purveyor of speech, Descartes disenfranchises the body from its involvement with signification."[12]

The Cartesian perspective not only performed an act of rhetorical dismemberment that excised the body from the symbolic world; it also severed the self from its corporate communal matrix that defined and constituted human identity. "The rationalism which, when carried to its logical though extreme conclusion, sees men only as isolated individuals for whom other men exist only as objects, also carries out a similar change in man's way of looking at the external world. In the human level, *it destroys the idea of community* and replaces it by that of an infinitely large collection of reasonable individuals who are all equal and all interchangeable."[13] The objective autonomy of the subject makes relationships with other members of the social order discretionary and at the disposal of individual initiative rather than presenting the prior existence of relationality as the inextricable social webbing that binds and defines and makes the autonomous person possible. The individual becomes the atomistic monad out of which the society is composed.

Edmund Husserl's phenomenology attempts to heal the violation of dissociation through the examination of the relationship between consciousness and experience. Within this mode of analysis, objects do not exist. All objects are *intentional* objects, for they are experienced by a subject before whom they appear. The term *intentional* finds extensive appropriation in Husserl, although the function it describes came from the original analysis provided by James. Although Husserl uses "intentional" as a corrective for Descartes's dissociative cogito, the term also locates phenomenology in the Cartesian ethos. *Intentionality* refers to the mental capacity to create an interior picture of external objects. "I can have no knowledge of what is outside me except by means of the ideas I have within me."[14] Intention, in medieval Latin, meant "picture or idea."[15] Ancient sources use the term in relationship to taking aim at a target, while the medieval Arabic scholar Ibn Sina used the term to describe the form that exists in the mind without matter.[16]

Husserl's phenomenology was radical, but only reconstructive, surgery, for he attempted to reconnect the isolated Cartesian cogito to the objectified world. His examinations of experiential subjectivity proceeded from the intentionality of all consciousness.[17] Paul Ricoeur's hermeneutic phenomenology addresses the issue that all subjectivity as source of being depends upon linguistic representation.[18] The subject defined by consciousness remains central to the phenomenological project.[19]

James, who provided Husserl and phenomenology with their founding principles and operative method—that consciousness cannot be examined apart from its intentional objects[20]—embarked upon the search for consciousness, the record of which his *Principles of Psychology* documents:

> Psychology, the science of finite individual minds, assumes as its data (1) thoughts and feelings, and (2) a physical world in time and space with which they coexist and which (3) they know.

> No one has even had a simple sensation by itself. Consciousness, from our natal day, is of a teeming multiplicity of objects and relations, and what we call simple sensations are results of discriminate attention, pushed often to a very high degree.[21]

James could not isolate the datum of consciousness apart from the *experience* of encountering its objects. The composition of this experience, however, could not be subdivided into distinguishable parts, subject-object, in the actual event of perception. "There is no manifold of coexisting ideas; the notion of such a thing is a chimera. Whatever things are thought in relation are thought from the onset in a unity, in a single pulse of subjectivity, a single psychosis, feeling, or state of mind."[22] The division of the two is not a property of the experience but a retroactively formulated and imposed organization of experiential data. "They [empirical positivists] know the object to be one thing and the thought another; and they forthwith foist their own knowledge into that of the thought of which they pretend to give a true account. To conclude, then, thought may, but need not, in knowing, discriminate between its object and itself."[23]

The terms James employed to describe the elements of experience as they are reflected upon after the fact approximate Husserl's use of noesis and noema. "What forms the materials into intentional experience and brings in the specific element of intentionality is the same as that which gives its specific meaning to our use of the term 'consciousness,' in accordance with which consciousness points *eo ipso* to something of which it is the consciousness."[24]

The act of consciousness that *intends* an object is noetic. The noetic possibilities, however, cannot be exhausted in a single act of consciousness. For Husserl, certain realms of being remained outside the variable acts of consciousness. For example, that which one experiences in perceiving a chair is a noetic act. What enables one to recognize the object that appears in one's dream, the thing one sits upon at the dinner table, and the apparatus that positions my body at this desk as I write is the ideal chair. "'In' each of these experiences there 'dwells' a *noematic* meaning, and however closely self-related, indeed, so far as a central nucleus is concerned, essentially self-same, the latter remains in different experiences, it differs in kind none the less when the experiences differ in kind."[25] The noema belongs to the ideal realm that bestows meaning (*sinn*) upon the objects of experience. The noema provides the "central nucleus," the sheer "objective meaning," which finds its occasion for realization in the individual noetic acts.[26]

In the analytic index to *Ideas*, Husserl lists the term *nucleus* next to the entry *noematic*. Husserl's use of the Latin term *nucleus* to describe the Greek *noema* reveals two dimensions of its importance to his project.[27] First, Husserl contends that the ultimate source of meaning, in contrast to the act of bestowing sense within the moment of perception, resides outside the actual experience and in the realm of ideals or noema. Second, his investigations depend upon the prior construction of human subjectivity, which remains his primary focus. The structure of Husserl's phenomenology relies upon residual Platonic and Cartesian elements: idealized realms outside experience and the bifurcation of subject-object poles of experience. Husserl's phenomenology provides a radical alternative to both Platonic and Cartesian idealities, but within the accepted frame of subjectivity. Husserl believed that he could uncover the essential structures of consciousness that generated or synthesized the infinite manifestations of perceived objects by turning reflexively from the things as they revealed or pointed to the internal essences of the cogito.[28]

Prior to Husserl, however, James attempted to isolate consciousness, the "constant play of furtherances and hindrances," in his thinking. In *Principles of Psychology*, James began his investigation with the assumption that consciousness resides within as an independent, nonmaterial entity he calls spiritual. His search, however, revealed no such immaterial thing: "it is difficult for me to detect in the activity any purely spiritual element at all. Whenever my introspective glance succeeds in turning round quickly enough to catch one of these manifestations of spontaneity in the act, all it can ever feel distinctly is some bodily process, for the most part taking place within the head."[29]

Upon closer scrutiny, the spiritual entity of consciousness is actually an activity inextricably related to his body, beginning with his sense organs. James's correlation between consciousness and corporeality expanded from the localized sensations to diffusion throughout the body.

> It [consciousness] may feel its own immediate existence—we have all along admitted to possibility of this, hard as it is by direct introspection to ascertain the fact—but nothing can be known *about* it till it be dead and gone. Its appropriations are therefore less to *itself* than to the most intimately felt *part of its present Object, the body, and the central adjustments,* which accompany

the act of thinking, in the head. *They are the real nucleus of our personal identity*, and it is their actual existence, realized as a solid present fact, which makes us say "as sure *as I exist*, those past facts were part of myself." They are the kernel to which the *represented* parts of the Self are assimilated, accreted, and knit on; and even were Thought entirely unconscious of itself in the act of thinking, these "warm" parts of its present object would be a firm basis on which the consciousness of personal identity would rest.[30]

If we return to Husserl's noema—defined as ideal nucleic sources of meaning that remain outside of experience—we note that James's description of consciousness includes similar terms: "nucleus," "kernel." The nuclei of consciousness in James's interpretation, however, are located *not* in the ideal realm beyond experience, but within experience as the nascent source of self.

James's investigation into consciousness uncovered corporeal and relational rudiments of the self rather than subjectivity. He avoided the Cartesian bifurcation of reality into subject-object poles that was the inevitable result of constructing subjectivity as an interior space, and consciousness as possessing inherent existence.[31] Unlike the Cartesian subject, which obtains the stable singularity of a homogeneous monad by eliminating the content of body and experience from its construction and representation,[32] James described the self—plural, unstable, and heterogeneously defined—through the variety of its bodily mediated experiences and relationships. Descartes stabilized the subject by mathematizing its boundaries[33] and eliminating the body. The subject depends upon autonomous axiomatic governance that excludes variability. Subjectivity, therefore, exists without modes, for its being is totalized exclusively in terms of thought.[34]

This hermeneutic phenomenological investigation into the religious experience of reconciliation begins not with Paul, but with William James. I propose to return to the intersection in James's conception of the individual expressed in *Varieties of Religious Experience* and *Principles of Psychology*, which present opposite constructions of the human agent of experience: in *Varieties*, the isolated, atomized individual of religious experience whose consciousness is mediated by subjectivity; and in *Principles*, a relational self and ontologically closer to the character of premodern religious experience and constructions of personhood. The emendation I propose to the methods of phenomenology of religion is to relocate the self as the mediation of experience and the relational ground of being as the source of human modality and the mediation of the ontological structure of the sacred. As presented in *Principles*, the various modalities of the self fulfill the methodological intentions of phenomenology of religion, and provide analytical richness and clarity to the interpretation of Paul's experience as one whose discovery of unanticipated dimensions of the sacred resulted in the transformation of identity, community, and his understanding of Divinity.

Phenomenology of religion, as a scholarly discipline committed to the description and interpretation of consciousness and the ontology of the sacred, derives as well as departs from the methods of Husserl. Terms such as *essence, subjectivity*, and *consciousness*, although redefined by scholars of religion, nevertheless indicate an ongoing interest in the religious subject's experiences. These terms also convey the continuing influence of Platonic conception upon the discipline, for which phenomenology of religion has been criticized.[35]

Scholars of religion, however, are neither unified nor invariable in their application of phenomenology. While scholars such as Mircea Eliade made the identification of a universal essence, the sacred, the interpretive aim of their work, their commitment to this methodological principle and the centrality it occupied in their discussions revealed the gravity of concern for understanding the meaning of religious experience to human subjects.

One of the limitations of the phenomenological method as employed by scholars of *Religionswissenschaft*, such as Rudolf Otto, Joachim Wach, and Gerardus van der Leeuw, is that their achievement of identifying the universal essence of religion in its various cultural manifestations resulted in the abandonment of the social context.[36] Charles Long identifies the achievements of phenomenological interpretations that address the relationship between ontological and experiential realms. He notes that the analytical studies these scholars created did not resolve the tension between the essential and the social:

> rather, they tend to state the problem more clearly, for, while each one in his own way envisages a step beyond the initial experience and behavior of *Homo religiosus*, the articulation of the relationship of religion to the other categories and dimensions of cultural life is stated abstractly and does not match their careful and refined analysis of the ontological structure of religious experience and expression. Thus, the practical side of the religious life, even when it is admitted to exist, does not seem to follow logically from their initial analysis.[37]

Within the theistic terrain of religious experience examined in this project, the various expressive symbolizations and enactments are the creative participation in the variable character of the holy or the sacred.[38]

If we are to account for the neglected and repressed interpretations of experience (praxis) as located in history and society, we must account for the body, community, and its modes of mediation in relationship to the sacred, for it is through embodied experiential subjectivity that our experience occurs and achieves personal and collective articulation. The phenomenological project, therefore, need not be abandoned, but it must be emended through careful attention to the following realm of experience: the holy interpreted in relationship to *Lebenswelt*. This relocation of a fundamental datum in religious experience redefines the sacred from that which is framed in terms of transcendental, Platonic essence to experiences that define and shape the interaction and perception of the immediate sphere of social existence. Husserl used the term *Lebenswelt* in two distinct but related realms: to describe the world of primary perceptions, and to describe the world of cultural forms: "It is pregiven to us all quite naturally as persons within the horizon of our fellow men, i.e., in every actual connection with others, or 'the' world common to us all. Thus it is . . . the constant ground of validity, an ever-available source of what is taken for granted."[39]

Husserl named this mode of consciousness as the natural attitude in which the world appears coherent and constant. The natural attitude "is that of straightfor-wardly living toward whatever objects are given, thus toward the world-horizon, in normal, unbroken constancy, in a synthetic coherence running through all acts. . . . We, the subjects, in our normal, unbroken, coherent life, know no goals which extend beyond this; indeed we have no idea that there could be others."[40]

Hans Blumenberg points out that this world described by *Lebenswelt* "has no modality."[41] Being possesses modes only in the actuality of "turning" (*tropos*), of moving from one structure to a different structure, one *Lebenswelt* to another. "It is precisely this incapacity to be otherwise which is not even considered in the life-world, since this idea presupposes the idea of the capacity to be otherwise."[42] The *Lebenswelt*, therefore, depends upon a unique epoche, for it exists by sus-pending every doubt concerning the existence and inevitability of this "world and its Objects."[43]

Husserl, however, was not ultimately interested in this world as an intentional object to be understood in phenomenological detail; rather the *Lebenswelt* marked a point of entry into consciousness that intentionally structures or con-stitutes it. The world, as theme, for Husserl pointed to the larger question, How do we have a world?

Husserl's description of a world as intersubjectively inhabited establishes a point of entry and a terrain for our project. Paul Ricoeur, whose hermeneutic phenomenology provides a valuable resource for this project, describes the limi-tations of and identifies the direction and boundary to the possibilities promised in Husserl's contribution. "Phenomenology is . . . caught up in an infinite move-ment of 'backward questioning' in which its project of radical self-grounding fades away. Even the last works [Husserl's] devoted to the *life-world* designate by this term a horizon of immediateness that is forever out of reach. The *Lebenswelt* is never actually given but always presupposed. It is phenomenology's paradise lost. . . . It is this that gives to Husserl's work its tragic grandeur."[44]

While this current project follows that movement of Husserl and Ricoeur, it does not share the momentum of unlimited, reflexive, regressive interrogation that leads to the lost horizon of pure consciousness. We awake to find ourselves cast out of the Edenic subjectivity of unmediated presence and thrown into the mediational realm of the world, objects, and self. Husserl's horizon of pure con-sciousness eludes our eidetic pursuit in the same manner that the horizon advances simultaneously with every step taken toward it.

Husserl, however, employed *Lebenswelt* also to describe the world of cultural creations. The first sense of the term, which appears in *Cartesian Meditations*, refers to the experience of immediate perception; the second, to the realm of cultural forms that mediate experience.[45] The phenomenology of cultural forms is cru-cial—Husserl's second sense of *Lebenswelt*—to the study of Paul, not only for its inclusion of religion as a cultural creation but also for addressing the character of being. For Husserl, the *eidoi* of perceiving are apodictic and unchanging.[46] The phenomenological task becomes one of identifying the necessary elements that are indispensable to particular experiences of intentionality: seeing, hearing, and spirit possession, for example. The eidetic structures of perception do not change.

A phenomenology of religion that interprets cultural structures, however, recognizes that these forms, which make religious experience possible, are historically contingent. Since the cultural *Lebenswelt* changes, phenomenology must deal with the eidetic structures of such change, the essential conditions of any and all cultural transformations.[47] That realm of *Lebenswelt* of importance to phenomenology of religion is *Mitwelt* (world-with). Max Scheler uses the term to describe the realm of human togetherness. This sphere of experience is prior to all other experiential realms, "a social reality which is the most fundamental category of human thinking. The 'thou' is, in this sphere, pregiven to the 'I' which knows itself only within the 'we.' Hence, 'community' is fundamental to the ego (*Eigenich*)."[48]

In the examination of Paul, the cultural form that provides the common denominator across his various transformative experiences is religious community. Both as a Pharisee and as an apostle, Paul evinces an enduring and passionate concern for the participation in and maintenance or creation of sacred communities. The composition and ethos of each, however, differ radically. In order to understand the alterations in communal modality, it is necessary to portray the relationship between Paul's self (or selves), its communal modalities, and his experience of the sacred, for reconciliation entails the transformation of each inextricably connected and interdependent realm.

Paul's struggle is neither the crisis of opposing will nor conscience. In Paul we encounter the crisis of creolization, for in the culturally heterogeneous composition of his identity and experience resides the sources of his religious creativity and his religious struggle that are responses to the condition of a Pharisee in the Hellenistic Jewish Diaspora.

The questions that guide this phenomenological recovery of Paul and his experience of reconciliation are as follows:

- What is the constitution of the self particular to Paul, his cultural condition, and his social location, and how does this definition of identity differ from those that have become the Western legacy of Augustine and Luther?
- What is the relationship between the experiential character of Paul's *Lebenswelt* and his sense of self as a Pharisee?
- What is his experience of the sacred with the community of Pharisees, or his sacred *Mitwelt,* and how are the boundaries and the membership of this community transformed by his mystical experiences?

We immediately face the difficulty of identifying the biographical material in the corpus of Paul's letters.[49] Paul, like Augustine and Luther, used autobiographical material for theological argument and reflection. New Testament scholars recognize that rather than constructing or working from a comprehensive theological system, Paul's letters address specific issues within specific and diverse communities.[50] Since his concerns are pastoral and practical, the mode in which his experiences are presented serve rhetorical purposes.[51] Jacob Jarvell contends that we have not one but three Pauls: "(1) the Paul of the Pauline letters; (2) the Paul of Acts; and (3) the Paul of the Pastoral letters."[52] In the face of fragmentary and ambiguous evidence, efforts persist in presenting a coherent narrative portrait of Paul.[53]

The approach in this project accepts the fragments, but instead of assembling them into a narrative or mosaic, forms that leave fissures to be filled with fabricated grout, I propose a phenomenological examination of *modes*. The root of the term is Latin *modus*, meaning "the measure with which, or according to which, anything is measured, its size, length, circumference, frequency, or class." In music, Greeks used the term to differentiate tonal organizations or scales such as Aeolian or Lydian. Each mode had an emotionally evocative character, which was inseparable from its mathematical intervals. The musical use of the term derived from the ancient Greek theories that attempted to differentiate styles of music according to tonal range, mood, and character (*ethos*) of the people from which the music originated. The Greek tetrachord fixed the beginning and end of each mode's range.

> Greek music must never be conceived in terms of any continuous scale—least of all—the harmonic series of our "just intonation." Its essential character lies in the logical priority of the fixed notes, which hold the melody between the iron girders of consonant progressions, over the contrasting flexible effects of the mobile notes, which bound various and irregular intervals, some hair-split, some widely gapped (and are no less mutable in the more evenly spread diatonic genus).[54]

Ancient Judaism, which shared the cultural influences of Near Eastern music, also employed modes within the services of the synagogues.[55]

Dorians were considered to be a dignified and masculine people, "stern and intense,"[56] like the mode by the same name. The Mixolydian is a mixture of the dignified Dorian, with the additional dimension of mourning, associated with the Lydian, attributed to Torebus from Lydia.[57] The Greek term, from which the Latin is translated, is *tropos*. The term includes the musical sense of *modus*, with the additional dimension of "style." *Tropos* also refers to habit, custom, manner, fashion, or guise. A *tropos* was a style that belonged to a particular ethos, Lydian, for example.

When musicians modulated from one *tropos* to another, the entire system of tetrachords changed. In other words, the entire style and structure of harmonic relationships (*harmonia*, "fitting together") changed from one *tropos* to another. *Hypertrophy* was defined as ascending or excessive modulation.[58] The turning of one system to another, however, is describes as *tropes*. Similarly, we understand our contemporary use of figurative language as *tropes*, or "turn, twist."[59]

The ambivalence of mode as "manner" or way in the sense of "how" one goes about living;[60] the sense of structural boundary or limit; and the movement of turning, twisting, as well as the use of figurative language are crucial to my application of the word as an interpretive term. No less crucial, and indispensable to the interpretation of religious experience, is the importance of religious emotions. A "mode" was a structure, an event, and an evocation of either a feeling or a host of feelings. Musical historian Donald Grout speculates that each mode might have been "a collection of melody types, phrases, rhythms, and even poetic forms which, taken together, could express a specific emotional quality."[61] Modes define and create a particular personality, affect, and way of being. Grout's definition of Greek modes as a richly layered, highly stylized music provides a common interpretive denominator between performance and presentation: both depend upon the related dimensions of *tropos*.

The relationship becomes illuminated when we place Grout's definition of mode (*tropos*) next to Clifford Geertz's definition of ideology as figurative language or tropes (*mode*): Interpretation often proceeds "with no notion of how metaphor, analogy, irony, ambiguity, pun, paradox, hyperbole, rhythm, and all the other elements of what we lamely call 'style' operate—even, in a majority of cases, with no recognition that these devices are of any importance in casting personal attitudes into public form."[62] Paul casts his personal religious experience into rhetorical modes or epistolary presentations of the self. In order to understand the manifestations of Paul's multiple selves, we must attempt to interpret the structure of the related worlds he inhabits. Since "the structures of one's world are the necessary conditions for the possibility of one's experience,"[63] we must include the multiple worlds and their different forms of communal mediation through and in which Paul moved.

The direction of this method, therefore, moves from the phenomenological to the ontological, through the interpretation of texts and cultural forms. Ricoeur plots two courses toward the ontological: the "short route" tread by Heidegger, who interrogated being directly; and, in contrast, Ricoeur's own longer path through "exegesis, history, or psychoanalysis,"[64] to "Being . . . metaphorical statements and narrative plots."

> I confess willingly that these analyses continually *presuppose* the conviction that discourse never exists *for its own sake*, for its own glory, but that in all of its uses it seeks to bring into language an experience, a way of living in and of Being-in-the-world which precedes it and which demands to be said. It is this conviction that there is always a *Being-demanding-to-be-said* (*un être-à-dire*) that precedes our actual saying which explains my obstinacy in trying to discover in the poetic uses of language the referential mode appropriate to him and through which discourse continues to "say" Being even when it appears to have withdrawn into itself for the sake of self-celebration.[65]

The priority phenomenology places upon experience and being as the archaic aim of its interpretive intentions finds epistemological cognates in psychology, anthropology, and theology. Psychology distinguishes between primary and secondary processes; Freud distinguishes between primary drives, aggression, and libido, and the secondary cognitive structures of ego.[66] Object-relations theory

denotes the difference between the nuclear self and its archaic internalizations and the cognitive functions of ego.[67] Anthropologists distinguish between
"emic" and "etic" as ways of describing indigenous meaning and patterns of
recognition, and those of outside observers.[68] Theology has held the distinction
between the experience of Divinity in the moment of encounter as *theologia
prima*, and the secondary formulations of doctrine and systematics as *theologia
secunda*.[69] Finally, phenomenology as a discipline proceeds as a first-level description and interpretation of experience, such as the work of Husserl, and the more
philosophical reflections on experience and ontology characteristic of the work
of Heidegger.[70] This investigation into Paul's experience of mystical transformation holds experience and being to be primary, while recognizing that experience
is always mediated through language, the body, and other cultural creations and
constructions, and is never found in an "uninterpreted" form.[71]

Paul's primary commitment is to the inclusion of the Greek Gentiles in
covenantal relationship with Jews gathered into the shared space of the sacred cultus into one holy community. This communal form is inseparable from the affective core of his intense mystical encounter with the holy, enthroned figure of his
ecstatic experience. Paul did not receive the full contents of this prophetic call during the moment of mystical rapture; rather, his encounter with the enthroned figure provided integrative healing through the exposure of his repressed and hidden,
therefore shameful, vulnerability to the empathic holy gaze of the one he would
eventually identify as the slain, resurrected, and ascended figure of the Messiah,
who looked upon Paul's exposed shame with compassionate scrutiny, leaving Paul
ruptured and whole: rupturing the primary defenses against shame—displaced
vulnerability, dissociated devaluation of unclean others, attenuated empathy that
allowed him to inflict injury upon others without affective resonance—and incorporating the unacknowledged narcissistic and social wounding into his personality, self-understanding, and understanding of the sacred. Paul became socially
integrated in the diasporic messianic community of Damascus, which provided
him with the interactive embodiment of his reconfigured self. Paul's rage was both
redirected and healed. While present, it was necessary to the cohesiveness of Paul's
personality, protecting the boundaries of this self from agents of permeable impurity in their acceptance of Gentiles and proclamation of a humiliated, powerless
Messiah. While his rage was necessary, its presence in Paul revealed the precarious
balance between his cultural intimacy and his cultic dissociation, a balance maintained by protective, projective elimination of vulnerability.

Chapter 2

Self/Shame Dynamics

Three Theories

In my preliminary discussion of Cartesian subjectivity, I noted that the construction of the subject depended upon the elimination of the body as the mediational basis of experiences and as part of the system of language. The subject is constituted in language by the personal pronoun, which allows for interchangeable substitutions with each new reader's perspective, since the subject is not situated or embodied in any particular material or social locus. The ontology of the subject derives from an ahistorical, nonexperiential realm of consciousness.

Husserlian phenomenology attempts to correct the Cartesian dislocation of subjectivity by restoring intentionality to consciousness. Objects lose their inherent existence and become intentional objects. Since they exist within the realm of experiential subjectivity, their autonomous "objective" status becomes bracketed or suspended in the epoche of phenomenological investigation.

William James, who provided the key insight to the phenomenological project through his understanding of intentionality, may also provide resources for a corrective to phenomenology's ontological subjectivity. The foundational logic upon which phenomenology unfolds its project is the effort to define the varied and multidimensional character of experience that transpires between the subject and the world. In the particular lineage of phenomenology that concerns us here, we explore the phenomenology of religion, the subject's experience of the sacred, and the cultural forms that mediate this realm of ultimate reality. Even though Husserl departed from the direction of Descartes's project summarized by his *zu den Sachen* (to the things), the structure of Husserl's phenomenology carries the ghost of Cartesian subjectivity. Noema, noesis, and eidos, as Don Ihde and Walter Ong have pointed out, derive from the Greek heritage of thought thoroughly rooted in visual modes of consciousness.[1] An ontological equation between thinking, seeing, and being operates in the Greek, the Cartesian, and the phenomenological systems. "Greek thinking was conceived in the world of light, in the Apollonian visual world. The Greek language expresses this identification of 'seeing' and 'knowing' by a verb which means 'appear,' 'shine,' in the present (*eidomai*), and 'I know,' properly, 'I saw,' in the past (*oida*). Thus the Greek 'knows' what he has 'seen.'"[2] C. M. Bowra contends that the Greek terms *eidos* and *idea* (notion or idea) are rooted in discrete observation of visible forms, hence Plato's comparison between eternal forms and the sun.[3]

Richard Rorty recognizes that Descartes's ultimate focus upon mind and its primary function of consciousness was an unprecedented development in Western thought. Descartes created a "conception of the human mind as an inner space in which both pains and clear and distinct ideas passed in review before a single Inner Eye. The novel was the notion of a single inner space in which bodily and perceptual sensations ('confused ideas of sense and imagination' in Descartes's phrase), mathematical truths, moral rules, the idea of God, moods of depressing, and all the rest of what we now call 'mental' were objects of quasi-observation."[4] From this alienated position of "inner space" wherein the subject resides, Husserl attempted to restore the connection between the subject and the object world, whose elimination, in part, constituted and made possible the very existence of Cartesian subjectivity.

We must ask how phenomenology would differ in the understanding of its project if it proceeded not from the investigation of experiential subjectivity and its concomitant ontology of consciousness, but undertook the examination of experience as mediated by the plurality of the selves, which owe their existence to a relational ontology. Rather than the foundational principle, *cogito ergo sum*, or *zu den Sachen*, the founding experience would be, *esse est esse necesse in propinquas*: "to be is to be unavoidably in connection." The starting point is not a principle or foundational tenet but an *experience*; to be alive or a human is to be inextricably bound in multiple human relationships that constitute one's being.[5]

The cogency of this phenomenological observation depends upon a severe departure from subjectivist ontologies that depend upon explicating degrees of consciousness, or theories of subjectivity that define the subject solely as a linguistic construction.[6] This affirmation derives its force from a fundamental datum of human existence: humans exist, live, move, and have their being only by virtue of other human beings.[7] Winnicott observed, "The infant and the maternal care together form a unit. 'There is no such thing as an infant,' [Winnicott quoting himself] meaning, of course, that whenever one finds an infant one finds maternal care, and without maternal care there would be no infant."[8]

The experiences of perception and the embodiment of a relational ontology are manifest in the enactments and expressions of the self. The reliability of the term *self* and the reality to which it possibly refers have undergone analytical assault and annihilation by some postmodernist thinkers.[9] Within the purview of this theoretical consideration, the self is the creation of language.[10] The self is socially and culturally constructed, not innately given at biological birth; it possesses coherency and consistency, is singular and stable, and is ultimately autonomous.[11]

I shall address this critique in the following discussion within three interrelated interpretations: The self as defined by (1) object-relations theory; (2) the psychology of William James; (3) shame theory.

OBJECT-RELATIONS THEORY: THE GENESIS OF THE SELF

While the birth and survival of the infant depend upon the presence of an adequately nurturant other, object-relations theorists emphasize that the experience from the perspective of the child has the unitary character of undifferentiated oneness. Theoreticians employ a varied vocabulary to describe the state: "symbiosis," "normal autism," "absolute primary narcissism," and "primary love."[12] Each of these terms refers to the infant's experience of the primary care provider as inseparable from the infant's own being. The relationship between the two is one of seamless continuity. D. W. Winnicott and Heinz Kohut and Ernest Wolf describe the other as a "subjective object" and "self-object," respectively, to indicate the mother as a predifferentiated participant in the child's psychic constitution prior to an autonomous relationship with an object.[13]

The child's self emerges from this experiential organum through its ability to make distinctions out of the totality of its experience. The character of the developing self will be deeply affected by both the role of internal structural agents and the caregiver's response to the neonascent self. Intrapsychic and interpersonal forces contribute to the establishment of the self. The degree to which these boundaries become stable, providing a coherent sense of well-being, or are poorly defined, existing on the verge of disintegration resulting in traumatic anxiety, depends upon the child's innate temperament and the quality of the interpersonal environment.

While theorists diverge in the degree of importance they assign to internal and external influences, they recognize the common function of introjection and projection as essential to the creation of boundaries and the experience of the self. "The structuring of the inner world begins from the very first. Incorporative aspects of the infant's global and undifferentiated experience precede the capacity to distinguish between self and object, but contribute a qualitative modification to the global experience. The experience is *good* or *bad* or perhaps both, and to the degree that it is unpleasurable, leads to primary attempts at externalization which organize the emerging lines of differentiation."[14] The child's undifferentiated experience is interrupted by discontinuity in the responsiveness of the mother. Infant omnipotence is gradually deflated by what Winnicott describes as the "good-enough mother."[15]

The punctuation of the child's experiential continuum into anxiety-provoking and tension-relaxing moments is accompanied by the presence of objects and/or parts of objects that are internalized as introjects. The introject acquires the capacity to substitute in whole or in part for the real object as a source of gratification or aggression. The schema derived from organizing activities becomes structuralized and acquires a quasi-autonomy of its own.[16]

Otto Kernberg's interpretation of introjects places them within the framework of Freudian structural theory. "Introjections, the earliest form of identification systems, may be considered as precipitants around which ego nuclei consolidate."[17] The child's ego organizes the experiences, which are accompanied by images, into pleasurable or unpleasant states. "The first ego state is probably one which the 'good internal objects' (the early positive introjections with mostly undifferentiated and fused self and object-images) and the 'good external objects' (such reality aspects of external objects which are really part objects) constitute the earliest defensive organization of the ego (the 'purified pleasure ego'), while all negative introjections are 'ejected' (Jacobson, 1964) and considered 'not me' one might also say that by the act of this ejection 'me' is established [Sandler, personal communication]."[18]

The primal emergence of the self is the product of paradox. The mechanism of projection that removes the painful introjects threatening the child's ego core, hence its existence, establishes the first boundaries between self and others; yet the emergent ego's movement is directed toward the restoration of narcissistic perfection. In other words, the ejection of negative introjects is not only the result of the "ego's incapacity to integrate introjection of dissimilar valences,"[19] but is an intentional effort to restore the experience of primal merger. The boundaries of the self-differentiation are the inevitable results of the attempt to eliminate the distinction between self and object. The fundamental and primary experience of the self, therefore, depends upon its ability to distinguish between tolerable and intolerable aspects of being, or the creation of boundaries within as well as between itself and the environment.

OBJECT-RELATIONS THEORY: THE EXPERIENCE OF SYMBOL

Winnicott and Kernberg also provide differing interpretations of the iconic dimension of experience. Kernberg examines the image as the child's internalization of the external world in the form of introjects that become part of the intrapsychic structure. Introjections consist of (1) object-images or object-representation; (2) self-images or self-representations; (3) drive derivatives or dispositions to specific affective states.[20] Since the introjects are charged with affect, the expulsion of introjects with a negative valence prior to the development of the child's verbal capacity makes the rudimentary establishment of the self an interpretive or hermeneutical act.[21] Separation of positive and negative valences, defined as splitting,[22] is characteristic of primitive mechanisms in the healthy child, and of regressive mechanisms in pathologic adults. For Kernberg, the development of a healthy ego involves the child's capacity to move from splitting to fusion of introjects with positive and negative valences. "From here on synthetic processes show an accelerated development. Integrative processes combining all kinds of introjections and identifications into the ego identity take place, and this expands and solidifies all structures of the ego."[23] The function and meaning of the iconic for Kernberg reside ultimately within intrapsychic structures.

For Winnicott, the locus of the iconic is neither exclusively intrapsychic nor external, but shares simultaneously in both interior and exterior realms. Winnicott's description moves toward perceptual experience and is therefore closer to a phenomenological interpretation of what he names as the "transitional object." "Transitional phenomena" refer to "the third part of the life of a human being, . . . an intermediate area of *experiencing*, to which inner reality and external life both contribute."[24] Although transitional phenomena begin to manifest from the age of four months to a year, they can be experienced throughout life.

The mother's incomplete but adequate compliance to the infant's needs and demands (the "good-enough" mother) interrupts the illusion that the object world represented by the mother's breast is inseparable and indistinguishable from the infant. Winnicott uses the term *illusion* to describe both the undifferentiated realm of the infant's experience of the breast, or any other object, and an internal object representation that the infant creates and experiences as real.

The mother's adaptation to the infant's needs, when good enough, gives the infant the *illusion* that there is an external reality that corresponds to the infant's own capacity to create. The infant perceives the breast only insofar as a breast could be created just there and then. A subjective phenomenon develops in the baby that we call the mother's breast. The mother places the actual breast just there where the infant is ready to create, and at the right moment.[25]

The gradual interruption of care results in disillusionment and the earliest eruptive distinctions in the creative and imaginary maintenance of a coherent sense of being. These eruptions precipitate the need for and movement toward transitional objects: breast, fingers, cloth, or any other affectionately cuddled object.[26] Transitional objects may vary since they are defined or constituted not by their status as objects but by the infant's experience of them. The object represents the infant's transition from a state of being merged with the mother to a state of being in relation to the mother as something outside and separate.[27]

The feelings that accompany the disillusionment and concomitant disentanglement of an object previously experienced to be inseparable from the infant are intensely ambivalent. The ambivalence of emotions enables and indicates a relationship with the real, or otherness: something that can be both loved and hated.[28] If we return to Kernberg's analysis of the healthy development from primitive mechanisms, which split positive and negative introjects, to the intrapsychic mechanism, which incorporates positive and negative valences into the ego structure through fusion, we can recognize that both the encounter with and the healthy adjustment to external reality precipitate and require the acceptance of polyvalent responses.[29] For Kernberg, the locus of integration is the intrapsychic structure of the ego; for Winnicott, the real emerges within the intermediate realm between mother and child, between the mature structure of the mother's personality and the emerging structure of the child: site of the symbol, or transitional object. Winnicott defines "symbol" as the union of the baby and the mother (or part of the mother) that emerges at the point of disunion: "It is at the place in space and time where and when the mother is in transition from being (in the baby's mind) merged in with the infant and alternatively being experienced as an object to be perceived rather than conceived of. The use of an object symbolizes the union of two now separate things, baby and mother, *at the point in time and space of the initiation of their state of separateness.*"[30]

Winnicott is describing the experience of both a material object that bonds self and other, and a site wherein their interaction takes place. The transitional object resembles the ancient Greek *symbolon* (*sym*, "together"; *bolon*, "throw"): "each of two halves or corresponding pieces, an identity token."[31] Winnicott's use of the term *symbol*, however, is not exclusively semiotic or representational, but experiential. "Symbol" describes an interactive social relationship made possible by a prior experience of nurture that enables the embodiment of polyvalent emotions within a created and creative *space*. Symbol, for Winnicott, is born of and exists *within* bonded human relationality.

Winnicott describes this interactive space as "the separation that is not a separation but a form of *union*. . . . I have located this important area of *experience* in the potential space between the individual and the environment, that which initially both joins and separates the baby and the mother when the mother's love, displayed or made manifest as human reliability, does in fact give the baby a sense of trust or of confidence in the environmental factor."[32] The self, therefore, is inseparable from the symbol: both are emergent, embodied structures that are enacted through imaginative interaction. The site of this activity resembles the liminal realm that exists between structures.[33]

I will return to the relationship of ritualized social interaction, symbol, and self, but at this point I want to stress that Winnicott emphasizes that symbols (transitional objects) belong to the in-between reality of creative interaction called "playing." In this sense, "playing" requires the bodily manipulation of objects within the imaginative and emotionally charged environment made possible by trust and caring between child and the primary caregiver. "Into this play area the child gathers objects or phenomena from external reality and uses them in the service of some sample derived from inner or personal reality."[34]

The interactive processes between child and mother, which generate self and symbol, are similar to and inseparable from the ritualized processes of cultural creation: both are formed within liminality. There is a direct development from transitional phenomena to playing, and from this to cultural experiences. "At this point my subject widens out into that of play, and of artistic creativity and appreciation, and of religious feeling, and of dreaming, and also of fetishism, lying and stealing, the origin and loss of affectionate feeling, drug addiction, the talisman of obsessional rituals, etc."[35] Winnicott believes that the relationship between transitional phenomena characterized by creative play and the creation of culture are universal processes.

For this project, I contend that the advent of the symbol indicates and enables a new mode of being: the self, which emerges between human beings within the intermediate realm of relationality and the simultaneous experience of interiority and exteriority made available by the symbol, which yokes differentiality into temporary coherency in the cathexis of polyvalent intensity. Neither the self nor its symbols is stable or enduring; neither is essential or innate. The self depends upon internalized enactments between bonded members of a community cultivated within the interpersonal and ritualized space of liminality. Symbols exist within the relational matrix defined as community, which is the site and source of the self.[36]

Phenomenologists, such as Paul Ricoeur and Mircea Eliade, as well as anthropologists like Victor Turner, have identified the multidimensionality of symbols as their distinguishing characteristic. Although their analytical terms are diverse ("multivalence," "plenitude," "heterogeneity," "polysemic," "polysemy"),[37] they bespeak a hermeneutical effort to avoid the reduction of language and being to univocality. "A symbolism that would be only a symbolism of the soul, of the subject, of the 'I,' is from the start iconoclastic; for it represents a split between the 'psychic' function and the other functions of symbol: cosmic, nocturnal, oneiric, poetic. A symbolism of subjectivity already marks the breaking-up of the symbolic totality. A symbol starts to be destroyed when it stops playing on several registers: cosmic and existential."[38]

On the other pole of symbolic possibility is proliferating polysemy. The inherent ambiguity of language, which resists our efforts of imposed categorical control, can multiply meaning into exponential instability: "an isolated symbol has no meaning; or rather, an isolated symbol has too much meaning; *polysemy* is its law."[39] Ricoeur suggests that since language is not inherently self-limiting, the limit upon its plenitudinous referentiality is to be found within community. "What then takes the place of polymorphic, naturalistic symbolism and dams up its wild proliferations is a typology of history exercised within the framework of the ecclesiastical community, in connection with a cult, a ritual, etc."[40] An ecclesiastical community has a sacred cultus with sacred symbols, which mediate the experience of the holy and enable its members to communicate and recognize the commonality of this sacred reality. I will explore the relationship between community and symbol later, but before proceeding to a brief discussion of Turner's analysis of symbols, I return to the question of symbol and its relationship to the self.

Ricoeur outlines two poles in the subversion of the symbol: fragmentation and infinitude. Fragmentation breaks apart the convergent polyvalences that a symbol "throws together." On the other pole, symbols that mean everything mean nothing at all. Tropes that transcend an identifiable terrain of meaning become unrecognizably hypertrophic.

A similar fate can befall the self. Let us place the symbol back into its relational matrix of the self and nurturant others. The symbol functions as a transitional object only within an environment that enables the child to experience distinctiveness in a context of relatedness. The transitional object holds the union of self and other together during the trauma of separation. If the environment fails the child, and the nascent self internalizes severely negative introjects, the transitional object loses its symbolic function. In other words, the child fixates on an object that no longer relates interior longing with external support, and self to other, but one that becomes a substitute for the lost object. Under these conditions the object serves as the "denial of separation." Winnicott uses the example of string as a failed transitional object: "As a denial of separation string becomes a thing in itself, something that has dangerous properties and must needs be mastered. When hope is absent and string represents a denial of separation, then a much more complex state of affairs has arisen—one that becomes difficult to cure, because of the secondary gains that arise out of the skill that develops whenever an object has to be handled in order to be mastered."[41] The potential symbol has become an idol, an object of mono- rather than multidimensionality. The boy stands over the object exercising power and control only because the object rent from its polyvalent matrix can no longer hold multiple realms together.[42] The fragmentation of the transitional object was the result of a premature rupture in the supportive relationships between caregiver and child, the environment in which the self emerges.

The other pole of polysemic infinitude has a corresponding modality in the self and assumes the form of multiple personalities. When the nascent self is subjected to intense, overwhelming, and ongoing violence, the creation of internal boundaries necessary for the formation of the self becomes interrupted and unstable. One response of the traumatized psyche is to fabricate multiple personalities, which act as personae or masks to present to a hostile environment. Integration is possible, under some circumstances, given the soothing presence of a reliable self-object whose empathetic responses to the victim allow for the internalization of a stabilizing other who can facilitate healing and unity of selves.[43]

Another, more religious way of understanding the poles in the self-symbol symbiosis is the relationship between the diabolic and demonic possession. The *diabolos* divides that which belong together; it is a divisive agent. The fragmentation of the *symbolon* is the disintegration of the multiple dimensionality of being and meaning: oneiric, cosmic, psychic, somatic, and relational.[44] The three temptations of Christ offered by the devil in the wilderness (a liminal terrain) can be interpreted as an effort to fracture the multiple unity of Jesus' relationship with God, God's word, and humanity. Each temptation is an agonistic hermeneutical dialogue over the correct action and correct interpretation of God's word. But both the words and the actions address the character of Jesus' relationship to the human community, to his human nature, and to God. If Jesus transforms stones to bread at the apogee of this fast, he nullifies the conditions that befall all mortals deprived of food and water. Similarly, if he calls upon angels to bear him up after throwing himself off the temple heights, he also chooses to dissociate himself from the consequences of gravity, thereby separating himself from the common fate of humanity. Finally, humanity becomes an object he will stand *over* if he will only stand *under* the devil. In rebuking the tempter, Jesus chooses to stand *with* humanity while embracing his own. Jesus' hermeneutical retrieval of the word of God from the singularizing interpretive manipulations of the devil restores the symbolic multivocality to sacred words, which is inseparable from preserving his membership in the human community with all its attendant vulnerabilities.

The Gospel of Mark provides an illustration of the relationship between uncontrolled polysemy and multiple personalities. The possessed resident of the Gerasenes lives in isolation from the rest of the community. Because he is removed from the relational matrix, his behavior, like his personality, has become unbounded, for he has resisted all communal attempts to control him: "and no one could bind him any more, even with a chain; for he had often been bound with fetters and chains, but the chains he wrenched apart, and the fetters he broke in pieces; and no one had the strength to subdue him" (Mark 5:3–4). These attempts, however, are not only isolating but also objectifying. The fetters have replaced human relationships. Jesus arrives with an itinerant healing community, which becomes community for the demoniac in the liminal realm outside the structure of the Gerasenes. "He replied, 'My name is Legion; for we are many'" (Luke 8:30). The demoniac's multiple personalities and violent behavior not only isolate him but make his true identity indecipherable to his community. Jesus' claim upon the demoniac stops the endless proliferation of multiple personalities. By bringing him into community, Jesus restores a recognizable humanity to him in a context of relational bonding that breaks the injurious cycle of self-abuse.

These two examples from Christian sacred texts illustrate the instability of the self, which, like the symbol, is subject to fragmentation or proliferation. Multiplicity, however, cannot be equated with disease any more than stability can be equated with health. The phenomenological investigation of William James led him to conclude that the self, by definition and etiology, is heterogeneous, multiple, and vulnerable to variability—the very qualities and characteristics that constitute and enable its development.

James defined the self, from a phenomenological perspective of experiential perception. Rather than a system of intrapsychic structures consisting of drives, defenses, and a semiotics as described by Freud, James's definition of the self exists within the concrete experiences of its multiple relationships of intentional objects of value:

> Understanding the Self in the widest sense, we may begin by dividing the history of it into three parts, relating respectively to
> 1. Its constituents;
> 2. The feelings and emotions they arouse,—Self-feeling;
> 3. The actions which they prompt,—Self-seeking and Self-preservation.[45]

Within this plurality, James identified three selves, each with varying character-istics that constitute the person: the material Self, the social Self, and the spiri-tual Self.[46]

James unfolds the description of the material Self as an ever-widening set of interconnected concentric circles. Beginning with the body, "the innermost part," he moves to its clothing, one's family (immediate and intergenerational), home, and personal property.[47] These are the material embodiments of the self.

The social Self consists of both a person's relationship within the various com-munities of one's social existence and the imago that belongs to each respective group.[48] James concludes that there must be multiple social selves, for "*a man has as many social selves as there are individuals who recognize him* and carry an image of him in their mind. To wound any one of these his images is to wound him. . . . [W]e may practically say that he has as many different social selves as there are distinct *groups* of persons about whose opinion he cares."[49] The imago held by a group, or by the person one loves, determines the script or plot of one's behavior. Maintenance of the imago shapes the character of relationships and expectations of one's actions that are inseparable from the maintenance of one's sense of self.[50] The key to the social Self (which is multiple by definition) is the person's awareness of himself or herself as seen through the eyes and evaluation of others. Another way of describing this insight is in terms of intersubjective knowledge. The phenomenological experience is one of knowing and feeling what another person thinks and feels as one's self becomes another subject's inten-tional object. In other words, one becomes the noema of another's noesis. This sense of self is crucial to my analysis of Paul, and I will resume the discussion of this aspect of James's thinking below. James, however, places a third self at the center of his consideration.

The spiritual Self comes closest to the contemporary conception of subjectiv-ity understood as consciousness and agency: "But whether we take it abstractly or concretely, our considering the spiritual self at all is a reflective process, is the result of our abandoning the outward-looking point of view, and of our having become able to think of subjectivity as such, *to think ourselves as thinkers*."[51] The spiritual Self resembles, at first, the radical reflexivity of Taylor's traditional West-ern subject, which functions apart from objects outside its center. We can feel, alongside the thing known, the thought of it going on an altogether separate act and operation of the mind. The spiritual Self "is felt by all men as a sort of inner-most centre within the circle, of sanctuary within citadel."[52] James identifies this realm as the "*self of all the other selves*."[53] His term, the "spiritual Self," designated that part of human existence independent of materiality, or material embodi-ment. "It is the source of effort and attention, and the place from which appear to emanate the fiats of the will."[54]

James seems to have described the function of the Cartesian cogito: the seat of cognition and agency that performs mental acts upon the material world. But James makes two fundamental qualifications in the independent existence of the spiritual Self. Thought, its distinguishing element, does not exist apart from its referents; and the acts of thinking are inseparable from the body's experience of acts of thinking. Earlier in his analysis, James separated the self from its attendant stream of thought: "Compared with this element of the stream, the other parts, even of the subjective life, seem transient external possessions, of which each in turn can be disowned, whilst that which disowns them remains."[55] James now explains thought, the agent of the "self of selves," in a similar description.

> A thing cannot appropriate itself; it *is* itself; and still less can't disown itself. There must be an agent of the appropriating and disowning [i.e., thought]. That thought is a vehicle of choice as well as cognition; and among the choices it makes are those appropriations, or repudiations, of its "own." But the thought is never an object in its own hands, it never appropriates or disowns itself.

> Its appropriations are therefore less to *itself* than to the most intimately felt *part of its present Object, the body, and the central adjustments*, which accompany the act of thinking, in the head. *These are the real nucleus of our personal identity.*[56]

The rehabilitation James has performed upon the Cartesian cogito, resuturing the dismembered body, which mediates the experience in the world, back into consciousness, is performed through the threads of intentionality.[57] James's interpretation of the bodily acts and effects of intentional acts of consciousness create what later thinkers such as Merleau-Ponty will describe as "the body-subject."[58]

James includes the bodily dimension of experience in the spiritual Self, and it is this conception of self that becomes the solitary receptacle of religious experience in *The Varieties of Religious Experience*. "Religion, therefore, as I now ask you arbitrarily to take it, shall mean for us *the feelings, acts, and experiences of individual men in their solitude, so far as they apprehend themselves to stand in relation to whatever they may consider the divine.*"[59] His selection of the spiritual Self is based upon the manner in which he chose to define the "self of selves" in *Principles of Psychology*, as acts of intentional consciousness appropriated as intimately felt parts of the body, "which accompany acts of thinking, in the head. *These are the real nucleus of our personal identity*, and it is their actual existence, realized as a solid present fact, which makes us say, 'as sure *as I exist*, those past facts were part of myself.'"[60]

The core self, while possessing agency and consciousness, is equated with feelings, for James the fundamental experience of individuation. James is guided by both theological and methodological principles in his work.[61] Here, both his Calvinist theological anthropology, "our responsible concern is with our private destiny, after all," and his analysis of feelings as the differentiating experience of the individual converge: "You can see now why I have been so individualistic throughout these lectures, and why I have seemed so bent on rehabilitating the element of feeling in religion and subordinating its intellectual part. Individuality is founded in feeling; and the recesses of feeling, the darker, blinder strata of character, are the only places in the world in which we catch real fact in the making, and directly perceive how events happen, and how work is actually done."[62]

In James's religious thought, the complex of consciousness, individuality, feeling, and body are confined to solitude and are private, lacking a social and public encounter with the Divine. The social Self, however, possesses a personal body but is not considered to be a primary site for religious experience. Can the social Self be introduced to the center of a phenomenological examination of religious experience of reconciliation?

SHAME AND PRIDE AS HERMENEUTICS OF RELIGIOUS EXPERIENCE

The clue to understanding the social Self, or relational self, as the mediation and subject of religious experience, appears in James's discussion of the "potential social self." The motivations for its behavior are based upon hierarchical sources of approval who serve as an "ideal spectator" to the person pursuing the creation of an "ideal social self." "Yet still the emotion that beckons me on is indubitably the pursuit of an ideal social self, of a self that is at least *worthy* of approving recognition by the highest *possible* judging companion, if such companion there be."[63]

James is describing not only singular authorities, but communities of confirmation in whose interrelational nexus the self sustains its being. Intercommunal movement is made possible by what is experienced as increasing degrees of approval by superior communal sources that sustain the self in the face of loss and disapproval due to the transition. James describes the multiple dynamics of interpersonal approval and censure:

> Those images of me in the minds of other men are, it is true, things outside of me, whose changes I perceive just as I perceive any other outward change. Both the pride and shame which I feel are not concerned merely with *those* changes. I feel as if something else had changed too, when I perceive my image in your mind to have changed for the worse, something in me to which that image belongs, and which a moment ago I felt inside of me, big and strong and lusty, but now weak, contracted, and collapsed. Is not this latter change the change I feel the shame about? Is not the condition of this thing inside of me the proper object of my egoistic concern, of my self-regard? And is it not, after all, my pure Ego, my bare numerical principle of distinction from other men, and no empirical part of me at all?
>
> No, it is no such pure principle, it is simply my total empirical selfhood again, my historic Me, a collection of objective facts, to which the depreciated image in your mind "belongs." . . . Indeed, the thing that is felt modified and changed for the worse during my feeling of shame is often more concrete even than this,—it is simply my bodily person, in which your conduct immediately and without any reflection at all on my part works those muscular, glandular, and vascular changes which together make up the "expression" of shame.[64]

This passage is quoted at length for the rich foresight into experience that others would later verify in their own work: phenomenologists such as Husserl and Max Scheler; object-relations theorists Mahler, Kohut, and Winnicott; research psychologist Silvan Tomkins; and shame theorists Helen Block Lewis and Donald L. Nathanson.

James begins the passage with a description of an experience that Husserl would later term "intersubjective":[65] "Those images of me in the minds of other men." This is the experience of not only being seen and known through the evaluative eyes of others, but also the experience of the self dependent upon and suspended in the felt moment of its interpersonal existence. The self then suffers a breach or interruption in the intersubjective continuum of its experience. This form of intersubjective knowledge is similar in effect to what Winnicott identifies as the "mirror role" of the mother in the child's experience of seeing "what she [the child] looks like is related to what she sees there [in the mother's face.]"[66] The difference between these conceptions is that the child is still in the process of internalizing the responses of the primary caregiver necessary for the development of intrapsychic structures. The modes of bonded intersubjective homeostasis, however, are similar in that the boundaries of the self and the symbiotic mode of coherence are similar.[67] The change in the image, from good to worse, and the accompanying deflation of the self are moments of "empathy failures"[68] between the self and ideal spectators. We will examine other possible responses to this failure below.

The reference to "my historic Me" is the poly-temporality of the self's existence, wherein its present mode is shaped by the cumulative weight of lived memory of its self before others, with the accompanying internalizations of those who have become part of its moments and structure, and the anticipation of future confirmation as well as the avoidance of possible denigrations of its experiences of part and past and present continuity. The self, therefore, is an internalized narrative selectively enacted within the presence and parameters of communal horizons. The key insight James provides, which has been enriched by the work of others, is that shame is located not in the pure ego but in the comprehensive sense of one's entire being, the self, which includes the automatic or involuntary reflexes of emotions and biological responses of the body. Shame, as I hope to demonstrate, is the indispensable human affect necessary for the creation of and existence in community.

SHAME THEORY AND AFFECTS

As an innately powerful agent of consciousness and behavior, shame is subject to multifocal examinations that struggle to comprehend its richness. I will summarize three: shame as (1) the subject of empirical psychological investigation; (2) portrayed in object-relations theory; (3) a cultural complex and code of behavior. I will integrate the three dimensions in the phenomenological interpretation of shame in the experience of Paul in chapter 4.

Empirical Definitions of Shame

The empirical positivist definitions of shame depend upon the theory of affects. The contemporary theorist credited with the major innovative research on affects as the foundational element in human behavior is Silvan S. Tomkins.[69] Affects operate within the human biological system as stimulus amplifiers intensifying the feeling and actions and awareness of one's responsiveness. Within his theoretical system, affects are constants that can be stimulated by a multiplicity of variables. Every human possesses nine affects, which Tomkins divided into two groups, one with a positive, the other a negative, valence.[70] The positives are *interest* or *excitement, enjoyment* or *joy*, and *surprise* or *startle*. The negative are *distress* or *anguish, fear* or *terror, shame* or *humiliation, dissmell, disgust,* and *anger* or *rage*.[71] Tompkins contended that affects were the biokinetic program for human behavior.[72]

"It is my view that affects are sets of muscular, glandular, and skin-receptor responses located in the face (and also widely distributed throughout the body) that generate sensory feedback to a system that finds them either inherently 'acceptable' or 'unacceptable.' These organized sets of responses are triggered at subcortical centers where specific 'programs' for each distinct affect are stored, programs that are innately endowed and have been genetically inherited. They are capable, when activated, of simultaneously capturing such widely distributed structures as the face, the heart, and the endocrine glands and imposing on them a specific pattern of correlated responses. One does not learn to be afraid or to cry or to be startled, any more than one learns to feel pain or to gasp for air."[73]

Tomkins's description confirms aspects of James's observations about the involuntary reactions to shame. The most important site of bodily manifestation for all the affects is the face, and while the entire body comes under the influence, the face remains the primary site for initiating and receiving the affect shame-humiliation. Once stimulated, each affect unfolds according to an invariable "blueprint," "program," or "script."[74] Shame-humiliation is activated by the painful interruption of another affect, interest-excitement or enjoyment-joy. When interest-excitement is triggered in a child by an object or activity that has arrested her or his attention, the affect amplifies this interest into a heightened interest-excitement. The child's eyebrows are lowered, the eyes fix upon and follow the object's movements, the mouth opens, breathing and heart rate may increase.

The shame-humiliation program begins at the point of painful interruption, not the elimination of interest-excitement or enjoyment-joy. "It is called into action when the organism remains fascinated by whatever had triggered its interest or remains desirous of communing with whatever or whoever might next have been a source of contentment, relaxation, or mirth associated with the affect enjoyment-joy."[75] The person turns away while desiring to turn back. In shame the individual wishes to resume his or her commerce with the exciting state of affairs, to reconnect with the other, to recapture the relationship that existed before the situation turned problematic.[76] Once initiated, shame follows the same sequence. Since the experience is painful, the subject turns away from the source, the eyes become downcast, neck and shoulders slump. This predictable pattern exhibited in all conditions of shame-humiliation is what Tomkins identified as affect: "the strictly biological portion of emotion" and pattern of elements.[77] Affects within Tomkins's system of analysis achieve a scientific identity since they are defined not according to the subject's experience but according to the observer's theory.[78]

The reduction of affect to functions within a biological system, free of cultural or social mediation, gives the empirical definition its universal character. Such a description renders affects as abstract, or "free of inherent meaning or association to their triggering source."[79] Shame-humiliation does not in and of itself directly describe the character of its precipitant origin—in other words, *what* we are ashamed *of*. Shame-humiliation, therefore, operates with the affect system in a manner similar to signs within a linguistic system. A sign, according to de Saussure, consists of the relationship between the signifier and the signified. The signified is the concept or image that a meaningful linguistic form, spoken or written, conveys as a signifier. "The bond between the signifier and signified is arbitrary,"[80] since the relationship between the two is shaped by convention, culture, or experience, not by nature. The signifier does not reveal any clues to the signified within its utterance or inscription, just as one cannot discern the origin or "trigger" for shame or any other affect by examining the affect's biokinetic unfolding or program. The relationship between the abstract affect, shame-humiliation, and its source stimulus is created and embodied in the bodily actions and interactions of the shame-filled self, just as the bond between signifier and signified becomes manifest in linguistic performance.

The contribution of Tomkins's theory to the understanding of affects in general, and shame-humiliation in particular, is outstanding. Yet his theory suffers the limitations inherent in all positivist empirical approaches to experience. Shame-humiliation interpreted as an abstract affect within a system reveals the severe distortions of human behavior that place ratiocentric cognition at the source of human motivation and behavior. Affects, according to Tomkins, are the primary source, a veritable demiurge of consciousness and behavior: "The cardinal feature of affect is . . . its ability to amplify anything with which it is linked; affect is responsible for attention. Anything that may be said to occupy our attention has taken center stage and become the subject of consciousness simply because it now has affective amplification. . . . [E]ach of the affects . . . produces its own quite specific form of attention and therefore its own form of consciousness."[81]

Affects do not enter human consciousness as "blueprints," or "programs," however; one does not experience the affect shame—one is ashamed *of* something, and this experience enters consciousness as emotion: "The move from affect to feeling involves a leap from biology to psychology. *To fit our definition of emotion an affect must be placed within a script or a story*" (emphasis added).[82] The story is the internal narrative of our cumulative memory including lived body memory, our experiences of what we came to associate with and understand as shame. As long as affect remains an element in a biophysiological system, constructed by a theory of its operation, shame is an invariable mechanistic sign; as a human emotion, shame enters language not as an abstract sign in a system, but as a symbol within a personal and collective narrative, subject to individual and communal interpretation. "The universal *linguality* of human experience . . . means that my belonging to a tradition or traditions passes through the interpretation of the signs, works, and texts in which cultural heritages are inscribed and offer themselves to be deciphered."[83]

We will later note that the experience of shame within a cultural system initiates scenarios that prescribe behavior in response to the offense. Unlike the biophysiological system, the linguality of experience leaves the meaning and interpretation of shame open to new interpretations, which transform the experiences of shame, as we will note in Paul's mystical and communal religious experiences. The tension between empirical positivists' and hermeneutical phenomenologists' interpretation of affect is not present within the experience of the self. One's internalized history of interactions with others converges upon and informs the moment of shame. It is the internalized past that object-relations theory attempts to recover, and to which we now turn.

Object-Relations Theory and Shame

As noted above in the discussion of object-relations theory and the symbol, the creation of the self is a primal prelinguistic interpretive act. Emotion, therefore, could be understood as an interpreted affect. Neither the affect nor the language of shame receives extensive analysis in object-relations theory. Andrew P. Morrison, however, contends that the work of one of object-relations leading theorists, Heinz Kohut, pays significant attention to the primal experiences of shame.[84] Before illuminating the embedded descriptions of shame implicit in theories of object relations, we must first describe Kohut's contribution to understanding the self's development.

The self, according to Kohut, is bipolar in that it has two mechanisms by which to establish a sense of coherence, or unity, what he names the "nuclear self." "This structure is the basis for our sense of being an independent center of initiative and perception, integrated with our most central ambitions and ideals and with our experience that our body and mind form a unit in space and a continuum in time."[85] The first manifestations of the child's initiative, which Kohut calls the "grandiose-exhibitionistic self," depends upon "his relation to the empathically responding merging-mirroring-approving self-object."[86] Winnicott describes the same mode as the "omnipotence of the infant,"[87] which is the creation of the "good-enough mother" responding to and reflecting back with loving approval and acceptance the infant's "spontaneous gesture."[88]

It is interesting to compare Kohut's description of the nuclear self with James's "Self of all other selves," or what he also calls the "Spiritual Self": "If the stream as a whole is identified with the Self more than any outward thing, a certain portion of the stream abstracted from the rest is so identified in an altogether peculiar degree, and *is felt by all men as a sort of innermost centre within the circle of sanctuary within the citadel, constituted by the subjective life as a whole.*" James also describes this self of selves as "the source of effort and attention, and the place from which appear to emanate the fiats of the will."[89]

If the mother fails to evince ample empathy for the child's grandiosity, hence failing to become the omnipotent self-object who enters and merges with the child's experience, the child suffers a narcissistic wound, an injury to the "nuclear self."[90] (Daniel Stern describes this realm as the "core self.")[91] Winnicott interprets the mother's empathetic failure to mirror and merge as the "substitution of her own gesture" for the infant's.[92] Alice Miller terms this process a "substitution" of the parent's unmet narcissistic needs for the infant's.[93] The less than good-enough mother creates a relationship that inverts the nurturant roles necessary for the emergence of the viable self.

In the face of empathic failure and narcissistic injury, the child can gravitate to a second pole or source for relational self-cohesion, "to the establishment of the child's cohesive idealized parent-imago (via his relation to the empathically responding self-object parent who permits and indeed enjoys the child's idealization of him and merger with him)."[94] The second pole is viewed as a "compensatory structure" since the mechanism continues to function in response to the inadequately nurtured, now wounded, self.[95] The means employed also depend upon secondary psychological functions such as rational operations or cognitive powers. The ego works toward the pursuit of ideals and optimum standards of behavior.[96] The compensatory actions in the example of male children who use achievements and skills to repair damaged self-esteem acquire these from the father, who is internalized as an "idealized self-object," or parental imago.[97]

This second movement is not without its price. Winnicott associates the empathic mirroring, unconditional acceptance, and adequate responsiveness to the needs and spontaneous gestures of the child's omnipotence with the "True Self." The failure of primary self-objects to meet the empathic needs of the child results in the creation of a False Self,[98] the result of the exposed and injured self. "[The] defensive function [of the False Self] is to *hide* and *protect* the True Self."[99] The False Self fulfills this purpose through "compliance to environmental demands."[100] The motivation to comply is the painful fragmentation of the self that does not have the availability of the soothing self-object to internalize for symbiotic coherency of the self. Disruption rather than continuity overwhelms its existence. "In practice the infant lives, but lives falsely. The infant remains isolated."[101]

The face is the key. "Nowhere else in the body can the anatomist demonstrate so many perfectly developed muscle groups packed together so well, each group served by its own specific nerve trunk. Many of the muscles of expression seem to have no function other than their relation to affect."[102] Tomkins noted that eye contact was the most intimate form of human connection.[103] Winnicott, Kohut, and Alice Miller all noted that behavior between mother and child, or any nurturant dyad, was formed face-to-face. Although the language of object-relations theorists differs from that of the research psychologists, both observed the same phenomenon: "During mutual gaze we feel attached. In the moment of shame, we feel shorn not just from the other but from all possible others."[104]

With the interruption or denial of the empathic gaze, the effects are not limited to the face; they are global. The self fragments, and the body responds in either the attenuation of feeling or explosive rage. The mother's interrupted or devaluing gaze not only disintegrates the experience of continuity within the nascent self, but becomes internalized as self-object, which would form the painful self-imago of the child. "The infant lives, but lives falsely." "Through the False Self the infant builds up a false set of relationships, and by means of introjections even attains a show of being real."[105] The compensatory adaptation of the False Self to its hostile environment ensures survival of the True Self, and the division or splitting of the self. Shame divides the self.

Shame splits the self since the internalized self-object's caustic or apathetic responses become a severely painful and intolerable element in the structure of the archaic self. Morrison points out that Kohut's description of narcissistic wounding, in terms of "disturbed self-acceptance," "dejection of defeat," "defective self," "mortification of being exposed," "guiltless despair," "hopelessness," "lethargy," and finally "nameless shame imposed by the ultimate recognition of a failure of all-encompassing magnitude,"[106] is Kohut's vocabulary of shame. The experiences of shame neither destroy the self nor prohibit its development. In order to experience shame, the self must attain a prior condition of adequate internal "cohesion"[107] and exist with a meaningful relationship. As noted above, shame compels the self to both turn away from and turn back toward the source of injury, while turning inward simultaneously in the heightened mode of anguished self-consciousness. Kohut recognized two modes in which the self seeks restoration: compensatory and defensive. What Winnicott and Miller describe as the False Self, Kohut describes as the defensive structure that covers over the wound to the core self in order to protect it from further injury.[108]

Compensatory structures and behavior attempt to repair the damaged self and injured esteem through the pursuit and internalization of ideals.[109] Winnicott and Miller integrate Kohut's two modes into one term that describes multidimensional movements. The False Self "hides" the True Self by compliance to external-social expectations ("environmental demands"): The False Self "is represented by the whole organization of the polite and mannered social attitude, a 'not wearing the heart on the sleeve' as might be said. Much has gone to the individual's ability to forego omnipotence and the primary process in general, the gain being the place in society which can never be attained or maintained by True Self alone."[110] Compliance, or what Miller calls the "idealized, conforming, false self,"[111] is the primary characteristic of the split self. Miller sees the split as the attenuation of sensitivity and authentic feelings, since true feelings become associated with vulnerability and woundedness at the core of one's being.[112]

If we return to Kohut's bipolar grandiose self and ideal self, Francis Broucek identifies the development of the grandiose self or the idealized self as "occurring only after the advent of objective self-awareness and as reflecting the greater men-

tal pain (shame) than normal in the developing child."[113] Broucek sees the idealized self (Winnicott's "False Self") as the attempt to hide the wounded self:
"Shame is the instigating force in the creation of the idealized self, and the construction of an idealized self always implies the coexistence of a devalued shame-
ridden self, which is in dynamic interaction with the idealized self."[114] The
diminished responsiveness to emotions, the split between the ideal self and the
rejected grandiose archaic self that remains hidden from and unintegrated into
the personality, yet all the while seeking object relations with which to merge, are
the reactions to the primal wounding of shame. As the False Self grows in social
sophistication, its capacity for adaptive protection of the nuclear self from shame
will mature. Vulnerability and the capacity to suffer narcissistic wounding will
become identifiable characteristics of the archaic True Self.

I propose that Paul manifests the behavior of one who has internalized
and enacted a commitment to an idealized self through his identity and membership in the diasporic community of Pharisees. His ability to maintain conformity to their ideals, I contend, serves the function of protecting him from
a painful self-conscious experience of an unacceptable and inadequate part of
his being (emic reference, later known as "thorn in the flesh"): not the guilt-
strapped struggling, unjustified spiritual hero before a relentlessly righteous and
just Deity who demands repentance. Paul's struggle is both the internal protection against archaic wounds to his nuclear self, and the communal protection
against devaluating interaction with derisive ideal onlookers of the Hellenistic
Diaspora, both sources of past and present shame-humiliation. Paul's mystical
experience is less a conversion and more the integration, hence emergence, of a
transformed self, a self wrought from the dissociated elements of its fragmented
heterogeneity and displaced vulnerability that once incorporated become the
core of his self and the source of his powerful need for the reconciled community
of Jews and Gentiles who together become the collective and cultural mediation
of the sacred.

Anthropological Definitions of Shame: Critique and Expansion; Shame Culture and Dyadic Personality

Biblical scholars have adopted models from cultural anthropology that distinguish guilt cultures from shame cultures. The difference between the two became
an established ethnographic paradigm in the work of Ruth Benedict and Margaret Mead.[115] Their classification system was based upon the identification of
the primary cultural mechanism governing behavior. "If culture depends primarily on external sanctions, it is considered to be a shame culture; whereas if it
depends on internal sanctions it is a guilt culture."[116] Their categories of classification derive from the application of Freud's theory of the intrapsychic structure of conflict between defenses and drives.[117] Guilt is described as the
transgression of the internalized prohibitive boundaries upon one's behavior, or
superego. Shame is the distance between the ego and ego-ideal.[118]

Traditions of literary and religious interpretations emerged based upon intrapsychic and cultural-geographic dichotomies. Eric R. Dodds identified the behavior of the Greek pantheon as shaped by the ethos of shame.[119] David H. Hesla employs the distinction between guilt and shame to illuminate the differences between ancient Greek tragedy and Elizabethan-Christian tragedy. In the former, tragedy is the inevitable result of inexorable consequences of impossible requirements upon one's personhood; the flawed execution of one's will defines the latter.

> The story (*mythos*, argument) which provides the plot of a Greek tragedy typically begins when a member of the aristocracy performs an act of wanton violence upon another member or members of the same class. . . . [T]he act is done in *hamartia*, in ignorance of the circumstances and consequences which it entails. Shame is the feeling that accompanies the recognition of the discrepancy between the good or ideal of *arete*, excellence, and the actuality of one's shortcomings. To be a mortal is to be a finite body and finite mind. . . . Shame therefore wants to disappear, wants not to be.[120]

Shame is ontological, while guilt is volitional: "The action of a Christian story begins, then, when a character possessed of a free will, and knowing what he ought and ought not to do, is tempted to defy the law of God or weakly to submit to a law other than God's. . . . [G]uilt requires four conditions: there must be a law; there must be knowledge of the law; there must be freedom to obey or disobey the known law; and there must be a violation of the law. Greek tragedy knows nothing of the first three conditions."[121]

In the orthodox tradition of Western theology and hermeneutics, Hesla places Paul within the lineage of willful captives and guilty thinkers: Augustine, Luther, and Calvin.[122] Gerhart Piers and Milton Singer have seriously questioned the creation and application of "pure" psychological categories to broad cultural patterns, while contending that evidence of shame and guilt can be found within the same cultural group.[123]

Recent biblical scholarship has continued to employ the anthropological paradigm, shame and guilt, as a comparative tool. The anthropologists upon whose sources these biblical scholars rely, however, have shifted their analytic perspective from the etic, or shame/guilt, to the emic, or honor and shame, with an emphasis upon the unifying principles of conduct and values *within* a specific culture. Julian Pitt-Rivers and J. G. Peristiany have designated the Mediterranean Basin as the culture site unified by the system of honor and shame, whose values and patterns of conduct have remained diachronically persistent.[124]

Biblical scholars whose work is informed by the anthropologists of Mediterranean culture have focused upon two dimensions of the honor and shame relationship: its code of conduct, and the dyadic personality. Pitt-Rivers provides a working definition of honor:

> Honor is the value of a person in his own eyes, but also in the eyes of his society. It is his estimation of his own worth, his claim to pride, but it is also

the acknowledgement of that *claim*, his excellence recognized by society, his *right* to pride.[125]

> Transactions of honour therefore serve these purposes: they not only provide, on the psychological side, a nexus between the ideals of society and their reproduction in the actions of individuals—honour commits men to act as they should (even if opinions differ as to how they should act)—but, on the social side, between the ideal order and the terrestrial order, validating the realities of power and making the sanctified order of precedence correspond to them.[126]

Pitt-Rivers's description of the personal and social aspects of shame is consistent with the descriptions of the phenomenon found in affect systems and object-relations theory, as well as in James.[127] "Transactions" also find an analogy in the biological "script" or "program" and the "imago" of ideal behavior befitting ideal image, mentioned in the preceding discussion.

One example of these transactions is the code of challenge-riposte. "Within the formal code the duel displays the principles involved: the offended party, judging that his honour was impugned, issued a challenge by which he invoked the honour of his offender and demanded satisfaction. The offender was obliged then either to retract and offer apologies (a course of action which was incompatible with the conception which many men had of their own honour) or to accept."[128]

The agonistic character of Mediterranean society is reflected at every level of ancient Greek society including deity, aristocrat, plebeian, and slave.[129] Bruce Malina and Jerome Neyrey have distilled this interaction into three scenes: challenge in terms of some action; perception of the message by both the individual to whom it is directed and the public at large; and reaction of the receiving individual and the evaluation of the reaction on the part of the public.[130] Honor/shame codes also govern hospitality transactions between hosts and strangers.[131] Honor, as a pervasive code of behavior, is described by anthropologist Edward Scheiffelin as a "cultural scenario."

> A cultural scenario is a series of events embodying a typical sequence of phases or episodes, which between its commencement and resolution effects a certain amount of social progress or change in the situation to which it pertains. The concept of cultural scenario differs from that of a ritual (which may, however, express or dramatize a cultural scenario) in that the cultural scenario is embodied in everyday, informal courses of action. It is empirically recognizable in the general procedure by which a people repeatedly approach and interpret diverse situations and carry them to similar types of resolutions. The situations themselves need not be similar; it is the similar manner in which they are interpreted, carried forward, and resolved that is important.[132]

The cultural scenarios of honor, together with the formal rituals and ceremonies that dramatically present and celebrate this sense of social order, constitute a world order or symbolic system.[133]

Anthropological analysis of honor as a cultural code or cultural scenario depends upon interpreting behavior as a manifestation of cultural categories governing behavior, or "scripts." These scripts can be explained in terms of ideology, indigenous self-justifying rationalizations that serve to "mystify," in Marxist terms, and preserve asymmetric relationships of dominant power.[134] This structural functionalist model, fundamentally Durkheimian, is adopted whole by biblical scholars from Mary Douglas and her work on symbolic systems, with Malina being the most consistent student of this approach.[135]

While this method provides a clear picture of behavior across numerous categories of cultural life: "purity, rite, personal identity, body, sin, cosmology, and suffering and misfortune,"[136] missing from its schema is an integrated interpretation of affective experiences of honor. When affect is considered, it is subordinate to behavior and ideology. For example, consider Pitt-Rivers's definition of honor: "It is a sentiment [affect], a manifestation of this sentiment in conduct, and the evaluation of this conduct by others, that is to say, reputation."[137] The participants within the cultural scenario, however, include only equals.

> When honour is impugned it can be vindicated. Yet the power to impugn the honour of another man depends also on the relative status of the contestants. An inferior is not deemed to possess sufficient honour to resent the affront of a superior. A superior can ignore the affront of an inferior, since his honour is not committed by it though he may choose to punish an impudence. A man is answerable for his honour only to his social equals, that is to say, to those with whom he can conceptually compete.[138]

Honor and shame are incontestably communal codes operating within the boundaries of distinct social affiliations. Pitt-Rivers's statement, "An inferior is not deemed to possess sufficient honour to resent the affront of a superior," is lacking in two indispensable realms of relationality: "not deemed to possess" begs the question, "by whom?"; and the definition overlooks the intersubjective reflexive character of honor and shame. I will address these two missing dimensions in the anthropological perspective in the next chapter. At this point, I want to stress that the phenomenological interpretation of shame and honor (pride) includes the estimation of one's esteem and personal value among equals, but far more crucial to shame (or the loss of honor) is one's relationship to hierarchical others and subordinates, rather than equals. In Paul we will see that empathic equality is the key to the cure for shame, subordination the key to honor (glory).

Critics of the ideological explanations provided by this definition have emerged from within the ranks of anthropologists. Their critique challenges the comprehensive claim upon honor as the predominant preoccupation of all Mediterranean people, and suggests that it is mainly a male matter, shame being the primary purview of women. Unni Wikan makes the counterclaim that honor "is bound up with male ideology and is not on a par with shame."[139] The feminine becomes the metaphor for expressing that which threatens masculine honor. "For the man who is 'dominated' sexually through his women, or who is bested in virile performance, is said to be 'shamed'; and this sense of shame conveys very strongly the conception of diminishment, of feminization, of being placed in the passive position of a woman, and therefore conceptually subject to homosexual assault. This diminishment is symbolised by the near-universal Mediterranean image of disgrace: the horns of the cuckold."[140]

Anton Blok explains the cuckold gesture as derived from the agrarian culture's animal husbandry of goats and sheep. The male goat's behavior is lascivious and promiscuous yet allows other billy goats access to his female. The ram however defends his exclusive privilege over his ewes. The goat, therefore, is the symbol of sin and shame (see Lev. 10:16; 16:5; Matt. 25:31–46), the ram, power and excellence.[141]

Gilmore offers an appropriate conclusion to the symbolic consciousness of the culture: "One may say confidently, therefore, that a common Mediterranean theme is the elevation of a demonstrated physiological masculinity, an ostentatiousness; 'indomitable virility,' to a paramountcy in the ascription of male social identity and reputation, whether we gloss this as 'honor' or by some other term."[142] The body, as I hope to demonstrate, will figure prominently in the expressions of shame and honor in the thinking of Paul. The body provides the fundamental metaphoric and metonymic vocabulary for the experience of each. I stress, at this point, that shame is inseparable from and dependent upon the experience, awareness, and symbolic mediation of vulnerability, as honor is dependent upon power.

The second and related terrain of anthropological investigation utilized by New Testament scholars is the definition of self particular to Mediterranean culture. Described as the "dyadic personality,"[143] "face-to-face societies,"[144] the term finds conceptual cognates in philosophy: the "relational self";[145] in psychology: "the social self";[146] in object-relations theory: the self;[147] and in the "we-self" of shame theorists[148] and phenomenologists.[149] The dyadic personality is characteristic of intensive communities whose interactions are governed by the shame-honor nexus.

> Honour and shame are the constant preoccupation of individuals in small-scale, exclusive societies where face-to-face personal, as opposed to anonymous, relations are of paramount importance and where the social personality of the actor is as significant as his office. When the individual is encapsulated in a social group an aspersion on his honour is an aspersion on the honour of his group. . . . In this type of situation the behaviour of the individual reflects that of his group to such an extent that, in his relations with other groups, the individual is forcibly cast in the role of his group's protagonist.[150]

If we set the anthropological descriptions of the dyadic personality within a more phenomenological interpretation of the experience of shame, the self appears to move between modalities of its collective embeddedness and isolation. Shame initiates the movement from the collective mode, the dyadic suspension of the self, that realm designated as "illusion" by Winnicott, to the fracturing of the relational nexus and the shattering of the symbolic. In the state of shame, one becomes the material embodiment of that which the community finds intolerable, offensive, polluting.

Anthropological definitions of honor and shame as cultural codes characteristic of dyadic personalities are helpful in locating Paul in the appropriate Mediterranean ethos. The primary emphasis of functional-structuralist renderings of shame/honor as a cultural script, which de-emphasizes the analysis of affective experience, leaves the cultural focus in need of phenomenological emendation. If we consider honor or the cultural patterning and ideological articulation of the emotion/affect pride, the theoretical definition provides a phenomenological point of entry.

Pride and shame are fundamentally social affects. They reside at the core of our existence and experience as relational beings. The affect pride begins with the affect interest-excitement, the result of an individual's intentional activity. The successful accomplishment of this goal triggers enjoyment-joy, creating a sense of pleasure and excitement that results in a global sense of competency. Pride is the creation of the competent self:

> Throughout life, any experience in which personal efficacy is linked with a positive affect will produce healthy pride. . . .
>
> Not only are we aware of having met or surpassed the standards we set for ourselves, but we feel that others share our pride and are happy for us. Somehow, then, pride moves from an individual experience, a solitary assessment *of* the self *by* the self, to a statement about the self-in-comparison-to-others. In the moment of pride I am willing to be—indeed, I want to be—seen and judged by my peers.[151]

In the mode of competency, the self's sensation of contentment is intensified by the presence of affirming and approving community. Pride is a pleasurable mode of self-awareness, one that returns the gift of approval from others through the mutual enhancement of joy. "We know . . . that others now admire us just as we once admired those who could do what we could not. At best, we will expect others to love us and to want contact with us just as we once wanted contact with those we admired. Pride is affiliative—it allows us to hoist the victors on our shoulders and share their triumph."[152] Community becomes the site and source of our memories and lived experiences of self-worth, our ideal internalized and enacted imago. The loss of this community would be a costly casualty: the loss of the self's relational matrix.

Shame in the anthropological literature appears as the binary opposite of pride (honor). The language of object-relations theory reflects and supports this oppositional understanding. For example, in dialogue with Kohut, Morrison interprets shame as the failure to met "the goals and expectations for the 'experience-near' shape of the ideal self." Kohut's term, "experience-near," referred to language, perspective, and experience that appropriate those of the human subject, while "experience distant" described the perspective of the outside observer, and the theoretical language that accounted for the empirical data in terms of a logically flawless system rather than the "essence" of the self.[153]

Morrison uses the term "experience near" to refer to the self's subjective perception of the "goal of perfection," and the fear of rejection that follows the failure to fulfill the ideal.[154] Anthropologist Unni Wikan appropriates the same set of terms to identify shame as "experience-near" and honor as "experience-distant."[155]

Affect theory, at first, appears to lend further evidence to shame as the dialectical other of pride. Shame leaves the self with the feeling of incompetency, pride creates the competent self.[156] "The joy in pride makes us public; . . . shame makes up private."[157] Pride is in victory, shame is in failure.[158]

A closer examination of shame, however, reveals that the affect is not binary but intermodal. Binary conceptions depend upon a bound set of opposite elements. The entrance of one element into consciousness simultaneously eliminates the other, not from activity, but from consciousness. The alternation between the two functions as an on-off switch. Shame, however, depends upon the prior engagement of the affects interest-excitement and enjoyment-joy. Tomkins defined shame as an "affect auxiliary," in that it modifies the intensity of other affects. "The innate activator of shame is the incomplete reduction of interest or joy."[159] "Notice that Tomkins does not claim shame to be an 'off-switch' for interest-excitement and enjoyment-joy. . . . Triggered by an impediment to positive affect is a highly amplified impediment to further positive affect."[160] Shame attenuates rather than eliminates the other affects and emotions.

If we examine shame as a mode of being constituted by biological and cultural determinates, shame proves to be an innate, universal, transcultural endowment with chromatic rather than singular negative characteristics. Carl Schneider, reflecting upon the various terms for shame in different languages, points out that French recognizes two dimensions, represented by *pudeur* and *honte*, and then quotes Karl Riezler: "*Pudeur* is shame felt before, and warning against, an action; *honte* is felt after an action."[161] *Pudeur* refers to the "positive restraining influence that the sense of shame—as modesty or discretion—plays in human experience."[162] *Pudeur* is that experience of shame we anticipate before acting immodestly, or what Schneider calls "discretion-shame." "The sense of shame recognizes what is the proper attitude, the fitting response. Shame, then, is not 'just a feeling,' but reflects an *order of things*. Furthermore, discretion-shame not only reflects, but sustains, our personal and social ordering of the world."[163] James Fowler describes this aspect of shame as the "custodian of a self *worthy* of respected membership in the group or groups that are essential to one's self-esteem and self-worth."[164] Discretionary shame establishes a boundary upon behavior, provides the basis of conscience, and preserves one's ideal imago.

Disgrace shame (*honte*) is the unanticipated, invasive entry of another's awareness of one's self as devalued, inadequate, repugnant: "A break occurs in the self's relationship with itself and/or others. The self is no longer whole, but divided."[165] The relational matrix, ruptured by shame, shatters one's ideal imago. Communal affiliation and affirmation are self- and symbol-making; shame is iconoclastic.

Fowler notes that the experience is precipitated by the failure to meet the standards upon which one's self esteem and personhood depend. The total self is found deficient. Guilt, by contrast, addressed only an aspect of the self; shame is global.

> Guilt . . . represents self-judgement occasioned by a particular act or a specific response to a situation. In guilt, one can separate the self, and questions of its overall worthiness, from its actions. In guilt there is an honest, self-condemnation of specific acts, based upon the specific violation of a principle or standard to which one is committed. Guilt can be addressed by repentance, apology, restitution (where possible), and forgiveness. In shame, however, it is a question of coming to terms with a lack, deficit or defect of the self *qua* self.[166]

I will address various practices for healing shame in the next chapter. The pain of disgrace, shame's intrusiveness, described as "searing," "burning," an "internal hemorrhage,"[167] is overwhelming. The response of the victim is to withdraw. The Indo-European root of the word "shame" is *kam/kem*: "to cover, to veil, to hide." The root of the definition points to the core of the experience of shame, which exposes the core of the person. Scheider points out that "*impudent* means shameless, while *pudic* and *pudenda* refer to the genital organs."[168] The shameful parts are the private parts of one's self that need to be protected and covered. The members of a healthy community become guardians of one another's vulnerability.

The instability of the self, its profound need for communal embeddedness, can compel the person to maintain his or her membership at the expense of authenticity. Conditions of empathic failure, described by Winnicott, may precipitate the development of the "false self," as mentioned above. Severe distortions in empathic mirroring may lead to a variation in the compensatory reaction described by Kohut. Fowler characterizes this distortion as "perfectionist shame."

> Fearing the threat of devaluation and unworthiness, s/he becomes particularly sensitive to the standards implicit in parental expressions of approval and disapproval. . . . [T]he child tries to construct a way of being a self designed to fulfill and exceed the parental ideals of worthiness and competence. Often the false self identity, the perfectionist self, is reinforced by the parents with the sanctions of religious and/or class ideals or moral superiority. Such children, rewarded by the conditional regard of their parents, often succeed well in the other socializing environments through which they move. Often it is not until much later in their lives that they begin to come to terms with the alienation from their own core-self—from their own authentic heart that resulted from their years of living out the perfectionist program they took on to meet the conditions of worth in the first little battalion of the family.[169]

Fowler's description of a particular religious personality, who aspires to and accomplishes a high standard of ethical idealism, aptly characterizes the personality of Paul the Pharisee. While we cannot account for the etiology of Paul's personality in terms of his relationship with his primary caregiver, since Paul's autobiographical statements fail to mention his mother, his membership in the

morally uncompromising sect of the Pharisees, the demands he placed upon himself, and the ethical standards he espoused and enforced as a Jewish leader of messianic communities in the Hellenistic Diaspora suggest that by both inheritance
and intention he found himself in religious communities that corresponded to
his archaic response to shame, both as a child and as an adult. The role of perfectionist shame in the interpretation of Paul's experience is significant, as I hope
to demonstrate in the next chapter.

I further hope to demonstrate the relationship between perfectionist shame
and what Fowler calls "shame due to enforced minority status."[170] The term
describes a form of ascribed shame:

> It has little to do with the personal qualities of the family or their children.
> It has everything to do with the social environment's disvaluing of some
> qualities over which they have little or no control. [W]here social discrimi-
> nations based on minority status have become part of a child's familial iden-
> tity, even before venturing forth into the world beyond the family the child
> will be impacted and will embrace a measure of shame due to enforced
> minority status.[171]

The term *minority* is a sociological term designating relative powerlessness and
victimization.[172] The political connotations of the term belong primarily to the
modern era. In the interpretation that follows, I propose to use the term *ethnic
shame* to identify the experience of Paul as a Jewish member of the Greek Diaspora. *Ethnos* is the Greek term for otherness, referring to those who were outside
the boundaries of the nation, the heathen. Jews of the Greek Diaspora used the
term to refer to those outside their covenantal community, but in proximity of
their Hellenistic environment, the pagan Greeks, or Gentiles (Ps. 2:1). Paul later
used the term to describe Gentile Christians in Rom. 15:27.[173] The term is a two-
way verbal mirror of otherness that reflects the attitudes of each group toward the
other in the shared setting of a common culture with distinct communities. The
juxtaposition of the ideals of perfection that characterize the personal strivings of
Paul, the diasporic Jew, and the communal consensus of the Pharisaical sect to
which he belonged, against the powerfully influential Hellenistic culture of the
Greek Diaspora provides the context for understanding the chromatic modula-
tions of shame, perfectionist and ethnic, at work within the mystical experience
of this messianic Jew.

Chapter 3

Augustinian and Lutheran Interpolations of Paul, and a Diasporic Revision

Interpretations of Paul's mystical experiences within the tradition of phenomenology of religion share an approach that is similar to those found within theological traditions of interpretation.[1] Both traditions place Paul within a genre of religious experience framed by Augustine (353–430) and Martin Luther (1485–1546). William James considers Paul as manifesting the symptoms of a "divided self," which he defines as "a certain discordancy or heterogeneity in the native temperament of the subject, an incompletely unified moral and intellectual constitution."[2] The particular variety of inharmonious heterogeneity from which Paul suffered is provided as an introductory example for James's discussion of Augustine: both saints suffer from a divided will with pathological intensity.

Rudolf Otto's interpretation of Paul appeared within the context of Otto's phenomenology of the holy (*Heilig*). Otto concluded that both the reformer and the apostle shared similar mystical experiences that yielded similar conclusions. Quoting Johann Arndt, the sixteenth-century mystic:

> By this heart-felt confidence and heart-felt trust man gives his heart to God utterly, reposes only in God, surrenders himself and attaches himself to Him, unites himself with God, becomes a sharer in all that is of God and of Christ, becomes one God with God. This is simply Luther's doctrine (his

41

fides as *fiducia* and *adhaesio*), clarified and raised to a higher power. These expressions might well be found in Luther's *Of the Liberty of a Christian;* indeed their meaning is to be found there. St. Paul says the same, only more forcibly still, in Gal. 2:20 and I Cor. 6:17.[3]

Otto characterized this experience as a union between a religious subject and an intentional transcendent holy object. Standing within the tradition of Christian interpretation derived from Paul's typology of the "old man" (Rom. 6:6) and the "new creation" (2 Cor. 5:17), Otto appropriates both Pauline and Lutheran terminology to describe "the very principle and essence" of Paul's encounter: "With it is given the new attitude to sin and guilt, to law and to freedom, and, in principle, 'justification,' 'second birth,' 'renewal,' the bestowal of the Spirit, new creation, and the blissful freedom of God's children."[4] Paul's experience also provides Otto with correlating examples of the two dimensions of the sacred: the *mysterium tremendum*, which Paul experiences as the "depreciation of 'the flesh' . . . the tragedy of sin and guilt"; and the *mysterium fascinans*, "the love of God, that bears the spirit beyond its boundaries into the third heaven."[5]

More recent phenomenologists of religion continue to draw upon this tradition of hermeneutical harnessing of Augustine, Luther, and Paul in the analysis of religious experience.[6] Both Ninian Smart and Patrick Bourgeouis assume the reliability of Luke's account of Paul's Christophany, an assumption that New Testament scholars no longer share.[7] In addition to their reliance upon the traditions of Christian theology, phenomenologists of religion bring an implicitly Cartesian influence and structure to the task of interpreting Paul.[8] Before we can proceed with the task of interpreting Paul's transformative experience and its relationship to his communities, we need to pose a set of questions to guide our inquiry into Paul's experience of mystical transformation and communal formation.

AUGUSTINE INTERPOLATIONS OF PAULINE EXPERIENCE

In approaching Augustine's reading of the person Paul, we need to remember that the ethical, the metaphysical, and the real are inseparable in the Neoplatonic structure of his understanding. His quest for virtue, in the Greek and Latin culture of late antiquity, was commensurable to conformity to an ultimate order of the cosmos. Augustine's failure at moral perfection not only alienates him from divine and personal approval, but leaves him estranged from his authentic self. For Platonists the realm of transcendent forms was the realm of ultimate reality. For the Neoplatonic Christian, the God of Abraham, Isaac, Jacob, and Paul resided beyond the forms.

Augustine's interpretation of Paul, especially his experience of conversion as portrayed by Luke, provided the primary hermeneutical lens through which Western civilization has come to know him. In discussing Augustine's departure from Plato, Charles Taylor describes this enduring method of self-portrayal and self-understanding as "radical reflexivity," and attributes its development and introduction to the fourth-century bishop of North Africa: "The step was a fateful one, because we have certainly made a big thing of the first-person standpoint. The modern epistemological tradition from Descartes, and all that has flowed from it in modern culture, has made this standpoint fundamental to the point of aberration, one might think."[9] The radicality of Augustine's "radical reflexivity" is the focus, and the optic metaphor is constitutive upon "experiencing our experiencing," or how we "become aware of our awareness."[10] Augustine, who struggled to disentangle himself from the persistent philosophical marking of his earlier Manichean formation, found his struggle reflected in Paul's as presented in the Epistle to the Romans.

Augustine, however, locates the site of this struggle not in the world, or the body, but in the interior regions of Paul. Plato, who saw the world as the site upon which one could look for clues to another realm that gave them form, the realm of the *eidos*, looked outward. For Augustine, the light is inner: "But as I groaned aloud in the weariness of my heart, all my anguish reached your ears. *You knew all my longings; the very light that shone in my eyes was mine* no longer. For the light was *within*, while I looked on the world *outside*. The light was not in space, but I thought only of things that are contained in space, and in these found no place where I might rest."[11]

The "outer" world, which had been the place where bodily pleasure and sensual appetites were indulged, becomes alien and hostile and offers neither refuge in his anguish nor reflection of himself. "What differentiates it from the outer light is just what makes the image of inwardness so compelling, that it illuminates that space where I am present to myself."[12] Augustine's sensual and tormented self, manifest in a sinful body, which had been the site of contestation between his sexual imperfection and the claims of Manichean moral perfection, found escape and deliverance in an unmediated interior realm. In his conversion experience, Augustine is instructed: "Close your ears to the unclean whispers of your body, so that it may be mortified. It tells you of things that delight you, but not such things as the law of the Lord your God has to tell!"[13]

Augustine now read Paul in a different light: "Now he will see in Paul nothing but a single, unresolved tension between 'flesh' and 'spirit.'"[14] "Flesh" and "spirit" become signs for the presence of two wills in one person. The two wills in Augustine correspond to the two laws, two natures, and, in reference to the above passage, two oracles: one of the body, the other of God. The Lord, unlike the body, speaks through the apparatus of the eye and its related media. Augustine's denial of his somatic oracle, whose utterances are translated as sinful desire, is accompanied by the privileging of "hearing" God "speak" by turning his gaze upon the written word: "So I hurried back to the place where Alypius was sitting, for when I stood up to move away I had put down the book containing Paul's Epistles. I seized it and opened it, and in silence I read the first passage on which *my eyes fell. Not in reveling and drunkenness, not in lust and wantonness, not in quarrels and rivalries. Rather, arm yourselves with the Lord Jesus Christ; spend no more thought on nature and nature's appetites.*"[15]

Augustine becomes present to himself to the extent to which he abandons the communion with his body. His desire for God is equally a desire for both an unmediated self and an unmediated presence of God, which he obtains by "an untroubled gaze, a most clean embrace; to see and to cling to Her [Wisdom] naked, with no veil of bodily sensation in between."[16]

The elimination of "bodily sensations" as a reliable means of knowing either true God or authentic self leaves only the realm of the interior as the site of divine revelation and self-disclosure. Augustine "then sees in Paul, and especially in Romans, the charter for the introspective self or the premier theological category, the setting for the drama of human will and divine grace. . . . Hence, for Augustine, *the inner life of man* is the sovereign arena of God's work of redemption, and the chief problem Paul addresses in Romans in the work of the law and grace."[17] Within the hermeneutical frame of radical reflexivity, Augustine re-creates the identity of Paul, no longer dependent upon social relationships, cultural particularity, or the body, since *Homo religiosus* finds authentic personhood in the interior presence of God. Radical reflexivity and interiority become part of a philosophical tradition that will culminate with Descartes, who relocates mind, identity, and ideas to an inner space.

Augustine's reading not only removed Paul from his specific world toward a transpersonal interior, but also redefined his identity from selfhood toward subjectivity. These seismic epistemological shifts will provide not only a different perspective, the vantage point of the "I think" that is "somehow outside the world of things we experience,"[18] but a different sense of what constitutes selfhood.

The Neoplatonic structure of Augustine's theology provided the metaphysical rationale for his inward turn. The cosmology of Plotinus provided Augustine with a unified order wherein all of creation emanated from a single ultimate source. The differentiated universe was structured upon three hypostases: "Beginning with the highest, there are the One or the Good; Intelligence, *nous* . . . ; and Soul, *psyche*. . . . These three *hypostases*, the One, Intelligence or *nous*, and Soul, are related by processes Plotinus calls emanation and return—*proodos* and *epistrophe*."[19] The material world, including the body, is the apogee of emanation (*proodos*), and therefore the least stable of all forms of being, for it is on the margins of disintegration or nonbeing. Embodied existence is subject to variability and plurality since it is furthest from the source of being, the One. Contemplation, as opposed to praxis, provides the means by which the soul, fueled by desire, may return to the source of its being. The source, the One, however, resides buried within.

> Augustine's *tu antem eras interior iutimo meo et superior summo meo* (thou wert more inward than the most inward place of my heart and loftier than the highest), with its suggested identification of the inward and the higher, strikes an authentically Plotinian note. As the soul ascends to the One, it enters more and more deeply into itself: to find the One is to find itself. Self-knowledge and knowledge of the ultimate are bound up together, if not identical. Ascent to the One is a process of withdrawal into oneself.[20]

Augustine's inward turn is dictated by the demands of the Neoplatonic metaphysical structure of being. Augustine's theology, however, made a major modification in Plotinian ontology. Platonic mimesis provided the identity between the knower (soul) and the known (the One) that resided within. Augustine distinguished between the soul and its life-giving source. Christian theology distinguished between Creator and creature, provided further differentiation to the distinctions Plotinus provided in Augustine's struggle with the Manichees. Christ was intimately immanent but not identical to the soul. While dwelling within, Christ transcended the soul.[21]

Two experiences within the context of Augustine's introspective journey toward the source of his being fundamentally altered the system of Plotinus and determined subsequent interpretations of Paul that persist until this day. Plotinian progress is fueled by contemplative desire and introspective omniscience. Desire and will bring one into conformity with the One.

> Withdraw into yourself and look. And if you do not find yourself beautiful yet, act as does the creator of a statue that is to be made beautiful: he cuts away here, he smoothes there, he makes this line lighter, his other purer, until a lovely face has grown upon his work. So do you also; cut away all that is excessive, straighten all this is crooked, bring light to all that is overcast, labour to make all one glow of beauty and never cease chiselling your statue, until there shall shine out on you from it the godlike splendour of virtue, until you shall see the perfect goodness surely established in the stainless shrine.[22]

Human agency is reliable for effective transformation. Through his own tortuous struggles, however, Augustine punctures Plotinian progress.

> So let every single person take a good look at himself, because in his letter Paul has placed a mirror, in which everybody can see himself. What the law commands delights our minds, and what the law forbids delights our flesh; and our minds and our flesh struggle together; mind struggles for the law, flesh against the law, and every single individual goes about with this quarrel going on inside him. The quarrel is taking place within the individual person. . . . But notice what the mind actually said: *I see another law in my members fighting back against the law of my mind, and taking me prisoner to the law of sin, which is in my members.* So the mind is being beaten by the flesh. Let it call on the Savior for help, and avoid the deceiver's trap. What a man the apostle was, what a great and mighty athlete of God. And yet he would be taken away as a prisoner, if the man who was crucified didn't come to his aid. Therefore, when he was in deadly peril, what did he say? *Wretched man that I am, who will deliver me from the body of this death,* so that I do not commit the iniquity that delights my flesh? *The grace of God through Jesus Christ our Lord* (Rom 7:23–25).[23]

The desires of the flesh impede and defeat the desires of the mind. "Law" in Augustine's discussion is not the symbolic patterns of social interaction and rule-governed behavior. Law becomes a theo-psychological marker for the intractable and inexorable parts of human behavior, against which the will cannot press into conformity with an objectified ideal: God.

Although Augustine divides this conflict between the mind and the flesh, the division is not strictly between noetic and somatic realms. These realms are not identical to later Cartesian categories of mind and body, but represent different appetites. Augustine's estimation of the mind's capacity for self-knowledge stands opposed to Plotinus's optimistic omniscience. Through contemplation, one discerns the difference between nous and the intelligible forms, and willfully brings one's being into conformity with the One.

> When you know that you have become the perfect work, when you are self-gathered in the purity of your being, nothing now remaining that can shatter that inner unity, nothing from without clinging to the authentic man, when you find yourself wholly true to your essential nature, wholly that veritable light which is not measured by space, not narrowed to any circumscribed form, not again diffused as a thing void of term, but ever unmeasurable as something greater than all measure and more than all quantity—when you perceive that you have grown to this, you are now become very vision. Now call up all your confidence, strike forward yet a step—you need a guide no longer.[24]

Augustine's introspection fails to uncover a pure and unified self. Instead, it reveals multiple manifestations of the self and his inability to determine any authentic one. "This memory of mine is a great force, a vertiginous mystery, my God, a hidden depth of infinite complexity: and this is my soul, and this is what I am. What, then, am I, my God? What is my true nature? A living thing taking innumerable forms, quite limitless."[25] The manifold self is unstable, infinitely variable, while the mind is finitely incapable of comprehensive self-examination or apprehension. "I cannot easily gather myself together so as to be more clean from this particular infection: I greatly fear my hidden parts, which Your eyes know, but not mine. . . . Behold, I see myself in You, my truth . . . but whether I may be like this, I just do not know. . . . I beseech You, God, to show my full self to myself."[26]

Luther will make the limitations of introspective consciousness central to his interpretation of Paul and works, which I will address below. The emphasis here remains upon Augustine's experience of the limitations of will and mind in his flawed efforts to obtain moral and ontological perfection. His struggle for salvation became an exploration of the limits of the power of will. Into the tension-wrought opposition between God's unfulfillable commands, the uncontrollable impulses of desire, and the potency and impotency of will, Augustine introduces the concept of *justitia Dei*, the justice of God. A brief summary of the background to this concept is necessary in order to understand its function in Augustine's interpretation of Paul.

The cluster of cognates for Hebrew *ṣdq* convey not only the sense "to justify," but include a soteriological dimension, rather than the strict administration of the law.[27] The verb appears in the causative form, conveying the discretionary power of Yahweh to bring the condition into existence. *Haṣdîq* more accurately implied to vindicate, to acquit, to declare to be right, or to give verdict in favor

of (Exod. 23:7; Prov. 17:6; Isa. 5:23; 50:8). The term refers to a covenantal understanding of properly ordered social relations and the commitment of Yahweh to
the preservation and deliverance of Israel.

> [W]hen God and Israel mutually fulfil their covenant obligations to one
> another, a state of *ṣdqh* exists—i.e. things are as they were intended to be. . . .
> Part of this "right order of things" is violated by the very existence of the
> poor and needy, and especially of the oppressed: therefore if *ṣdqh* is to be
> established, God must deliver these unfortunates from their plight. It is this
> aspect of the Hebrew concept of righteousness which proves so intractable
> to those who would understand *ṣdqh* as *iustitia distributiva*.[28]

Justice within this Hebraic view is both law and rightly ordered relationships.
The Greek translation of the Hebrew Bible, the Septuagint (LXX), employed the
term *dikaiosynē*. The semantic slippage between the two linguistic fields becomes
manifest in several areas. "Indeed, *dikaiosynē* simply cannot take on the meaning
of 'mercy' or 'benevolence' associated with *ṣdq(h)*."[29] McGrath points out that
dikaiosynē, when used with a personal object, implies that one's cause is unjust,
and therefore punishable. Rarely does the term indicate vindication. Septuagint
usage, however, is predominant in the context meaning "to justify."[30] In Greek
diasporic Jewish communities, the term acquires new meaning in order for it to
be understood.

Augustine's biblical sources are Latin, a translation twice removed from the
Hebrew Bible, and once from the Greek Bible. Prior to Augustine, patristic theologians took little interest in justification as a central theological issue. Krister
Stendahl explains that these ante-Augustine interpreters recognized that Paul
used the terms to address specific issues of intracommunal conflict between Jews
and Gentiles.[31] McGrath also provides supportive arguments that include the
unfinished form of the Christian canon, the threat posed by Gnosticism, and the
absence of Jewish Christians as contributing factors.[32] Theologians prior to
Augustine held the power of the will as sufficient to enable humans to accom-
plish good. The Latin translation of the Greek *dikaiosynē* into *iustitia* relocates
the quality or merit upon which one is justified from conference to possession.
The Latin linguistic and cultural contexts create a distinctive anthropology of
freedom of the will, self-determination, and merit that incurs divine obligation.[33]

Augustine amplifies Paul's discussion of justification within the context of
both the Latin philosophical anthropology and legal context of individual agency
and responsibility, out of his personal experience of failed efforts at moral perfection. Sin, for Augustine, is not transgressive acts (i.e., sins), but an ontological condition (i.e., Sin). The locus of the struggle is not primarily relational but
volitional. "They, however, must be resisted with the utmost ardor and vigor who
suppose that without God's help, the mere power of human will in itself, can
either perfect righteousness, or advance steadily towards it."[34] Grace liberates the
captive will, and restores volitionality in compliance with divine demands.
"'Being justified freely by His Grace' [Rom 3:24]. It is not, therefore, by the law,

nor is it by their own will, that they are justified; but they are justified *freely by His grace*—not that it is wrought without our will; but our will is by the law shown to be weak, that grace may heal its infirmity; and that our healed will may fulfill the law, not by compact under the law, nor yet in the absence of law."[35]

Justification by faith becomes a theological doctrine as well as the disposition that cultivates the sensibilities of transcendental, as opposed to relational, receptivity. "Justification" signifies an ontological alteration of the human being through one's participation in the life of God, or the Trinity, in Augustine's theology. The fundamental ontological conception of both the human condition and human being places sin, being, grace, and God within the realm of substance. Augustine removes justification to the realm of the essential, thus making a subjective experience of self-definition constituted by volitionality the ground for the revelation of a radically different and divinely dependent sense of self. Justification, therefore, is essential for Augustine, relational for Paul.

Augustine's graft of Paul's epistolary biographical fragments into his *Confessions* dislocates Paul's identity from the relational realm to the autonomous realm. I will provide an extended description of the concept of self below. The crucial distinction here between subject(ivity) and self resides within the epistemological and ontological status of world as object in the definition of each.

LUTHER'S INTERPOLATION OF PAULINE EXPERIENCE

Augustine pressed Paul into mirroring the anguish of a divided soul torn by opposing wills. Luther's reading of the Pauline epistles, Romans in particular, shaped Paul into an overwhelmingly guilt-burdened soul in search of soteriological surety. Luther's adult religious formation in an Augustinian monastic community conditioned him toward intense introspective examinations of conscience. He also inherited Augustine's conviction that original sin nullified the power of will to bring one's depraved condition into conformity with divine will or to a condition of faith without the intervention of grace.[36]

Luther's intense preoccupation with the guilt-afflicted conscience and the inherent inability of consciousness omnisciently to oversee all sinful transgressions represent sharp departures from Augustine and Paul. Like Augustine, Luther concludes that human will unassisted by God is impotent. But Augustine affirmed the cooperative role of the will, liberated by grace, in the human-divine effort to become whole.

> For an act of choice is not just a matter of knowing what to choose: it is a matter in which loving and feeling are involved. And in man, this capacity to know and to feel in a single, involved whole, has been intimately dislocated. . . . The vital capacity to unite feeling and knowledge comes from an area outside man's powers of self-determination. Thus, for Augustine freedom can only be the culmination of a process of healing. The most fitting image of the freed will, will be one full of motion, the baffling resilience and

activity of a great fire, that can rise up again when beaten by the winds of adversity. The idea that we depend for our ability to determine ourselves, on areas that we cannot ourselves determine, is central to Augustine's "therapeutic" attitude to the relation between "grace" and "free will." It is the connection of the two, in a single healing process, that occupied all Augustine's attention.[37]

In the Neoplatonic frame of his understanding, the Christian dissolved the distinction between choosing the good and doing good. The good, human participation within the good, delighting in goodness, and consciousness of the good become a unified reality. The choice is not between good and evil, but between the real and illusions. Reality is qualitative. For Luther, the terrain of internal struggle shifts from the will to the conscience.[38] The source of Luther's painful sense of personal inadequacy and his critical indictments of the late medieval church's inadequate theology and practice of reconciliation derive from the relationship between conscience, consciousness, and efficacious works.

Luther's personal struggle for soteriological security took place within the larger structure of the Thomistic theology of penance, its accompanying Aristotelian metaphysics, and the ritual system of penitential practice. David Steinmetz identifies two penitential traditions that coexisted during this period.

> The first tradition stressed the importance of the disposition of the penitent in the confessional, the sincerity and completeness of the penitent's confession, and the necessity for finding a competent and sensitive spiritual advisor. The other tradition stressed the authority of the Church and its sacraments, the power of priestly absolution, and the consolation which the faithful can find when they turn their attention away from themselves and focus on the efficacious rites and ceremonies of the Church.[39]

Dietrich Kolde, an Augustinian friar who authored a popular catechism in German (1480), represented the first tradition. His pastoral theology exercised impressive influence upon Luther.[40] The core of Kolde's teaching stressed the crucial importance of the contrite condition of the penitent as the proper and necessary disposition for the efficacious reception of the sacrament. The successful functioning of this system depended upon the penitent's consciousness and memory, for all sins needed to be confessed in exhaustive detail. Equally important is the confessor's capacity of discernment, since he bore responsibility for determining the sincerity, hence quality, of the contrition. Kolde stressed both the importance and the inadequacy of atoning works for providing satisfaction for the offenses against God: "groaning, crying out, begging help, giving alms, private mortification of the flesh, sharp clothes or belts around the body, or by disciplines, or vigils, or humbly going on pilgrimages."[41]

The tradition that placed primary importance in the reliability of the mediating structures of the church was represented by the Augustinian observant John of Paltz, who also authored works on practical pastoral theology during the early 1500s.[42] Since the sacramental effectiveness depends upon the priest, rites and the authority of the church, Paltz emphasized the attrition, rather than the contrition, of the penitent. The minimal sign of necessary attrition was the willingness of the penitent to enter into the rite of confession.

The theological tension between the personal disposition and structural mediation operated within the larger frame of Aristotelian metaphysics as interpolated by Thomas Aquinas. Aquinas accounted for the process of change that occurred in the transmission of grace to the repentant sinner. The penitent provided the material cause: his or her disposition (contrition or attrition), confession, atoning penitential works. The confessor provided the formal cause in the act of absolution. Together, as material and form, they created a sufficient "sign" or sacrament. If the penitent failed to be sufficiently contrite, the church's form provided the compensatory grace that resulted in sacramental efficaciousness. Aquinas nevertheless stressed the priestly role of "reading" the necessary signs manifest by the penitent.[43]

Driven by both a passionate desire for divine approval from a wrathful God and an obsessive attention to his own sinful inadequacies, Luther remained haunted by both the sins he consciously committed as well as those beyond the scope of his awareness. Since his understanding and conviction weighed heavily upon the personal responsibility of the sinner for the efficacious mediation of penitential grace, Luther remained disturbed by the pressure of his forgotten or unrecognized, therefore unconfessed, sins.[44]

The inherent limitations of finite consciousness provided one source of Luther's affliction. One had to be conscious of one's sins in order to confess them and perform the atoning works. Even if the conscious mind possessed infallible recall and omniscient awareness of sins, Luther would have remained scourged by his punitive conscience. The role of conscience in Luther's theology derived from the painful role it performed throughout his life: "the will is the power to act (*virtus operandi*), whereas the conscience is the power to judge (*virtus iudicandi*)."[45]

In Luther's anthropology, the conscience belongs to the flesh of humanity and to the law of God. As part of the flesh, the conscience acts according to what it sees and feels. The conscience detects the individual acts of transgression against the law of God and judges them as discrete sins. As judge, the conscience can condemn or acquit. Since the transgressions are acts of the will, atoning prescription demands willful acts. The offense and the recompense share the same foundation:

> He [a monk] depicts God to himself as enthroned in His heaven, tailoring cowls, shaving heads, and manufacturing ropes, coarse shirts, and wooden shoes. And then he imagines that whoever clothes himself in these not only merits heaven for himself but can also help others get to heaven.
> They only pile laws upon laws, by which they torture themselves and others and make their consciences so miserable that many of them die before their time because of excessive anguish of heart.[46]

The conscience presumes not only the freedom of the will but its unlimited power to perform works that are ultimately pleasing to God. Conscience imputes qualities of potentiality to the will that this faculty does not possess, while demanding a quality of meritorious performance that leaves it unsatisfied.

The psychological pattern of neurosis is apparent and has been adequately diagnosed.[47] Luther's analysis provides a dimension of theological insight that makes his dilemma similar to the agony and insight of Augustine as he emerged from his Manichean entanglement.[48] In Luther's theology, the conscience is inseparable and identical to God. God, therefore, is known through the immediate experiences of one's tortured (in Luther's case) interiority rather than mediated through the structures of the church. The God of Luther's conscience is a deity of immanence and immediacy, devoid of transcendence and alterity. The conscience prohibits and denies the mitigating claims of revelation entrusted to the authority of the church and the efficacious operation of the sacraments administered by priests within the rite of reconciliation.

To participate in the "experience" of forgiveness, the Catholic system required the penitent to partake in the ritual acts of confession, absolution, and penance, all of which were practical manifestations of faith. Faith, in this context, became the enacted submission to the authority of the church. Faith, or the assent to the dogmatic reliability of the church's instruction, operated within the symbolic system of hierarchical communication and community: the presence of Divinity mediated and diffused throughout various interrelated signs and actions, human and material.

The medieval sacrament of penance consisted of a tertiary symbol:

> At the outer layer, or superficial level, there was the evident activity of the penitent's confession and expression of contrition and of the confessor's imposition of penance and absolution. This level was sometimes referred to as the mere sign. At a deeper level was the penitent's genuine contrition, which would include the purpose of amendment of life by turning away from the sin in practice. That was referred to as the reality to which the outer sign pointed, but which was in turn a sign of a still deeper reality. It would also be possible to place at this level the specific grace of the sacrament disposing the penitent to contrition. At the deepest level or inner core of the sacrament was that which was the ultimate reality and did not point any further, namely God's forgiveness.[49]

Penance, or what Luther pejoratively referred to as "works," was a sign that connected the extra-ritualistic activities of contrition with those priestly actions of absolution performed within the rite, to the interior disposition or sensibilities of receptivity toward the sacramental mediation of grace.

Luther's reading of Paul's epistles and personal identification with the apostle's (imputed) struggle for divine deliverance from the law ruptured the mediational structure of divine presence. Seeking refuge from his relentlessly injurious conscience, Luther found solace not in the structures of the church, its priestly power to absolve sins, or the power of the individual's will to perform the exhaustive acts of atonement. Luther took no comfort in any mediational structure, personal, priestly, or corporate. "In the grapplings of his introspective conscience, he picked up Paul and found in him God's answer to his problem, the problem of the West, and the problem of the late medieval piety of the West."[50]

> I greatly longed to understand Paul's Epistle to the Romans and nothing stood in the way but that one expression, "the justice of God," because I took it to mean that justice whereby God is just and deals justly in punishing the unjust. My situation was that, although an impeccable monk, I stood before God as a sinner troubled in conscience, and I had no confidence that my merit would assuage him. Therefore I did not love a just and angry God, but rather hated and murmured against him. Yet I clung to the dear Paul and had a great yearning to know what he meant.
>
> Night and day I pondered until I saw the connection between the justice of God and the statement that "the just shall live by his faith." Then I grasped that the justice of God is that righteousness by which through grace and sheer mercy God justifies us through faith. Thereupon I felt myself to be reborn and to have gone through open doors into paradise. The whole of Scripture took on a new meaning, and whereas before the "justice of God" had filled me with hate, now it became to me inexpressibly sweet in greater love. This passage of Paul became to me a gate to heaven.[51]

Luther found solace in immediacy.

Luther's reading of Rom. 1:17, along with 3:28, became a hermeneutical key to the entire Scriptures. Luther's translation of Rom. 3:28 is: "a man is justified by faith alone [*sola fide*]" (cf. RSV: "a man is justified by faith apart from the works of law").[52] *Sola* points not only to the grace of forgiveness apart from the institutional structures of mediation, but to the solitary, asocial character of Luther's religious experience. Even though his understanding of this experience comes by way of his reinterpretation of Paul's letters, the context in which the text is situated is no longer the hermeneutical community of the local church, or the magisterium, but the individual reader. Luther's act of interpretation ushers him into the immediate presence of God: "through open doors into paradise," and the "gate of heaven."

His rejection of ritual semiotics redefined religious experience and faith. Luther's amplification of the important role of unmediated experiences of divine presence would eventually influence subsequent traditions of theology and inform methods of phenomenological interpretation of religion.[53] "Faith" becomes a reference to the personal direct experience of God. Luther's description of his experience, interpreted through Romans, became the foundational Protestant theological principle: "Justification by faith was thus a term for a religious experience whose primary characteristic was faith or trust springing from direct encounter with the redeeming presence of Christ."[54]

Unmediated divine presence within personal experience, rather than liturgically and sacramentally mediated presence within ecclesial structures, is ephemeral and unpredictable, eluding intentional invocatory or iconic control. Faith, in the mode of "justification," referred to only one realm of Luther's experience of the Deity: *deus revelatus*. This Deity breaks the cycle of condemnation created by the conscience, which equated its punitive judgments with the totality of God. Luther's affliction, therefore, derived from the undiminished and unrelieved presence of a relentlessly present and unaccepting Deity, devoid of transcendent alterity. Luther's religious experience, subsumed under "justification," released him from the oppressive presence of an encapsulating and condemning Deity. The experience of forgiving presence, however, provided the basis for the concomitant experience of God's absence, *deus absconditus*. "Faith" became the unifying term that referred to both the experience of God's accepting presence and God's inscrutable absence.[55]

Luther's exegesis of the terms for "justice," "justification," and "justify," as they appear in Paul's Romans, derived from his early translations of Psalms 70 and 71.[56] Within the Latin translation of the Psalter, the Hebrew term for "righteousness," *sedaqah*, appears as *justitia*. Cicero's definition of justice as "that which each person received according to what each deserved" informed the Latin term. The individualistic and distributive emphasis in the Latin distorted the Hebraic definition, which operated within the context of the divine-human covenant.[57] Luther recovered these connotations of divine compassion and covenantal commitment to salvation through the utilization of "faith" (*fides*) as an interpretive theological term, *one that is rooted in and derived from his personal religious experience.* "Faith," a term Luther radically altered and expanded by his personal encounter with God, restored to the truncated Latin sense of *justitia* the Hebraic valence of God's mercy and salvation. "Perhaps unwittingly, Luther returned to an understanding of the 'righteousness of God' close to that of the Old Testament: *justitia Dei, justitia salutifera!*"[58] His religious experience informed his tropological reading of Scripture: *Sic iustita tropologice est fides Christi* (thus righteousness in a tropological sense is faith in Christ).[59] His experience also informed the creation of a set of interlocking master and meta-tropes that have dominated New Testament exegesis until recently. Luther, turning to Romans 3 and reading it against his religious experience and exegesis of Psalm 71, finds three dimensions in the term *justified* instead of one:

> First, when he punishes the unrighteous, for then he shows himself as righteous and righteousness as manifestly acclaimed by the punishment of our unrighteousness. . . .
> Secondly, in an indirect and relative way as in the case of opposites which, when they are placed next to each other, are more enhanced in their individual character than when each stands by itself. In the same way, God's righteousness is the more beautiful, the more detestable our righteousness is. . . .
> Thirdly, when he justified the godless and infuses his grace or when one believes that he is righteous in his words. For by such believing he justifies, i.e., he reputes as righteous. This is why this righteousness is called the righteousness of faith or of God.[60]

Faith, in Luther's reconstruction, operates privately within the transcendental realm of the divine-human relationship. His radical iconoclasm made the interior experience of divine presence the basis for interpreting all signs, Word and Sacrament. The Word of God, as Scripture, became the sole external sign that contradicts the singular voice of a condemning conscience: God. This singular objective sign, however, depended upon the internal, subjective correlative for verification. The internal experience of divine acceptance, which Luther called the Holy Spirit,[61] confirmed the scriptural interpretation. Experience "reads" Scripture. Faith becomes existential trust, unsupported by objective social, literary, or ritual symbols and practices, when the interior experience of divine presence becomes unobtainable. In both realms, *deus revelatus* and *deus absconditus*, faith became redefined as subjective and radically reflexive.

Luther's negation of the soteriological importance of works also removed this ritualistic praxis from the symbolic realm. Works are no longer penitential signs of reconciliation, but the enacted response to one's vocation. The former is directed toward God, the latter toward humans.[62]

Augustine's and Luther's reconstructions of Paul may be summarized as follows: Paul becomes the introspective heroic archetype in the struggle of opposing wills for Augustine, and the sin-sick soul in search of God for Luther; his predominate concern is for individual salvation and the forgiveness of sin; the site of the conflict between his bondage to sin (law: opposing wills to Augustine; unplacable demands for works for Luther) and the encounter with God (grace) is the interior realm wherein both God and self become manifest; the body becomes the oracle of sinful utterances (Augustine), and the site upon which penitential acts are performed (Luther); Paul's body becomes both transhistorical and transcultural, no longer socially embedded or defined; "justification by faith" displaces ritualistic-symbolic mediation of Divinity and self; Paul's identity shifts from one that is relationally mediated and socially constructed to one that is understood in terms of interior location and unmediated experience.

In other words, Paul becomes progressively *less* a self and more of a subject. Why, we must ask, have the force and influence of Augustine and Luther persisted and prevailed in the (mis)interpretation of Paul? Equally important, why have "justification by faith" and the accompanying categories of "law" or "works," along with "grace," become the theological categories for interpreting Western Christianity in both the professional realm of the academy and the pastoral realm of ministry? I cannot completely answer these two questions in this current project. A few tentative answers and trajectories, however, are relevant. Although both Augustine and Luther experience the Divine in ways that are less socially and ritualistically mediated, emphasizing interior, subjectively affective encounters, the range of the sensory realm progressively narrows. Augustine *hears* the voice of God through the song of a child, directing him to *read* Paul in Rom. 8:13–14; Luther *reads* Rom. 1:17 and is ushered into the presence of God. The interior realm, understood as a location that does not include the body, all of its senses, and the relational ties and experience of community, becomes the site of divine revelation and the disclosure of a new identity.

Augustine and Luther encounter the Divine in the midst of crisis. Precipitated by what? Although separated by over a millennium, their individual crises belong to an enduring tradition of self-definition in Western civilization. Both men are heirs to and agents of a cultural definition of identity rooted in volitionality. Agency and power of intentionality, seated in the consciousness and determinacy of the individual, reside at the heart of the Western project. The crisis experienced by Augustine and Luther is the result of the encounter with insurmountable and uncontrollable limits to their ability to determine and enact an acceptable sense of self. For Augustine, the problem of an opposing and intractable will prohibits him from entering into the state of moral perfection: the cessation of carnal delight, desire, and activity. "I had turned my eyes elsewhere and while I stood trembling at the barrier, on the other side I could see the chaste beauty of Continence in all her serene, unsullied joy, as she modestly beckoned me to cross over and to hesitate no more."[63] Augustine willfully desires to cross over, but the "barrier" that prohibits his consummation with Continence does not succumb to his willful intentions. "The mind gives an order to the body and is at once obeyed, but when it gives an order to itself, it is resisted. The reason, then, why the command is not obeyed is that it is not given with the full will. So there are two wills in us, because neither by itself is the whole will, and each possesses what the other lacks."[64]

Augustine's experience with the interior visitation of the Divine resolves his crisis in the creation of a new identity.

> "Can you not do what these men and these women do? Do you think they find strength to do it in themselves and not in the Lord their God? Why do you try to stand in your own strength and fail? Cast yourself upon God and have no fear. Cast yourself upon him without fear, for he will welcome you and cure you of your ills." Somehow I flung myself down beneath a fig tree and gave way to the tears which now streamed from my eyes, the sacrifice that is acceptable to you. (Psalm 50:17)[65]

Augustine discovers another source of power that will assist in the struggle toward moral completion. But he experiences this power at the limit of his own powerlessness. While maintaining the centrality of agency and willful determinacy, Augustine's sense of self now incorporates dimensions of relinquishment and submission.

Luther's struggle as the repentant sinner responsible for penitential works also defines him in terms of agency and willful determination. The limitations he experiences, which threaten his sense of self, are the result of the failure of his volitional activity to quell his conscience. His interior experience of divine presence alters his identity from the condemned agent incapable of performing divinely pleasing works to the forgiven recipient of divine grace, which is the fruit of the sacrificial works of Christ. Luther, like Augustine, experiences a new unconditional Deity and a new identity in the relinquishment of power.

> Inasmuch as every created being gives such testimony, it cannot happen that one who is full of his own righteousness can be filled with the righteousness of God. He fills only those who hunger and thirst. Whoever, therefore, is satiated with his own truth and wisdom is incapable of comprehending the truth and wisdom of God, for they can be received only in emptiness and

vacuum. Let us, therefore, say to God: Oh, that we might *willingly* be emptied that we might be filled with thee; Oh, that I may *willingly* be weak that the strength may dwell in me; *gladly* a sinner that thou mayest be justified in me, gladly a fool that thou mayest be my wisdom, gladly righteous that thou mayest be my righteousness![66]

Luther's stress upon willful emptiness, willful weakness, parallels Augustine's throwing himself down and yielding to tears, both of which are pleasing to God. Volitionality remains central to their experience and understanding of Paul, even in the willful relinquishment of will. Their actions, which lead to personal salvation, find reflection and inspiration in the kenotic trajectory of the preexistent Christ, who becomes incarnate through the willful relinquishment of power. This grand and enduring mythos is central to Western Christianity's doctrines of atonement.[67] In moving across the boundaries between the metaphysical and the physical, transcendent and immanent, divine and human, unseen and visible, Christ also provides continuity across distinct and separate realms of identity. Atonement conceived as a narrative of transactional movement from power to powerlessness would exert enduring appeal within a civilization that idealized the power of will and made individual agency central to morality and identity. A kenotic conception of Christ and atonement addresses the crisis of volitionality as continuity to those whose primary sense of self seeks integrity, coherence, and continuity in personal agency.

CREATING A HERMENEUTICAL CONTEXT: PAUL AS DIASPORIC PHENOMENON

Resolving the questions and issues of Paul's identity, cultural composition, and relationship to first-century Judaism is inseparable from the struggle to interpret the phenomena of the Jewish Diaspora and its relationship to Palestinian Judaism. The geographical, religious, and interpretive terrain pertinent to this part of the study E. P. Sanders defines as follows: "'The Diaspora' is short for 'the Greek-speaking Diaspora of approximately 100 BCE to CE 100': the Diaspora reflected in the writings of Philo, Josephus, many of the books of the New Testament, some of the Apocryphal or Deutero-canonical works, and a large number of the 'Old Testament Pseudepigrapha.' On a map, one may draw a curving line from Alexandria to Rome, skipping only Palestine."[68]

The Palestinian lacuna preserved in Sanders's cultural cartography has been closed by contemporary scholarship. Richard Batey, John Dominic Crossan, F. Gerald Downing, and Burton Mack portray Palestine during the period in question as inundated with and inseparable from the Greek culture and literature that characterized the regions of Jewish settlements beyond Palestine.[69] In the struggle to clarify the relationship between hinter- and homeland, scholars assigned the designation of "Hellenism" and "Judaism," respectively. These dipolaritous terms defined opposing centers of religious and cultural gravity in early scholarship.[70]

"Judaism" (*Ioudaïsmos*) first appears in the first-century BCE propaganda literature intended to strengthen the unity between Egyptian diasporic Jews and those living in Palestine under Hasmonean rule.[71] *Ioudaïsmos*, as used by the redactor of Jason of Cyrene's second version of the history of the Maccabees, describes the heroic efforts of Judas Maccabeus to remove the Seleucid army from and end the profanation of the temple. "Jason makes it clear that their [Jason the Oniad, Menelaus, and their followers] deadly sin was not greed or civil strife, but neglect of the Torah in their uncontrolled mania for Hellenism."[72] The unintentional irony is evident in the authorship and the linguistic function of the term "Judaism," and, as we shall see, the operational "Hellenism." Jason of Cyrene, who composed the work that became 2 Maccabees, is considered to be a Greek-speaking Jew from outside Palestine. Unlike 1 Maccabees, written in Hebrew, 2 Maccabees is composed in Greek. While his attitude toward Greek civilization is hostile, the conventions he uses to exhort the Jews toward observance of the Torah depend upon the understanding of Greek rhetoric and cultural attitudes of his diasporic readers.[73]

> Jason the Cyrene narrated the history of Judas Maccabaeus and his brothers, of the purification of the greatest of temples and the dedication of the altar, and also was against Antiochus Epiphanes and his son Eupator, and of the manifest interventions from heaven in favor of those who vied with one another in fighting manfully for Judaism: few though they were, they took the spoils of the entire country and drove out the barbarian hordes and recovered the world-renowned temple and freed the city and reestablished the laws which were on the point of being abolished. (II Maccabees, 2:19–22)[74]

The term *Ioudaïsmos* is found in neither the Hebrew Bible nor the Talmud, two sacred texts, but is the creation of a Jewish, Greek-speaking author/editor.[75] In the passage above, the term operates in oppositional distinction to "barbarian," from the Greek *barbaros*, "non-Greek, foreign."[76] The rhetorical effectiveness of the two terms depends upon the identification with and the familiarity of the diasporic reader with the ideals of Greek culture and the history of that civilization's struggle to defend itself from, in particular, the Persians. "Judaism" displaces the position previously occupied by the term "Hellenism." "Judaism" supplants the implicit reference to the Hellenes and acquires the ennobling character of the previous Greek victors. By subverting the standards of the alien culture of the Greeks, and by bringing them into service against the Hellenistic, the rhetorical strategy places the Greeks in the same linguistic position reserved for the *barbaros* and its denegrative connotations.

Hellenismos is a Greek term "and is limited to the philologically unobjectionable dominance of 'common Greek' as opposed to dialects and barbarisms."[77] Hengel contends that the term operates within the limits of linguistic distinctions, but the cultural valuations (and devaluations) are inextricable from the term. *Hellenismos* as "pure Greek" is used in opposition to *barbarikos*.[78] Second Maccabees is the earliest example of the expanded use of the term to include the adoption of a foreign culture and its inevitable idolatry and apostasy from Judaism. Again, the word operates as an oppositional boundary term between cultural styles, political power, and an indication of purity in the cultic identity of the Jews in relationship to the temple. The rhetoric establishes clearly discrete and unequivocal polar territories of identity.[79]

The strategy of the rhetoric, however, again depends upon the diasporic reader's familiarity with Greek culture and a common horizon of values and meaning between Jews and Greeks in whose culture and civil life they shared. By placing *Hellenismos* in the position of the *barbaros*, *Ioudaïsmos* (Judaism) acquires the valorization that Greeks reserved for their own sense of self and cultural superiority. Goldstein notes that the Greeks retained the memory of fifth-century war against the Persians and the betrayal of those who became complicitous with Cyrus, the ruler of the Medes. Acts of collaboration with the ruler of the Medes were described as "Medize." The implied antonyms of "Medize" and "Medism" were "Hellenize" and "Hellenism," which would mean "be loyal to the Greek cause."[80]

The author and audience of 2 Maccabees not only possessed an intimate knowledge of Greek culture and history, but the strategies employed in the narrative reveal a structure of consciousness among Jews in the Diaspora whose values and sense of self are intimate with and dependent upon intersubjective knowledge of the dominant culture. We will return to this relationship between intersubjectivity and language, but for now, it is important to note that "Diaspora" refers not only to culture, region, and language, but to a peculiar and distinct structure of consciousness.

Scientific appropriations of the term *Hellenism* were attempts to describe the development of new cultural forms that were the result of invasive interaction between Greek and oriental traditions. "It was J. G. Droysen who first gave the term 'Hellenism' the significance it now bears, by transferring it to the epoch of Greek expansion in the Orient which begins with Alexander the Great. [Quoting Droysen:] 'Greece, invading the life of the world of the East and fertilizing it, developed that Hellenism, in which the paganism of Asia and Greece, indeed antiquity itself, was destined to culminate.'"[81] The history of analytical applications of this term often has more in common with the strategic intent of 2 Maccabees than with Droysen's more nuanced sense of innovation. Droysen viewed the culmination of Hellenism as the integration of diverse cultures into a grand unity. Scholars in the nineteenth-century disciplines of history and religion would term the development *syncretism*, while students of the New Testament would readopt the oppositional tandem of "Judaism" and "Hellenism."[82]

Diaspora Judaism, and its cognate Palestinian Judaism, is understood as the religious tradition that shares the undiluted continuity with ancient Judaism, and most importantly protected from the corrupting influences of Greek culture. Diaspora Judaism therefore becomes the religion of lesser concentrated influence distorted by its exposure to an overwhelming and surrounding culture of Hellenism.

According to this interpretive schema of distinct realms of influence, Paul and the religion he promulgated become the manifestation of ancient faith preservation and regeneration, or symptomatic of diasporic adulteration. The following examples are representative of the latter:

> Did Paul rightly understand the law as the saving principle of the old covenant? I think that we must answer this question in the negative, for in my opinion Paul succumbed to a characteristic distortion of vision which had its antecedents in the spiritual outlook of Judaic Hellenism.[83]

> The question is, how could it have been possible for an adherent of a Judaism that was quite uncontaminated by foreign influences to create a religion (or give the impetus to and assist in the creation of a religion) which was to a considerable extent non-Judaism and which after no very long time became a half-Jewish, half-pagan faith? . . . it is clear that a man who spoke and wrote excellent Greek, and frequented Greek and Hellenized cities, would naturally hold, even if he were not conscious of the fact and did not mean to do so, any number of religious opinions which a purely Palestinian Jew like Jesus could not have held, since Jesus never went beyond the borders of his own land.[84]

Now consider the following as an example of Paul as an impermeable vessel of Judaism.

> Paul belongs to Late Judaism. Whatever he received in the way of influences such as Comparative Religion [syncretism] takes account of came mainly through this channel. The suggestion that apart from this he might be personally and directly affected by "*Oriental*" influences calls for very cautious consideration. . . .
>   It is further to be remarked that Late Judaism was no longer in his time *so open* to external influences that any and every kind of religious conception which was floating about anywhere in the Orient could necessarily impose itself on Paul's mind through this medium. The period of assimilation was, speaking generally, at an end. . . .
>   A still further point is that any one whose thought moves in the Apocalyptic system created by the books of Daniel and Enoch is not so much exposed to, as withdrawn from, the action of free *Oriental influence*. He is already *saturated* with those elements in regard to receptivity which *the Jewish mind* possesses and the tendency to assimilation, and possesses it not as something *foreign* to himself but as *Jewish*. *Apocalyptic tends to produce in him immunisation as against further syncretistic infection.*[85]

In the first two passages, by Schoeps and Klausner, respectively, Paul's location in the Greek Diaspora is a highly threatened position. His identity as a Jew, defined by his relationship to Torah and covenant, is at risk since his immersion in the surrounding Greek culture no longer affords an accurate interpretation of the sacred traditions.

Klausner's commentary moves toward imagistic depictions of the threat. The concluding phrase associates the purity of Palestinian Judaism, represented by Jesus, in terms of geographical borders. The logic of this reasoning depends upon equating boundaries with purity. The antithesis, therefore, equates the Diaspora as a permeable or even breached boundary, which subverts the integrity of religious identity and exposes its host to the impurity of foreign influences. Droysen's vision of Hellenism as a source of cultural fertility here reappears in the form of mongrelized offspring, or monster (half-Jewish/half-pagan).

Schweitzer's passage, the last and most graphic of the three, presents the problem of diasporic influences in terms of symptomatology. Again the issue of boundaries moves throughout the text ("Judaism . . . no longer open to external influences"). As with the others, the location endangers, but Schweitzer adds the metaphoric dimension from cellular biology to describe the effective mechanisms by which healthy resistant boundaries of distinctiveness are maintained. The apocalyptic, Schweitzer's crucial contribution to understanding Paul's mysticism and identity as a Jew,[86] operates osmotically as a source of higher concentration to maintain the cerebral cellular walls of religious integrity against the Asian contagion. Schweitzer's conception of "syncrestic" as the toxic strain of influence is remarkably similar to the attitudes of German scholars in the nineteenth-century discipline of *Religionswissenschaft*. Herman Usener described the development of new religions, which were the results of syncretism, as *Religionsmischerei*.[87] Usener "regarded the phenomenon of syncretism as an unprincipled abandonment of the faith of the fathers," a statement that the Maccabeans could recognize.

The categorical distinctions between Palestinian Judaism and diasporic/Hellenistic Judaism, which shaped the interpretive struggle to define Paul and Pauline Christianity, collapsed under the analysis of W. D. Davies.[88] Davies resolved the tension between the polarities by reshaping the relationship between Palestinian and diasporic culture from dichotomy into Hellenistic continuity.

> Two things stand out clearly, however, first, that Palestinian Judaism is not to be viewed as a watertight compartment closed against all Hellenistic influences: there was a Graeco-Jewish atmosphere even at Jerusalem itself, and, secondly, we can be certain that Judaism in the period before A.D. 70 was not as reserved and cautious as it afterwards became. There is thus no justification for making too rigid a separation between the Judaism of the Diaspora and that of Palestine, and particularly is this true in the case of a man like Paul whose home was, most probably, a bit of Jerusalem outside Palestine.[89]

Davies's method demonstrated that the "Hellenistic" material in Paul is actually derived from the traditions of Palestinian Judaism, a Judaism permeated with Greek cultural influences.[90] While most modern scholarship on the Diaspora and Paul does not maintain the earlier dichotomies, they have a way of reappearing and informing the thinking of scholarship which denies their reliably. Consider the following:

> Although in Palestine as a whole, with its numerous Greek cities, Hellenization became general and penetrated by numerous byways even into Hasmonean Jerusalem, Jerusalem Jewry was strong enough to defend itself, to counter force with force, and intellect with intellect.[91]

> If the entire judicial framework was Hellenistic, it was natural that the principles of Hellenistic law itself should have penetrated Jewish life.[92]

> An intensive penetration of the territory [Palestine] began especially during the long rule of the vigorous Ptolemy II Philadelphus (282–246 BC).[93]

> A further indication of the penetration of Greek thought into Jerusalem is the claim that the Jews were related to the Spartans through Abraham, which presumably arose as early as the third century BC among circles which were well-disposed towards the Greeks.[94]

> The penetration of Greek education into Jewish circles in Palestine began in analogy with the expansion of the Greek language as early as the third century BC.[95]

> The emphasis on discontinuity springs, in part, from the Christian view that post-biblical Judaism was a debased religion. In part, however, it is merely the result of focusing on new influences that were penetrating Palestine.[96]

Each author of the preceding passages supports the hellenization thesis over the dipolartous conception of Judaism uninfluenced by Greek cultural hegemony. But the influence of Droysen and the persistence of latent theological Protestant images reveal the presence of a metaphor-metaphysic.

In this figurative portrayal the operative tropes of virginity and fertilization, purity and defilement, implicitly control the ordering of the relationship between the two cultures. Although these interpretive tropes are governed by theological and ideological commitments, they also point to another possibility, or, perhaps, more accurately, a difficulty. The struggle for an adequate language for diasporic phenomena reveals the problematic within the traditions of Western thought faced with variable forms and heterogeneous structures.

E. P. Sanders recognizes the interpretive issues regarding the relationship between Paul and Judaism. Sanders describes the method utilized by comparative religion:

> the history of the comparison of Paul and Judaism is a particularly clear instance of the general need for methodological improvement in the comparative study of religion. What is difficult is to focus on *what* is to be compared. We have already seen that most comparisons [by New Testament scholars] are of reduced *essences* (faith versus works; cf. liberty versus law, a spiritual religion versus a materialistic and commercial religion and the like) or of *individual motifs*. Neither of these constitutes an adequate category of comparison.[97]

We have seen that in phenomenological traditions, including phenomenology of religion, the investigation of essence provided a means of describing the invariable beneath the variable appearances, and creating an integrated understanding of religion and religious being. Sanders's criticism of the motific approach is that it ignores the context and significance of discrete elements within the religion as defined as a comprehensive system. Function and operation are eliminated by the comparison.[98]

Sanders poses a corrective to this neglect, a reorientation upon which his analysis of Paul proceeds:

> A pattern of religion, defined positively, is the description of how a religion is perceived by its adherents to function. "Perceived to function" has the sense not of what an adherent does on a day-to-day basis, but of *how getting in and staying in are understood*. The way in which a religion is understood to admit and retain members is considered to be the way it "functions." This may involve daily activities, such as prayers, washing and the like, but we are interested not so much in the details of these activities as in their role and significance in the "pattern": *on what principles are they based*, what happens if they are not observed and the like. A pattern of religion thus has largely to do with the items which a systematic theology classifies under "soteriology." "Pattern of religion" is a more satisfactory term for what we are going to describe, however, than "soteriology." For one thing, it includes more than soteriology usually does: it includes the logical beginning-point of the religious life as well as its end, and it includes the steps in between. The better descriptive term is "pattern of religion."[99]

Sanders's alternative method proposes several foundational assumptions that govern his interpretation and shape his results. Perception, for Sanders, is primarily cognitive, unlike the phenomenological use of the term to describe an organic experience that unifies intellection, affect, and bodily mediation. The central cognitive operation is comprehending the basis upon which belonging and relatedness operate: "getting in and staying in." Then Sanders makes an interesting shift from the implicitly practical activities implied by "getting in" and "staying in." The former clearly refers to rituals of initiation that provide enacted passages into the community, family, or nation or ritualistically confirm one's inherited kinship, while the latter addresses identifiable behaviors, ritual, ethical, social, that maintain and reinforce one's participation and solidarity with the group. Sanders, however, does not found his method upon traditional Durkheimian functionalism, but makes yet another qualification: "but we are interested not so much in the details of these activities as in their role and significance in the 'pattern:' *on what principles are they based*."

Principles, in Sanders's method, operate as a boundary mechanism, a linguistic demarcation of point of entry ("getting in"). The highly cognitive character of this marker organizes the field of religious phenomena into propositional classifications. Boundaries are established according to the *principles* that distinguish one from another. Sanders, in effect, brackets praxis and makes an *eidetic* reduction of religious phenomena to *noetic* principles. He then provides a clarifying analogue, comparing the functional principles to the role of a category in systematic theology, "soteriology." The subtext to Sanders's methodological description is replete with pragmatic performances: "getting in" rituals of initiation (baptism, bar mitzvah), "staying in" rites of communion (Eucharist, atonement). The explicit naming of soteriology provides a theological analogue or emblem for his pattern or principle. His qualification of the term, however, is based on its inadequacy as a comprehensive description of his methodological principle: "it includes more than soteriology," a logical beginning point such as initiation in terms of ritual. But religious logic could point to several different beginnings, including mythology, cosmology, protology, and "the end" of religious life funeral rites, or eschatology.

If we follow the clue provided by Sanders's analogical illustration, one possible conclusion is that Sanders's methodological principle is actually a theological method based upon theological principles. Compare the following description of their origin:

> The emerging evangelical faction of Wittenberg, associated with Martin Luther, chose to define itself in relation to an explicitly doctrinal criterion: the doctrine of justification by faith alone. . . . The affirmation that the doctrine of justification is the *articulus stantis et cadentis ecclesiae* confirms the importance of this doctrine to the self-definition of the Lutheran church, as is evident from Luther's ecclesiological criterion concerning the identity of the true church.
>
> Once the Lutheran church became established as a serious and potentially credible alternate to the medieval church, self-definition through doctrinal formulations once more became of crucial importance to the catholic church. The significance of the Council of Trent lies in its perception of the need for the catholic church to define *itself*—rather than define *heretics*—at the doctrinal level. Earlier medieval councils had tended simply to condemn heretical opinions, thus defining views which placed those who entertained (or were prepared to admit to entertaining) them as heretical, and thus lying outside the bounds of the church. In other words, they defined who was *outside* the bounds of the church, on the assumption that all others, whose views did not require definition, were *within* its bounds. The Council of Trent, in discussing the doctrine of justification felt obliged to do more than simply censure Lutheran ideas: it defined catholic ideas with unprecedented clarity. In an extensive series of anathemas, Trent defined who was outside the bounds of the church; it also, however, provided a remarkably comprehensive statement of catholic doctrine, thus providing an explicit definition of the intellectual (and hence the social) bounds of the church.[100]

The principle, or in Sanders's term, "pattern of religion," that the heretical protesting community chose to establish its identity over and against the magisterial church of Rome and the power of its papacy, was "justification by faith." One's identity or usual point of entry into Protestant community was no longer mediated by a ritual or graphic icon or symbol, or by the ecclesial structure itself, but by a confessional proposition. This theological pattern is a form of Protestant orthodoxy applied to the study of comparative religion.[101]

Sanders concludes the description of his method by arranging the motivational order of human behavior into one which places the priority upon cognition.

> A pattern of religion, while not being the same as systematic theology and while not having to do with many of the speculative questions of theology, *does* have to do with thought, with the *understanding* that lies behind religious behaviour, not just with the externals of religious behaviour. Thus from cultic practice one may infer that the cult of a given religion was *perceived by its adherent to have a certain function* in their religious life. It is the adherents' *perception* of the significance of cult that is important, as well as the fact that the cult was observed.[102]

This passage is tension-filled for several reasons, most of which are beyond the scope of this project. Two are pertinent. Sanders makes an analogy between the manner in which systematic theology organizes its materials around key categories of understanding: "soteriology," "pneumatology," "grace," "atonement," and "sin," for example, are concepts that shape both the ordering of theological projects *and* religious behavior. Theology, thus understood, is a cognitive, discursive form of intellection.

The analogue to systematic theology understood in terms of cognitive principles applied to "patterns of religion" is religion understood according to the interpretation of the underlying cognitive principles that determine religious behavior. We should note that Sanders has chosen a particular definition of theology upon which to base or clarify his method. Theology, thus understood, privileges understanding over experience ("behaviour"), and has become the primary expression of religion in the modern academy. Historically this definition of doing theology has been considered secondary, in contrast to theology understood as the experience of God.[103] We shall return to this issue later. My point, at this moment, is Sanders's decision to locate himself in relation to a specific understanding of an activity called theology, with a ratiocentric locus.

The second issue is the disparity between the description of the first part of Sanders's analogy of theology/religion as conception and its application to the example he provides. His use of the term "perceived" as the analogue to "understanding" and "thought" are at odds with one another. Perception is not the analogue to conception. Further, perception performs a central function in the phenomenology of Merleau-Ponty and Scheler, both of which inform the method of this project. The phenomenological use of the term points to an experiential realm that both precedes and eludes comprehensive systematic cognition. Although Sanders uses cultic activity as an example, and much of his discussion on Judaism and Paul addresses religious praxis, religious experience remains in the background.

Sanders's emphasis upon cognition over perception and conceptuality behind experientiality applies not only to "patterns of religion" but also to Paul. In addition to the Reformation orientation in his methodology, the priority Sanders gives to the ratiocentric ordering of Paul's identity and behavior indicate the reliance upon an "Enlightenment anthropology."[104] According to this view, one understands (correctly), then behaves accordingly (properly). This theonoetic primacy can be found throughout much of modern scholarship on Paul.[105] Sanders's declaration of his methodological intentions helps to clarify the critical questions before us: (1) who is Paul, not only in terms of cultural composition of his identity and his social location; but related and perhaps more important: (2) how do we define and interpret his sense of identity, or more precisely, his sense of self?

The questions are both crucial and complex, for Paul is one of the sources of our understanding of personhood in the West as well as the subject of our inquiry. Along with Augustine, Luther, and Descartes, Paul has figured in the philosophical and theological projects to disentangle the individual from the collective, one of the major projects and achievements in the Western intellectual and political tradition. While we cannot recount or outline the genealogy of his monumental accomplishment, some summary statements that shape traditional interpretations of Paul are necessary in order to reinterpret him. (One of the ironies is that Paul as a source of inspiration of this emancipatory project may have suffered the fate of having the integrity of his self obscured and unrevealed in the resulting concept of individuality he inspired.) Augustine's interpretation of Paul, especially his experience of conversion as portrayed by Luke, provided the primary hermeneutical lens through which Western civilization has come to know him.[106]

Paul's struggle is neither the crisis of opposing will nor conscience. In Paul we encounter the crisis of creolization, for in the culturally heterogeneous composition of his identity and experience reside the sources of his religious creativity and his religious struggle that are responses to the condition of a Pharisee in the Hellenistic Jewish Diaspora.

Chapter 4

A Phenomenology
of Reconciliation

Transformations of Self and Sacrality

A phenomenology of religion that interprets those experiences of Paul that inform and constitute his embodiment, enactment, and articulation of reconciliation address the experiential terrains of mystical transformation, the creation of ethnically heterogeneous community, and the facilitation of intracommunal reconciliation. Informed by the preceding discussion, my interpretation proceeds according to an understanding of Paul as a self whose consciousness is determined by relational modes of being, shaped by communities located within the Hellenistic Jewish Diaspora. What is the convergent relationship between these elements and the modalities of the sacred that Paul experiences?

Our points of entry through which we attempt to move toward the realm of the sacred are the two related realms of the *Lebenswelt* as defined by Husserl: the structures of the pre-given world, and the cultural forms that mediate Paul's consciousness.[1] The first or more classic phenomenological sense of the term is used in this context to define the pervasive Hellenistic world that enveloped Paul and other Jews of the Greek Diaspora. The second sense of *Lebenswelt* is referred to here as the *Mitwelt* or the immediate relational nexus that shaped Paul's basic consciousness and his most fundamental sense of self. The *Mitwelt* is the realm of self-consciousness: not only the awareness of one's self, but that consciousness

shaped by beings in relationship to one another and dependent upon both proximity and communion for its existence. "Community," or what Ferdinand Tön-
nies referred to as *Gemeinschaft,* that intimate circle of bonded togetherness,
approximates Scheler's *Mitwelt,* but cannot serve as a synonym. The *Mitwelt* is
not only a social category but the primary form of shared consciousness, feeling,
and morality.[2] The *Mitwelt* is the intersubjective composition of community that
enables the collective interactions of a distinct group to create the transparent
ordering of experience called their "world."

As noted in chapter 3, the *Lebenswelt* of Jews in the Greek Diaspora was suf-
fused with Greek culture. "It was impossible for the Jews of the Diaspora to escape
being profoundly affected by the civilization of their adopted lands. Greek ideas
and customs penetrated their lives. Even Hebrew thoughts and religious conceptions came to the young generation through the medium of Greek translations."[3] Hellenistic cities were sites of cultural exchange, especially those of the
Eastern frontier.[4] Antioch, for example, contained Greek inscriptions, while
the population outside the city spoke Aramaic.[5] "Josephus wrote his history of
the Jewish War in Aramaic for the benefit of the Eastern diaspora."[6] While the
first few generations of immigrants maintained their Hebrew and Aramaic
tongues, Greek eventually became their native language. The translation of the
Torah into Greek during the third century BCE became "a mighty agent in the
fusion of the Hebraic and the Hellenic strains that modified the creative spirit of
the subsequent generations."[7] The translation in effect sealed the Diaspora's
Lebenswelt for those Jews born into its unity of perception. Paul, as a first-century
(CE) child of the Diaspora, developed the perception of one both related to and
rent from the seamless cultural consciousness of the dispersion.

While almost every datum of information is contested about Paul, and the
resolution of the biographical variables are beyond this project's scope, this interpretation proceeds in accordance with the following plausibilities. Paul (formerly
Saul), a Jew born of Aramaic- and Hebrew-speaking Jewish parents of the tribe
of Benjamin, living in the eastern Diaspora, perhaps Tarsus, became a member
of the holiness sect of Pharisees and persecuted fellow messianic Jews who
accepted the humiliated and murdered Messiah, Jesus, as the fulfillment of apocalyptic promises to Israel, and extended, by his death and resurrection, the
covenantal inclusion of the Gentiles through the prophetical call and apostleship
of Paul.

Paulos, according to Joseph Fitzmyer, is a Roman name appearing here in
Greek.[8] *Saulos* appears only in Acts (7:58; 8:1; 9:1). The name *Paul* is rare among
residents of the eastern Greek dispersion who are not Roman, "and does not occur
at all among contemporary Jews."[9] Hengel notes that the translation from the
Latin *cognomen* to Greco-Roman *nomen* occurs when Paul moves "from a Jewish-
Christian to a pagan environment as missionary to the Gentiles" (Acts 13:9).[10]
As used by Luke, the name marks the traversing of ethnic boundaries, and
the transformation of relationships, identity, and vocation. The term "a Hebrew
born of Hebrews" implies both reference to vernacular traditions and nativity.

F. F. Bruce suggests that "Hebrews," as opposed to "Hellenists," attended syna-gogue services conducted in Hebrew but spoke Aramaic at home.[11] Philo's use of the term "Hebrews" includes Aramaic.[12] "In the dispersion throughout the Graeco-Roman world, the Hellenists [natives of the Greek Diaspora] would be the majority of resident Jews while the Hebrews would be recent immigrants from Palestine or members of families which made a special point of preserving their Palestinian ways."[13] The term also appears, in part, during Paul's epistolary debate with his Corinthian opponents (2 Cor. 11:22) to emphasize descent from aboriginal ancestors born in Palestine.[14] Benjamin was the only patriarch born in the land (Gen. 35:17). By lineage and language, Paul could lay claim to promi-nent status both in the Diaspora and in Israel.

Although the conservative tendency in modern scholarship reverses the tradi-tional academic and confessional trust in the reliability of Luke as a historical source and privileges Paul's own epistles as data, Luke's contention that Paul's Hebrew name was Saul correlates with Paul's epistles that he belonged to the same tribe as his royal patronym (Rom. 11:1, Phil. 3:5).[15]

Jürgen Becker affirms the reliability of Luke's report of Paul's origin: the city of Tarsus in Cilicia (Acts 9:11; 21:39; 22:3).[16] In so doing, he aligns himself within a struggle to claim Paul for either Tarsus or Jerusalem.[17] W. C. van Unnik divides Paul between these two cities, allocating Tarsus to his birth and youth, Jerusalem to "the springtime of life."[18] Becker argues from linguistic evidence that Paul was of the Diaspora rather than Palestine: "The Greek language of Paul is not only free of harsh Semitisms (and thus was hardly learned later as a foreign language, for example, in Jerusalem) but also follows independent Greek style."[19] U. von Wilamowitz-Moellendorf supports Becker and concludes that Paul did not imitate Attic models or Asianic styles: "This Greek of his [Paul's] is related to no school and follows no model but comes directly from the heart . . . and yet it is still just Greek, not a translated Aramaic . . . this makes him one of the clas-sicists of Hellenism."[20] Paul indirectly lends evidence to the Tarsus thesis in his argument in Philippians. In an effort to establish his claim to be of Jewish lin-eage, he fails to mention Israel or Judea in the context of 3:5.[21]

The increasing consensus seems to favor Tarsus as Paul's city of birth, develop-ment, and citizenry.[22] Paul's family could have emigrated from Palestine, and while maintaining a strong relationship through language and allegiance with the land, became part of a strong Jewish settlement in a thriving Roman city.[23] Scholars cite as evidence for the Palestinian inheritance of Paul both continuity between the Greek cultural presence in Israel and the Jewish Greek Diaspora, as well as his self-identification as a Pharisee (Gal. 1:13–14; Phil. 3:5).[24] Günther Bornkamm argues that Paul must have spent extended time in Jerusalem to have received training in the traditions of the Pharisees, since evidence is lacking in support of Pharisees in the Diaspora.[25] While scholars acknowledge the paucity of material on Pharisees before the destruction of the Temple in 70/71 CE, that Paul never-theless was trained, behaved, and thought as a Pharisee has become an operative interpretive principle.[26] I will continue the discussion on the Pharisees and their relationship to Paul below. The issue raised by the question of Diaspora Pharisees addresses the relationship between Paul and his Hellenistic environment. This question has also been approached through the status of Paul's language.

"This brings us to the most characteristic feature of Paul the Jew. Paul was to the last a pious Bible Jew, a Septuagint Jew."[27] The language of the Septuagint (LXX) was Koine Greek, the vernacular of Jews in the Greek-Roman Diaspora, including Paul.[28] The LXX employed Greek idioms to express Hebraic conceptions of divinity and existence. For example, Hebrew *Shaddai* becomes Greek *pantokrator*; *Elohim* is *Theos*,[29] which also subsumes the Tetragrammaton. Calvin Roetzel qualifies the transparent translation of the Hebraic religious ethos into the Greek: "even though the translators may have striven to remain true to the spirit of the Hebrew text, certain Greek ideas inevitably crept into their translation."[30] The unintentional, albeit inevitable, permutations of the Greek moved the LXX toward the abstract and away from the concrete Hebrew. Compare the Hebrew "I AM WHO I AM" (Exod. 3:14) to LXX's "I am the Being" (LXX).[31]

Paul's intentional use of the LXX reveals his locus as a Diaspora Jew intimate with the language of the text from childhood.[32] Yet his method of textual interpretation and argumentation point toward Hebraic, Pharisaic patterns of thinking.[33] Paul makes extensive reference to the Hebrew Bible in the authentic Pauline epistles.[34] "Sometimes his quotations are in verbal agreement with both the LXX and Hebrew, sometimes with one against the other, and sometimes against both."[35] Paul's compositional and argumentative style moves creatively between Hellenistic rhetoric and Hebraic forms and interpretations.[36] Doty summarizes Paul's intercultural craft of letter making precisely:

> Paul seems to have had a sense of freedom in literary matters corresponding to the freedom in theology that many commentators have noted. Instead of remaining tied to literary models, for instance, he combined non-Jewish Hellenistic customs with Hellenistic Jewish customs, and created a form which cannot be equated with either tradition. The most obvious place in the Pauline letters where this fusion can be identified is in the very first part of the typical Pauline letter, in the phrase "Grace to you and peace. . . ." This phrase includes a modification of the stereotyped "greetings!" of Hellenistic letters (*chairein* becomes *charis*, "grace") and the characteristic "peace" (*shalom*) of Jewish letters. (. . . The letters created for Acts do not demonstrate this fusion of terms, but have normal Hellenistic openings.)[37]

Robin Scroggs provides further evidence of the amalgamated genealogy of Paul's epistles identified with rabbinic hermeneutics and argumentation derived from the Pharisees, and styles of argumentation associated with the philosophical school of the Stoics.[38] Romans 1–4 and 9–11 are a homily shaped by expositions of Hebrew Scriptures (Gen. 15:6; 21:12), which are in turn illuminated by other passages of Scripture, or by the use of a *gezerah šawah*. Thus Ps. 32:1–2, "Blessed is he whose transgression is forgiven, whose sin is covered, blessed is the one to whom the Lord will not reckon sin,"[39] is used to interpret Gen. 15:6: "Abraham believed God, and it was reckoned to him as righteousness." Through the use of *elogisthē* ("reckoned, accounted," Rom. 4:3, 23), *logizetai* (4:4), and *logizesthai* (4:24), Paul transforms Abraham from patriarch of Israel to paradigmatic anomaly who simultaneously serves as founding father of faith (*episteusen*) for both Jew and Gentile: "The purpose was to make him the father of all who believe (*pisteōs*) without being circumcised and who thus have righteousness (*dikaiosynēn*), reckoned (*logisthēnai*) to them, and likewise the father of the circumcised who are not merely circumcised but also follow the example of the (*pisteōs*) which our father Abraham had before he was circumcised" (Rom. 4:11b–12).

Paul's Pharisaic method of textual weavings, or midrash, through the linguistic agency of *pisteōs* and *elogisthē*, traverse the boundaries between texts (Gen. 15:6 and Rom. 4:3; Exod. 33:19 and Rom. 9:15; Lev. 18:5 and Rom. 10:5; Deut. 30:12–14 and Rom. 10:6–9), in an effort to traverse the boundaries between his Greco-Roman Jewish and Gentile congregation.[40]

Interspersed between what Scroggs identifies as one homily (Rom. 1–4, 9–11) is yet another that does not conform to the preceding or following in either content or method. Romans 5–8 follows the structure of the diatribe, which derived from Greek philosophical methods of argument associated with the Stoics.[41] The diatribe also influenced Hellenistic Judaism prior to Paul's adaptation to his immediate context.[42] The quotations from Hebrew Scripture, numerous in Rom. 1–4 and 7–11, become sparse, while the use of *Christos* more than doubles.[43] Paul employs the diatribe style—a series of rhetorical units linked by repeated phrases, or alternating questions and answers:

> For those whom he foreknew he also predestined . . .
> and those whom he called he also justified;
> and those whom he called he also justified;
> and those whom he justfied he also glorified. (8:29–30)
>
> Are we to continue in sin that grace may abound? (6:1)
>
> What then shall we say?
> That the law is sin? (7:7)
>
> What shall we say then?
> Is there in justice on God's part? (9:14)

Romans contains, therefore, two distinct homilies for two distinct groups ("I am now turning to speak to you Gentiles," 11:13), in order to create one unified body. In other words, Paul utilizes the resources of cultural distinctiveness in the cultivation of a new cultural unity. Vernon Robbins describes this function as the "bi-cultural nature of the rhetoric" in service to the "transformation of the multiplicity of different social and ethnic/cultural value systems into a unity."[44]

The form (*morphē*) of the Pauline epistle is neither purely Judaic nor Hellenistic: "witness . . . the struggles of New Testament commentators to determine whether a particular passage is intended for Jews, for Greeks or for both."[45] In

Paul's effort to create an intercultural heterotopias *ecclesia*, he calls upon his unique formation as a diasporic Jew, heir to both Pharisaic and Hellenic legacies of intellection, in order to create a heteromorphic epistolary: a *kainē morphē*.

Paul's proclivity toward and competency in creating new forms from diverse sources has become commonly recognized and accepted in New Testament scholarship. As might be expected, scholars have enlisted a variegated vocabulary in the effort to describe this phenomenon: "In Paul Athens and Jerusalem are *strangely mixed*";[46] "peculiar *mixture* of Jewish and Greek elements," "peculiar *blending* in him of all sorts of elements of Jewish and Hellenistic origin";[47] "bi-cultural," "wanderer between two worlds";[48] "a *blending* of these [Hellenistic-Jewish, Judaism-Hellenism, Palestine-Greek] worlds";[49] "fusions";[50] "synthesis."[51] Most of these terms provide descriptively neutral or positive implications. The same phenomenon can also be described in devaluative terms, such as "syncretism" and "apostasy."[52]

We have now reached a hermeneutical juncture at which the questions we pose proceed to examine the relationship between Paul's letters and the composition and character of his communities, or Paul's letters and the person, Paul, or the relationship between the letters and enduring theological questions. Each hermeneutical terrain has been identified with a major scholar and school of interpretation. Rudolf Bultmann certainly remains largely associated with the third topos, wherein Paul appears as the first great Christian theologian.[53] More recently, the question of Paul's identity has been raised from the perspective of Jewish history, redressing the neglect, censor, and scholarly disinheritance of Paul qua Jew by the Jewish intellectual community.[54]

Contemporary biblical scholarship turns sharply in the direction of the intersection between text and social order. This method is not without its antecedent champions, such as Deissmann and Dobschütz.[55] More recent scholarship relies directly upon the methods of sociology and anthropology to interrogate the texts of Scripture as social documents. John G. Gager describes this method in service to his examination of the Christian construction of the social world and world-maintenance: "the processes whereby a given new world is brought into being and seeks to establish itself in competition with numerous other worlds . . . The method I will follow in succeeding chapters is to examine specific problems in terms of theoretical models from recent work in the social sciences. In each case the model has been formulated independently of Christian evidence. My procedure will be to test them against information based on early Christian documents."[56]

The scholarship of Bruce Malina utilizes anthropological models to understand the cultural creations of Christians as a social group: "nature," "gender," group identity, symbolic behavior. The method proceeds in a manner similar to that described by Gager, but arrives at a different yet related concern. "For texts are the end products of languaging, and languaging is a form of social interaction. People 'language' each other to have some effect. The best a contemporary biblical scholar might offer Bible readers is a way to get back to the domains of reference which derive from and are appropriate to the social world from which the biblical texts derive. The problem, then, is how to move from a text to the social system that endows the text with meaning."[57]

The procedural direction of the interpretive investigation from text to the social matrix that creates a particular text is inversed by recent developments in rhetorical criticism. This methodology moves far beyond the mono- to the multiple social and cultural situations that are encoded in a single text. Vernon Robbins, Burton L. Mack, and Jerome H. Neyrey are primary practitioners of this emerging hermeneutics, which Robbins defines as: "(a)rhetorical-literary features internal to the text; (b) intertextual aspects of the text; (c) social and cultural dymanics in the text; and (d) ideology."[58]

Phenomenology in general and phenomenology of religion in particular place a different set of questions before the texts, proceed in a direction similar to the sociological (from text to beyond the text), yet aim to uncover the ontological realm as revealed in the relationship between various modalities of being and consciousness. The theoretical frame within which a religious-phenomenological investigation proceeds is determined by the person's experience of the sacred. "It is the task of interpretation to show that the form of interpretation is relative to the theoretical structure of the hermeneutic system being considered. Thus, the phenomenology of religion deciphers the religious object in rites, in myth, and in faith, but it does so on the basis of a problematic of the sacred which defines its theoretical structure."[59]

Phenomenology's point of entry into this investigation are the various creations of human existence, cultural symbols, "rites," "myths," "faith" (by which Ricoeur refers to religious experience), sacred texts. Phenomenology depends upon an inseparable organic relationship between language and experience. Unlike some postmodern theories of language that are founded (despite postmodernist's antifoundationalism) upon a "differential theory of knowledge"[60] in which language is both nonrepresentational[61] and non-referential,[62] at best enclosed within its system, at worst, caught within the generativity of perpetual indeterminacy.[63] Since there is nothing "outside" language—understood as system—consequently there is no radical distinction between signifier and signified—the signifier "has no constitutive meaning."[64] "Now the structure of the signifier is, as is commonly said of language itself, that it should be articulated. This means that no matter where one starts to designate their reciprocal encroachments and increasing inclusions, these units are subjected to the double condition of being reducible to ultimate differential elements and of combining them according to the laws of a closed order."[65]

Since language never belongs to anything "in the world" outside its system of operation, language refers to more language, texts to other texts, in a "chain of signifiers that the meaning 'insists' but that none of its elements 'consists' in the signification of which it is at the moment capable."[66] Language and, consequently, "being" come into existence as a result of the radical displacement of the subject *by* language. In other words, being, which phenomenologists have known as the source of language, and which can be known *through* language, is the creation of the subject's absence. "The 'being' referred to is that which appears in a lightning moment in the void of the verb 'to be' and I said that it poses its question for the subject. What does that mean? It does not pose it *before* the subject, since the subject cannot come to the place where it is posed, but it poses it *in place* of the subject, that is to say, in that place it poses the question *with* the subject, as one poses a problem *with* a pen, or as Aristotle's man thought *with* his soul."[67] The subject, now serving as the linguistic placeholder for its absent being, cannot be known, nor can it know the real. Being and language are dismembered; the subject is born of its cleavage.

I believe it to be possible to retain one of the insights of Lacan without hopelessly surrendering being to exile wherein the language that implicitly poses the most basic questions of being's existence forever remains incapable of answering its questions.

Phenomenology's understanding of language takes issue with theories of language that posit language as a system. Ricoeur provides a critique: "A linguistic analysis which would treat these significations as a whole closed in on itself would ineluctably set up language as an absolute. This hypostasis of language, however, repudiates the basic intention of a sign, which is to hold 'for,' thus transcending itself and suppressing itself in what it intends. Language itself, as a signifying milieu, must be referred to existence."[68] Ricoeur is suggesting that as humans we can conceive of language as a system, but that as language users we do not *experience* the comprehensive simultaneous differentiations of signifier/signified. The ontological relation of language to language-using beings is reference, not reification.

My own observations concerning the various theories of knowledge dependent upon de Saussure's theory of language concur with Ricoeur. My first question, however, is posed not to language as a system, but to the very existence of the system. In other words, what is necessary for its existence? What must language first become in order to enter into systemic arrangements?

We first note that de Saussure, Lacan, and Derrida depend upon a delimitization of language's operation in order to build their theories. To stabilize language's behavior, they must first impose a powerful reduction upon its innate polysemic character that confines its behavior to the semiotic level of sign. This a priori operation, which must precede all others, requires an unacknowledged position of linguistic privilege and an exercise of power, power to define and control language as such. This position, implicit in each of the respective author's discussions, renames the unacknowledged position of linguistic privilege; "unacknowledged" since the foundational theory of "language as system" is not considered constituted or constructed, but dis- or uncovered. Possessing the characteristics of independent empirical operational existence, the other possible modalities of language are invisibly bracketed. Theirs is an over-standing of language since the discretionary use of power to confine language to the systemic boundaries of the sign reveals a certain mode of being in the world that remains unarticulated but embodied in the application of their theory.

Phenomenology of religion begins its investigation not at the point of standing over signs through the exercise of power, but at an understanding of symbols that exercise power over the religious subject. Through this experience of language at the level of symbol, phenomenology enters its investigation of various modes of being within the structures of the sacred. Ricoeur referred to the sacred as "problematic" in relation to theoretical structures. I will examine the further implications of its problematic nature below. The dimension that concerns us at the moment is the problematic nature of the sacred in relation to linguistic theories. That mode of being most distinctively characteristic of the sacred is otherness or alterity: sacred means set apart for worship. The sacred exists both within and beyond the boundaries of human experience and comprehension as well as within and beyond the limits of language. For example, the Tetragrammaton YHWH refers to the God of Israel, but the letters are only placeholders since the name of God is never uttered in completion, since no human word can adequately signify the transcendent nature of the holy. In the Christian tradition, the apophatic mystics, such as John of the Cross, Gregory of Nyssa, Meister Eckhart, and Jacob Boehme, refer to God by denying the referential adequacy of language.[69] The New World traditions of Christianity among enslaved members of the African diaspora share this apophatic dimension in the spirituals:

> He's so high, you can't get over Him
> So low, you can't go under Him
> So wide, you can't go round
> You got to go right through the door.[70]

All of the members of these various religious traditions depend upon language to express their encounter with the sacred, while pointing to a dimension of the sacred that eludes language.

The linguistic character of symbols is attested by the fact that it is indeed possible to construct a semantics of symbols, that is, a theory that would account for their structure in terms of meaning or signification. Thus we can speak of the symbol as having a double meaning or a first and a second order of meaning. But the nonlinguistic dimension is just as obvious as the linguistic one.[71]

Ricoeur carefully distinguishes between the theory of the symbol that mediates adequately and the one that mediates inadequately the Sacred and the experience of the holy. The theory he describes as follows: "Symbolic signification, therefore, is so constituted that we can only attain the secondary signification by way of the primary signification, where this primary signification is the sole means of access to the surplus of meaning. The primary signification gives the secondary signification, in effect, as the meaning of a meaning."[72] The sign, therefore, serves as a medium or entrance into the nonlinguistic realm of the symbol, which transcends the sign in its inexhaustible plenitude, yet retains the sign as a marker of opacity.

A concomitant moment from the symbol's mediation and participation in aspects of sacred being occurs in the direction of the experiencing self. The realm that resides ultimately beyond human comprehension or signification is the source of religious experience.

Finally, the symbolism of the sacred, as it has been studied, for example, by Mircea Eliade, is particularly appropriate for our meditation on the rootedness of discourse in a nonsemantic order. Even before Eliade, Rudolf Otto, in *The Idea of the Holy*, strongly emphasized the appearance of the sacred as power, strength, efficacity. Whatever objections we might raise about his description of the sacred, it is valuable in that it helps us to be on guard against all attempts to reduce mythology linguistically. We are warned from the very beginning that we are here crossing the threshold of an experience that does not allow itself to be completely inscribed within the categories of logos or proclamation. The numinous element is not first a question of language, if it ever really becomes one, for to speak of power is to speak of something other than speech even if it implies the power of speaking. This power as efficacity par excellence is *what does not pass over completely into the articulation of meaning.*[73]

Language assumes the quality of holiness as spoken or written with regard to its participation in and submission to this set-apart realm of power. What distinguishes language in this mode is that its speaker or scribe is *not* in control of its use: the scribe as he commences to inscribe a new Torah prays over each letter; the priest who implores God's mercy and forgiveness in the cleansing rite of preparation before praying for the descent of the Holy Spirit as he elevates the host for its consecration and transformation; the church mother in the Afro-Baptist tradition who prays that the "words of my mouth and the meditation of my heart be acceptable in Thy sight, O Lord, my rock and my redeemer."

The "language" that comes closest to approximating the peculiar character of the Holy is ecstatic speech or glossolalia. This utterance, often sounded at worship or unexpectedly in prayer or baptism, is nonrepresentational, nonreferential, and neither sign nor symbol. It is the voice of the Spirit in the awe-fullness of her power to displace recognizable human speech and personality.[74]

This describes only one movement in phenomenology of religion's investigation of the relationship between language and the ontology of the sacred. A concomitant movement along with the symbol's mediation and participation in the sacred occurs in the experiencing self. Modes of being are determined by modes of experiencing that which appears before, or reveals its presence in, hierophantic, semantic, or visionary disclosure. Phenomenologists of religion understand the relationship between symbols that reveal the order or structure of the universe and human existence to be inseparable. One reveals the other's mode of being. "There is no self-understanding that is not mediated by signs, symbols, and texts."[75]

Unlike the theories of Lacan and Derrida, who view linguistic referentiality as dependent upon a logocentric metaphysics of presence, which owes its existence to repetition or an illusion, the phenomenological attitude takes the metaphysical as a point of entry into the examination of experience. Metaphysics is a secondary order of expression of a primary realm of experience whose efforts to "testify," to borrow a term from the sacred cultus, as to the veracity of its lived moment has bodied forth in symbol, gesture, icon, or terrifying shriek. "Experience is not reducible to metaphysical categories, but metaphysical categories are exemplified in experience."[76] Language, text, or the sacrificial action performed before the altar can be "turned back on the immediate experience of the self."[77] The crucial question becomes, why does language provide access to and knowledge of authentic being for Ricoeur, Eliade, Long, and Otto, but not for Derrida, Lacan, and de Saussure?

One possible response to this question may come from examining a representative passage by Lacan that serves as a parable for his thinking. Parables disrupt the given accepted order of reality in order to reveal another order of things in our midst.[78] Lacan's parable is also a tragic parody, for it reveals an inescapable condition or plight for all humanity. For Lacan, the symbolic belongs entirely to the realm of culture, which functions as a language, a play of signifiers, the chain of the signified. The symbolic realm is the only realm inhabited by humans, who create its play of differences and who are encompassed and enclosed by its determinates.

> Symbols in fact envelop the life of man in a network so total that they join together, before he comes into the world, those who are going to engender him "by flesh and blood"; so total that they bring to his birth, along with the gifts of the stars, if not with the gifts of the fairies, the shape of his destiny; so total that they give the words that will make him faithful or renegade, the law of the acts that will follow him right to the very place where he *is* not yet and even beyond his death; and so total that through them his end finds its meaning in the last judgement, where the Word absolves his being or condemns it—unless he attain the subjective bringing to realization of being-for-death.[79]

Embedded in Lacan's text is the nativity from Matthew's Gospel (2:1–23), but his allegorical parody is built upon the inversion of the narrative. Matthew's Mosaic interpolation of Yeshuah, however, aimed at inscribing him into the sacred traditions of the Torah and Prophets, is read through Lacan's essentially Greek philosophical displacement of the Hebraic: Logos overshadows Messiah. Lacan's choice of a particularly Hellenic, though unvoiced, reading of the nativity is necessary to his narrative inversion.

In Matthew, the representatives of the Gentile kingdoms come to worship the "king of the Jews" (Matt. 2:2). "Worship" here is *proskynēsai*, to fall down or fall at another's feet. Matthew's text is itself embedded with humorous irony. The star that led them had taken a wrong turn to Jerusalem instead of Bethlehem. The wise men are not wise enough to find the newborn King, and they fall down and worship an infant when they do. In Lacan's reading, the men retain their status as representative rulers of the world, but here understood as a dominating and dominical system of the signified that rule the world. The gifts become chains of linguistic-social-cultural creations that determine everything about our humanity, including gender (e.g., "to be engendered").

In a footnote Lacan identifies "flesh and blood" as the binary chain of the linguistic system that orders human existence through language understood as the play of differences. He cites Lévi-Strauss, *The Elementary Structures of Kinship*, as the source, a work that makes universal claims for the binary system of cultural production. Yet "flesh and blood" is also the first indication of Lacan's unacknowledged conflation of Matthew's and John's Gospels. John completely eliminates the human origins of Jesus, displacing Matthew and Luke's Oedipal triangle of Jesus, Mary, and Joseph with the prexistent, metaphysical, only recently enfleshed Logos. "He was in the world, and the world knew him not. He came to his own home, and his own people received him not. But to all who received him, who believed in his name, he gave power to become children of God; who were born not of blood nor of the will of the flesh nor of the will of man, but of God" (John 1:10–13). Lacan unmasks the totalizing Logos upon which Western civilization is built as a creation of "flesh and blood," human rather than a received or divinely revealed order.

Lacan's parable returns to Matthew in the following clause: "so total that they bring to his birth, along with the gifts of the stars," is an entire cosmic order into which the child, all children, are encompassed, an ultimate and inescapable order with divine sanction and protection, including the realm of "nature" and even the illusion of the imagination: "if not with gifts of the fairies." For Lacan, even fantasies and the realm seemingly outside the domain of human culture, or nature, are culturally determined, "the shape of his destiny." "They," the interlocking chorus of fathers whose acts and utterances are love, leave only two alternatives to the son(s): submission or rebellion as he either conforms his behavior to the inculcated desires of the father's order, or transgresses that order.

"The law of the acts that will follow him right to the very place where he is not yet and even beyond his death":[80] the birth of the subject comes only through its radical alienation from authentic being in the resolution of the Oedipal stage. "The very place where he is not" is both the predetermined social location that provides only the illusion of an individual, and the locus of the subject that stands in the place where being is absent. "[S]o total that through them his end finds its meaning in the last judgement, where the Word absolves his being or condemns it." The "Word" is the direct reference to the entire process and system of divinely attributed and sanctioned order, which masks the principles of its human operation and its human cost in self-alienating subjectivity. We can, therefore, reread the opening verses of John's Gospel as a preamble or revealed declaration of the governing principles of human-created *Lebenswelt*: "In the beginning was the Word, and the Word was with God, and the Word was God. He was in the beginning with God; all things were made through him, and without him was not anything made that was made" (John 1:1–3).

The nativity, in both the Oedipal family and its religious reifications, is actually a death of authentic personhood whose only potential hope for authenticity is the embrace of "being-for-death." Neurosis, mental illness, and criminal behavior are all symptoms of refusal of one's true condition. The symbolic, if my exegesis of Lacan's parable is adequate, mediates everything but the experience and knowledge of one's self, eternally suspended by insatiable desire. "Our relation to language is ambiguous because it kills us in order that we may live; only in the alienating ambience of the symbolic, the linguistic and cultural realms can we become subjects; but as subjects severed by the signifier, we are necessarily cut off from the real, which 'is beyond the automaton, the return, the coming back, the insistence of the signs by which we see ourselves governed by the pleasure principle.'"[81]

As stated earlier, Lacan's theory depends upon a prior operation performed upon language that by eliminating its innate polysemy allows it to function within a closed system. The subject that comes into creation born of radical somatic and relational alienation is sustained only by its entry into the larger linguistic system or cosmos or culture. Suspended beyond access to experience is the phenomenal realm, including the phenomemon of the self that depends upon the interactive presence of others. The other, during and after the mirror stage, distorts and denies true reflection and knowledge of one's self, and becomes only a mediation of alienation, the divide between the subject and its desires. Language conceived as a system of signs is as fundamental to the creation of the alienated subject (a redundancy) as the concept of drives is necessary to the creation of Freud's intrapsychic topography.

We will proceed to examine Paul and his experience of the sacred within the understanding of being and its relationship to its created forms, including language as interpreted by phenomenology of religion. We will then return to Lacan's theory of the mirror as the mask of being and the invention of alienated subjectivity.

PAUL AND THE EXPERIENCE OF EMERGENT CREOLIZATION

The intentional objects of Paul present to us are his letters. These, however, contain references to mystical and ritual experience, to myth and the composition and maintenance of the sacred cultus. We will examine each of these in turn. The key to understanding Paul's transformations and theirs lies within his peculiar consciousness as a diasporic Jew. Paul's primary mode of being is best understood as that of a *creole*; his consciousness, *creolian*; and the process by which he tries to cultivate and impart its sensibilities to others I refer to as *creolization*. Paul's emic term for the process of creolization is *katallagē* (reconciliation).[82]

"Creole" as a hermeneutic phenomenological symbol is especially well suited for the purpose of disclosing ontological dimensions in Paul's experience, for the term is particularly, though not exclusively, associated with diasporic phenomena. Although it was eventually adopted by the academic community as a scientific term of linguistic and cultural analysis, its earliest appearance was used to describe New World nativity. The term and the practice is one of adaptation to the local, immediate environment, the process of domestication associated with making animals and people suitable to their new environment.[83] Spanish *criollo* embodies the process it describes since technically the term is a New World variation (corruption) used by aliens to describe a process that enabled them to make an unknown place both familiar and inhabitable.

The earliest use of the term describes Europeans born in the New World, in particular the first generation of children born to Spanish settlers in the Caribbean.[84] The term appears during the same century in English and French, applying to the same New World development: "An English Native of St. Christophers, a Cirole, as we call all born of European Parents in the West Indies [1697] . . . the Whites may be divided into two classes, the Europeans, and Creoles, or Whites born in the Country."[85]

The eighteenth-century usage begins to apply to the language spoken among the New World population, as well as to native rather than imported slaves.[86] Linguists distinguish between pidgin and creole language. A pidgin is a language that develops as a result of the initial encounter between two different groups with "neither knowing anything of the language of the other." The encounter and struggle to communicate create a third language. The resulting language, called a substrate, derives its lexicon from the original languages, while the phonology and grammar are new developments. Since the lexicon (termed "input") is limited, pidgins are often referred to as reduced or simplified versions of their parent languages.[87] "A pidgin, by definition, is nobody's native language: it is learned by linguistic adults as a second language."[88] An example is *Tok Tsion* (talk pidgin), which is the language resulting from the encounter between English explorers and settlers and the natives of Papua, New Guinea.[89]

The technical definition of a creole language is similar to that of a pidgin. Both are characterized by their derivation from superstrate languages, with the substrate exhibiting limited or restricted input (or smaller lexical base).[90] The creole emerges as a new language with its own identity with at least two characteristics that distinguish it from the pidgin: the creole language "is equivalent to pidginization *plus* the creation of form-meaning relationships which serve the creator's (learner's) communicative and expressive needs, but which cannot be explained as having been 'acquired' from the input. The forms themselves come from the input, but the meanings they convey are provided by the learner and are not those they have in the input."[91]

The innovations and developments that alter the creole language in relationship to the pidgin have their origins in the different experience of the language speakers:

> Unlike a pidgin, which functions only as an auxiliary contact language, a creole is the native language of most of its speakers.[92]
>
> Pidgins are nobody's first language, while creoles must be someone's first language.[93]
>
> Pidginization is second-language learning with restricted input, and creolization is first-language learning with restricted input.[94]
>
> In some cases communities composed of individuals of diverse first languages have taken a pidgin as their common language, and have raised chil-

dren for whom it is native. When this happens, we cease to call the language pidgin and say that it is *creolized*.[95]

Pidgin is a linguistic object that its creators bring into a world that is already established by a previous set of linguistic practices. The transition from pidgin to creole is the movement from a second language to a new *Lebenswelt* for those to whom it is aboriginal rather than invented.

Within the context of the New World French diaspora, the term *creole* was eventually applied to anyone born in the New World whose parents originated in the old world of Europe or Africa.[96] The term, therefore, was applied equally to slaves, settlers, and white or colored members of the population. The term referred to geographical nativity rather than social designations or race.

Cultural anthropologists and historians, borrowing both the terminology from linguistics and the indigenous term from New World diaspora records, have applied the term in their scholarship on the New World African diaspora.[97] Linguists, anthropologists, and historians, while differing in their technical use and application, nevertheless share a common range of terms to describe the term. Such terms as "mixed language," "hybrid," "hybridize," "hybridization" "convergence," and "mixture" are frequently employed by linguists, while "heterogeneity," "mixed," "borrowing," and "exchanging" are found among anthropologists and historians.

To fashion a hermeneutical tool out of the term for my own purposes, I want to pay particular attention to the following aspects of the multidimensional complex that composes the phenomenon "creole":

> *Authentic*: in New World African diaspora communities, "creole" indicates authenticity in language use and demonstrated affect. To "break away" into Creole is to go "natural," to "be real." The sudden turning away from a standard language (French or English, for example) into Creole is also a departure from a social norm of behavior. The scene becomes a moment of unveiling, a sudden casting off of the mask of prevailing social decorum as defined by hegemonic cultural codes, and an emotionally charged disclosure of true feelings and opinions, a moment fraught with risk.[98]

> *Transgressive*: Creole depends upon both an intimate and a practical knowledge of social and linguistic norms, especially in diasporic conditions of cultural hegemony. The language comes into creation by transgressing established norms of usage while retaining older forms, with meanings redefined according to new experience.

> *Innovative*: Creolization is the realm of new cultural creation at the boundary between older cultures.

T. H. Breen describes the process of New World African slaves coming to adjust to the diaspora: "these early Blacks successfully created new cultures that were part African and part American. They transferred some customs familiar to blacks throughout West Africa. The slaves also negotiated compromises, invented new rules and languages and learned how to deal with whites; in short, they crafted complex social orders in the face of great personal deprivation."[99] Yet within the domain of the innovative a moment arises wherein an emergent structure appears that was not determined or simply predicated upon the antecedent ones.[100]

Breen describes the violent dimension of cultural exchange within which the creative response of displaced Africans and their New World descendants generated new cultural forms. At the other end of the spectrum, during the early colonial period of seventeenth-century New England, African slaves and European settlers, both aliens in the New World, engaged in a less violent form of cultural exchange:

> within specific, semi-isolated localities it was possible for individuals to negotiate social status on the basis of various attributes, only one of which was race. Just as persons had not yet formulated precise rules governing interaction with members of their own race, so too they had not determined a rigid etiquette for interracial encounters. Cultural boundaries were therefore remarkably fluid, and under these conditions borrowing occurred in ways that would became less common, even non-existent, during the eighteenth century.[101]

Creolization is the creative process that depends upon permeable boundaries of interaction that allow for the invention of new cultural forms, new sensibilities, and transformation of consciousness. The term in its New World context eventually came to refer to the offspring who constituted a class of people descended from parents of European (white) ancestry and parents of African (black) ancestry, either slave or free people of color. The history of New Orleans is paradigmatically creole.

The process of creolization continued demographically and culturally: after the Civil War, the white groups became racially and culturally speaking ever more *exclusive*, whereas the "gens de couleur" community continued to be *inclusive*, accepting in its fold the issue of racial and cultural mixing. Hence, in the course of the nineteenth century, the francophone "creole of color" group grew and incorporated (i.e., creolized in the sense of "making native") African American, Native American, Italian, German, and other traditions, whereas the "white creole group" declined; it either calcified and atrophied or assimilated to an American ideal of racial and cultural purity.[102]

The colored population, creole and black, stratified yet interactive, became the catalytic incubator of new aesthetic forms that resulted in the transformation of American culture: jazz (Louis Armstrong), Caribbean (Wild Magnolias, Neville Brothers), rhythm and blues (Fats Domino, Professor Longhair), and the music of the sanctified church associated with the work of its native (holy) sister, Mahalia Jackson. The primary characteristic of this diasporic phenomenon is the multidimensionality of its intersubjectivity and the new-found consciousness of the fundamental heterogeneity of its relational being.

Its importance as a hermeneutical symbol for the interpretation of Paul's various related religious experience resides in the ambiguity of the term as one of the empirical (etic) analysis *and* its "experience-near" (emic) description of consciousness. It is possible to manifest the cultural embodiments of creolization to an outside observer without possessing the consciousness of one's location at the intersection of cultural convergence. This is the condition of Paul the Pharisee. As a Pharisee neither Paul's language nor his consciousness is creole. Paul speaks in Koine. Understood as language, koines are neither pidgins nor creole. "What characterizes them [koines] linguistically is the incorporation of features from several regional varieties of a single language. . . . Another feature that distinguishes koinés from pidgins . . . is that they are never detached from the languages they issue from. That is, Common Greek as spoken at the beginning of the Christian era (but already 300 years old) in Jerusalem, Corinth, and Rome, would not be discontinuous from Attic Greek which was its base."[103]

As noted above in the discussion of Paul's capacity to generate new epistolary, Paul possesses the linguistic ability and cultural consciousness to address both Greek Gentile and hellenized Jew within a single letter. Yet this same capacity and resources were not at his disposal to create a new community of Greeks and Jews within the shared cultic space prior to his mystical encounter with the crucified and risen Yeshuah. The radical introduction of inclusive heterogeneity into his consciousness as the indispensible core of his authentic personhood marks the emergence of creole consciousness. This is the condition of Paul, Apostle to the Gentiles. If creolization is the consciousness of and commitment to the embrace of heterogeneous identity, then we must attempt to account for Paul's movement from homogeneous community and its concomitant lack, and therefore displaced unconscious heterogeneous selfhood, to interethic community and the accompanying incorporated creolian consciousness.

MODES OF FORMATIONAL EXPERIENCE

We do not know enough about Paul's childhood or adolescence to place him within a developmental frame of analysis. Even possessing such, the information would belong to a different project. We can suggest correspondences between probable experiences and variable modes of consciousness. If we organize our interpretive frame in the manner of Greek musical modes, which provide a range of tonal variation and possibilities rather than diatonic sequence of fixed progressions, one possible way of conceptualizing Paul's experience is as follows:[104]

> *Formation*: those experiences of nurture, both adequate and inadequate, performed upon us within the primary spheres of family, synagogue, and sectarian fellowship before we are aware of its inculcation; consciousness is shaped through interaction and internalization before we are conscious of its occurrence.

> *Conformation/Confirmation*: actions initiated by the individual within the relational matrix of one's formative experiences that embrace and commit one to the form and consciousness one has received: *Mitwelt*. The ambiguity in

the spelling is deliberate to indicate both those religious rites and practices that confirm us in the certainty and reliability of our received world to which we now intentionally conform.

Reformation: standing apart/against either that which we have become, or the behavior or social arrangements or discourses of others. This is often understood as counterdiscourse to the dominate discourse and associated with countercultures and dominate cultural conflict.[105] Reformational positions can be oppositional without being confrontational or violent toward opposing groups, such as sectarian movements and personalities—Anabaptist, for example.[106] Reformation has an additional dimension when examined from the perspective of intracommunal relationships. Although nonconfrontational and nonviolent in intercommunal relationships, reformational positions can turn violently inward toward members of their own sect, or those identified as heretical while belonging only to the community in general. See, for example, the Nation of Islam.[107]

Transformation: powerful yet transitory moments whose effects alter personality, perception, and identity indelibly. Although these moments can be anticipated, desired, or even prepared for, they are not discretionary or volitional; they can only be received, not grasped; eluding discursive description they often remain ineluctable, ineffable, and inexorable. They can be associated with mystical disciplines, but are not dependent upon them.[108] Transformational experiences can either be contained within orthodox boundaries, such as Augustine's, or trangress them, such as Paul's. Ritual transformations can alter status and ontology without altering fundamental categories of perception and social epistemology, while mystical transformations can alter perception without changing one's status and ontology.[109]

Again I stress that these terms are modalities rather than categories of linear development. Mystical transformation can occur at any moment, or not at all, while reformation may be a lifelong process. What I have not included, for reasons that I hope will be made evident below, is the term *deformation*. This is the experience of violence, through psychological abuse, physical assault, or social-status devaluation. I propose that prior to Paul's transformational experience, his perception and responsivity lack affective empathy for those who are subject to his persecutions. Therefore, the reality portrayed in deformative experiences exists beyond Paul's pretransformative conciousness.

CONFORMATION: A PHARISEE IN THE DIASPORA

The Pharisees provide our point of entry into the examination of Paul's experience of the sacred prior to his mystical transformation and the formation of new communities. The Pharisees embody the paradox of Judaism's encounter with Hellenic culture. On the one hand, they were a reaction against the forces of religious compromise caused by the Greek presence and Jewish embrace of Hellenic culture. Their origins as a scribal class in opposition to the Sadducees during the reign of Hyrcanus I (135–104 BCE) led to civil war as recorded by Josephus in his *Antiquities*. "If, then, we ask ourselves what the distinguishing characteristics of the Pharisees were as revealed by the structure of events, we are struck by the fact that they had been responsible for promulgating *nomina* for the people. . . . [T]he Pharisees were active, aggressive, and determined protagonists of a system of laws uniquely their own. . . . [T]hey are ready to resort to violent rebellion when these laws are endangered."[110]

While they reacted against the intentional compromises with hellenization, they adopted Greek cultural creations in their resistance to Greek hegemony. Pharisees were familiar with Greek literature; they mstered and prayed in its language.[111] Several thousand Greek words entered the Talmud, while the term for their textual exegesis, "*gezera shawa*, translates *sunkrisis pros ison*."[112] "Indeed, the supreme council of the Great Synagogue (or Great Assembly) of the Pharisees was modelled in its organization on Hellenistic religious and social associations."[113] In their attempt to establish their legitimacy as heirs to a divinely revealed oral Torah, they appropriated the Greek method of formulating a chain of antecedent sages "in which the teaching of the founder was transmitted from generation to generation by successive scholars."[114] As with the written revelation, the Pharisees received the oral Torah from Moses. "Rabbinic literature richly attests to extrabiblical traditions, and the Mishnah tractate *Avot* ('Fathers') gives a chain of transmission that presents in detail what Josephus had said in summary: they 'observed regulations handed down by former generations.'"[115]

W. D. Davies provides an insight beyond the formal level of identifying the transmission of cultural forms. "The Pharisees also—in order to be respectable and respected—wanted to establish their pedigree or spiritual ancestry."[116] Both in the form they borrowed from the Greeks, whose influence they also opposed, and in the influence they intended to exercise over Israel, the Pharisees sought the simultaneous recognition of Greek and Hebrew. Davies's statement indicates not only the extent to which Greek values had become Jewish values, but that even sectarian Pharisees evaluated their status through Greek eyes.

By absorbing Greco-Roman institutional models such as the boule (council meeting), Greco-Roman modes of deductive reasoning, and Greco-Roman examples of lawmakers, sages, and philosophers, the Pharisees enabled their followers to be in congruence with Greco-Roman civilization without loss of their Jewish identity.[117] Although the Pharisees were a Palestinian development, the form of community they developed would be well suited for Jews zealous for the law yet embedded in the Jewish Diaspora of Greco-Roman territory.

The cultural ambivalence is also embodied in their name (*perushim*, "separatists," in Hebrew; *Pharisaoi* in Greek) which expresses their commitment to resolve such tensions into monovalent exclusivism.[118] The Hebrew and Aramaic root *prsh* means "separate" and "interpret."[119] The Sifra Midrash uses *parush* to translate *parush qadosh*, or "holy": Lev. 11:44: "Ye shall therefore be holy; for I am holy."[120] "The command to the Jewish people is that they should be as far removed from everything which corrupts or contaminates as is God himself. Lev. 20:26: 'I have separated you from other people that you should be mine alone.'

Consequently, the earliest rabbinic commentaries on the verse, including Sifra, extended the verse so that it reads: 'You shall be holy and separated, even as I am holy and separated.'"[121]

The separation is from all that is polluting. "Holiness and impurity are at opposite poles."[122] Jacob Neusner reveals the metaphor that orders the relationship between these two conditions:

> Two important ideas about purity and impurity come down from ancient Israel: First, purity and impurity are cultic matters. Second, they may serve as metaphors for moral and religious behavior, primarily in regard to matters of sex, idolatry, and unethical action. Purity furthermore closely relates to holiness. The land is holy, therefore it must be kept clean. It may be profaned by becoming unclean. Reference to the symbols of purity and impurity comes, in the Hebrew Bible, chiefly in priestly writing, whether legal, or prophetic, or historical.[123]

As Mary Douglas explains, purity is a matter of order, and Neusner indicates that the Pharisees derived principles of a divine order from the temple and its priesthood. The Pharisees defined themselves in proximity to the hierarchy of "cultic cleanness" according to the rules of behavior governing the priests who tended to the sacred functions of the temple. Their primary ritual act was to eat unconsecrated food in a state of ritual purity.[124] The table fellowship provided the basis for the ritualized enactment of a holy community or *haberim* (neighbors). The Pharisees relocated the center of holiness from the temple to the table, and considered every Jewish home to be "like the table of the Lord in the Jerusalem Temple."[125] The table became an altar, the meal a sacred ceremony. Pharisees therefore observed the practices designed to separate them from possible pollution, including meals, marriage, and Gentiles.

In the Diaspora, the tension between a ritualistically established exclusive identity based upon strict observance of Torah and table fellowship and the encounter with Greek culture would be heightened. "The basic problem in the Jewish Diaspora was how to maintain the Jewish tradition in an environment dominated by Gentiles. The people who made up the majority in Babylon and other centers of exile were, for better or worse, 'significant others,' and Jewish identity would inevitably be modified by interaction with them."[126]

Interculturated Hellenic Jews could either relax the boundary between themselves and Gentiles or, in the case of the Pharisees, heighten it. The tension would be between demonstrating to Gentiles the significance and importance of Jewish "wisdom, learning, literature, history achievements, and godliness of their own,"[127] while at the same time being severely criticized by Gentile Greeks as misanthropic. As E. P. Sanders and J. N. Sevenster point out, Greco-Roman authors were especially critical of Jews for their refusal to eat in the context of Gentile fellowship.[128]

John Gager critically challenges Sevenster's evidence and conclusion. He contends that accusations of separateness served as a rhetorical ostensible for other issues, that Jews were not "aloof and separate." Once we lift the veil of polemics, we find not a "people apart with their own customs and religion which admitted little intermingling with their Greek neighbors, but a people both in and of their world."[129] While detailed evidence of diasporic Pharisees is unavailable, they were certainly a minority within a minority, therefore highly self-conscious about their practices and beliefs that separated them from both pagan Gentiles and less observant Jews. They would become even closer in their table fellowship and sense of bonded commitment to one another. "Internal rules, such as food rules, kept the intimates of the groups united to one another and distinct from gentiles and even from other Jews with whom they constantly had to interact and with whom they competed."[130] Neusner interprets such rules and restrictions as indicative of both ongoing interaction with Gentiles and heightened protective watchfulness against polluting encounters.[131]

Against Neusner's conclusion that the definitive center of Pharisaical community was table fellowship and ritual purity based upon the relocation of the Temple's holiness to a communal diffusion, E. P. Sanders has maintained critical (at times personal) opposition. "It is not true that Pharisees would not come into contact with others. They took part in civic life and associated with other members of society. Paul, a Pharisee, persecuted early Christians, and so must have come near them."[132] Sanders, for all his extensive scholarly labors to refute Neusner and to correct the portrait of the Pharisees, nevertheless misses the fundamental point. While he is perhaps correct in noting the difficulties Pharisees, especially in the Diaspora, would encounter trying to avoid unclean encounters, his approach fails to reveal what is at stake. For as extensive and familiar as Diaspora Jews might have come to be with pagan Greeks, Pharisees—including Paul—however, *did not experience the presence of the sacred in their mundane and profane encounters with the Gentiles!* The point is crucial if we are to understand the relationship between Saul the Pharisee and Paul the Apostle.

Established phenomenology of religion valorizes experiences of heightened intensity or ecstatic moments in the selection and interpretation of data. The selection may be either discrete rituals (such as initiation rites, exorcisms, cosmic renewals) or mystical encounters.[133] William James, as noted in chapter 1, distinguished between "personal religion" of primary experience and the "second hand" of "tradition," by which he meant rituals, ceremonies, and doctrine.[134] W. W. Meissner stands within the "tradition of the fathers" in his psychological interpretation of the same.[135] When we divest ourselves of a protestantized view (which is ironically present in Meissner), we encounter a broader variety of religious as well as mystical experiences. Alan Segal suggests an alternative interpretation: "For Paul and his generation, ritual was not an empty form. Even for Hellenistic Jews—living outside of Pharisaic authority and having to deal with the problems of acculturation and assimilation—ritual, like prayer and certainly more than philosophy, became symbolic of the deepest religious commitments because it was characteristically and unambiguously Jewish."[136] Ritual for Paul, therefore, performed the crucial and life-giving *ergon* of creating and maintaining a *kosmos, koinonia,* and *autos.* As Neusner indicates, the metaphor-metaphysic informing the task of world ordering were derived from Levitical priestly codes and the spatial orientations of the temple. The rituals, from a position of external observation, created a sacred locus around which and in reference to which all of life's activities became oriented.

Both cultivating the self and creating the sacred are activities in boundary establishment, based upon symbolic systems of purity. Douglas describes the relationship between the ancient priesthood, its cultic activities, and the creation cosmology of Israel. The primary cosmogonic act of Yahweh in the Priestly documents of Genesis 1–11 is separation.[137] Cosmogony is a matter of establishing categories that distinguish the elements and items that constitute a comprehensive unified order[138] and the elimination of ambiguous characters or anomalies. Since anomalies confuse or blur the boundaries of the established order, an order established through separation, "hybrids and other confusions are abominated."[139] Douglas then quotes Lev. 18:23: "And you shall not lie with any beast and defile yourself with it, neither shall any woman give herself to a beast to lie with it: it is perversion"; and Lev. 19:19, "You shall keep my statutes. You shall not let your cattle breed with a different kind; you shall not sow your field with two kinds of seed; nor shall there come upon you a garment of cloth made of two kinds of stuff." These materials, animals, or human conditions, such as menses, leprosy, seminal emissions, creeping, crawling, swarming animals, nocturnal birds, which traverse or transgress divinely ordered categories, threaten the entire cosmic order. Holiness, according to Douglas, consists of both separation and completion or perfection (in the sixteenth-century use of the English term). "To be holy is to be whole, to be one; holiness is unity, integrity, perfection of the individual and of the kind [class]. The dietary roles merely develop the metaphor of holiness on the same lines."[140]

This cosmogonic paradigm is re-created in the cultic rituals and extended from temple rules to sex rules and food rules into "a single system which sustains the whole moral and physical universe simultaneously in their systematic interrelatedness."[141] Rituals establish, protect, and restore the order portrayed in the liturgical or sacred narrative.[142] Yom Kippur, for example, is a ritual enacted by priests within the cultus that not only purifies the people of Israel from sin but also restores order to the entire cosmos.[143]

Douglas interprets this material in the tradition of Durkheim, who sees the religious activity as an epiphenomenon of human patterning and meaning making. The system, as noted above, operates comprehensively and simultaneously in much the same way that a linguistic system operates simultaneously. Neusner, however, closer to a phenomenological sensibility, understands the temple to be the center from which all power emanates and all being gravitates. The system coheres not by symbol but through the presence and power of the source of all being, Yahweh, whose cosmic/earthly seat rests in the sanctuary of Jerusalem.

To summarize, according to Douglas, holiness in ancient Judaism consisted of the separation of all elements within a comprehensive order wherein all elements that conform to their proper category are designated as pure and included within the realm of the holy, which is separated from anomalous elements that are designated impure and excluded from the sacred. According to Neusner, holiness derives from one's participation in cultically sanctioned activities and orientation toward the temple. Holiness relates to proximity to the sacred presence of Yahweh around which all of creation and human activity converge.

Both definitions, one empirical-functionalist, the other phenomenological, are helpful in interpreting Paul's life as a Pharisee. Ritual, understood as a boundary-creating activity, played a crucial role in maintaining the identity of Diaspora Jews. "The stress on purity rules as boundary creating mechanisms is typical of minority groups who are striving to keep their identity and bring about change in a strong society."[144] But Paul's experience of holiness was not only a categorical function of ritualistically maintained boundaries. Here is where Neusner's phenomenological interpretation is helpful. Holiness is also defined and experienced in relationship to the temple, which is the center of the universe. Human beings are only able to enter the presence of Yahweh in a state of purity. In other words, experience of purity is dependent upon the experience of the divine presence.

If we define mysticism as not only the heightened and intense states of divine-human encounter, but the experience of the immediate presence of God, then Paul, as part of table fellowship of Pharisees and the daily fulfillment of the ritual acts of Torah observance as well as Torah reading and interpretation, experienced what Max Kadushin termed "normal mysticism."

> The ordinary, familiar, everyday things and occurrences constitute occasions for the experience of God. Such things as one's daily sustenance, the very day itself, are felt as manifestations of God's loving-kindness, calling forth *Berakot, Kedushah,* holiness, which is nothing else than the imitation of God, is concerned with daily conduct, with being gracious and merciful, with keeping oneself from defilement by idolatry, adultery, and the shedding of blood. Although the experience of God is like none other, the *occasions* for experiencing Him, for having a consciousness of Him, are manifold.[145]

Paul employs the language of purity "to describe and maintain the new boundaries of the Christian community"; it is therefore "likely that he was familiar with Jewish and perhaps Pharisaic purity rules."[146] Paul's use of purity language, however, is inseparable from the presence of Christ.

We can, therefore, conclude that Paul's experience of the sacred was in the presence of the fellowship of other law-observant Jews in the Diaspora, the fulfillment of ritual prescriptions, and the interpretation and reality of Torah. These experiences would also have the conceptual formulations described by Douglas wherein all elements conform to their proper taxonomic categories, including Jew and Gentile. Paul's experience of the sacred would be in accordance with the experienced values of a community who understood its interactive relationships, shaped in accordance with Torah.

Understood as either a mode or a category, neither interpretation of Paul's experience of the sacred included table fellowship with Greek pagans, or any breached or transgressed category of classification. The shape and content of the holy would root Paul's sense of self within the boundaries of his law-observant fellowship founded upon an identity based on exclusive otherness, homogeneous community, and fixed boundaries between sacred and profane.

Douglas points out that *tebel* in Lev. 18:23 (also Lev. 20:12), translated in the RSV as "perversion," means "confusion" or "mixing." By the same logic, Lev. 13:12–13 portrays a person with leprosy to be clean when the disease has covered his body entirely. "The person whose skin turned entirely white no longer suffered an improper mixture."[147] Heterogeneity would threaten the established order of wholeness (integrity) and leave one defiled in the presence of the holy.

CONFORMATION: A PHARISEE IN THE DIASPORA (A PHENOMENOLOGICAL INTERPRETATION)

As a Pharisee in the Diaspora, Paul lived both in the communal mediation of sacral alterity, whose boundaries, maintained by strict observance of food and fellowship, put them in distinct opposition to the Greco-Roman social order, while belonging to the Pharisees, whose form of fellowship, Greek language, and methods of interpretation and cultural life tied them intimately, if not always consciously, to the Greek Gentile world.[148] That which consciously derived from Greco-Roman culture was made holy and acceptable through its incorporation into the community for sacred purposes: Greek hermeneutics for the sake of halakah; Greek language in order to translate Torah; Greek social forms in order to form a purified community.

The cultural complex of Paul was governed by the codes of honor and shame (see chapter 3). Paul was intimately aware of these cultural values and practices, as he demonstrates in Romans: to those who, by perseverance in doing what is good, seek for glory (*doxan*) and honor (*timēn*) (Rom. 2:7) glory and honor and peace (Rom. 2:10) one vessel for honorable (*timēn*) and another for dishonorable (*atimian*) use (Rom. 9:21).[149] Although we do not know about Paul's early life, his extensive familiarity with the vocabulary that expressed the values of a shame and honor society indicates that such values shaped his maturing consciousness.

Although his formation took place within a Jewish community, his consciousness was informed by both the values of the larger society and his ethnic community. If the values of his adult life as a Pharisee point to early experiences, we might use them to enter into his interior realm. Paul writes in Philippians that he was "circumcised on the eighth day of the people of Israel of the tribe of Benjamin, a Hebrew of Hebrews; as to the law a Pharisee, as to zeal a persecutor of the church, as to righteousness under the law, blameless" (Phil. 3:5–6). Paul uses the term *blameless* in several letters (1 Thess. 3:13; 4:3–7; Phil. 1:10; 2:15; 2 Cor. 12:21; Rom. 6:19; 16:19). Here he expresses an exceptional commitment not only to the law but to perfection under the law. The same enthusiasm and ideal is expressed in Galatians: "I advanced in Judaism beyond many of my own age among my people, so extremely zealous was I for the traditions of my fathers" (Gal. 1:14).[150]

While these expressions indicate continuity between Paul's enthusiasm as a Pharisee and his commitment to the mission to the Gentiles, they also may be archaic strata of the nascent self whose evolution depends on adequate empathic mirroring from primary self-objects (see discussion in chapter 2). Empathic failure results in narcissistic wounding and the precipitation of compensatory structures characterized by the identification with and attachment to ideals and the idealization of a second parental self-object, usually the father. Paul describes himself as being far more a zealot for the traditions of his paternal ancestors. If Paul suffered archaic wounding, the familial and communal environment shaped by the ethos of the Pharisees, with an emphasis upon strict observance of Torah, would have provided the support and structure compatible with his need for idealization and perfection.

The idealizing mode of the bipolar self can achieve viability, and the compensatory response to inadequate empathic mirroring should not be symptomatically assessed as pathological.[151] Paul's testimony of himself as blameless indicated the reservoir of the affect pride, which both his accomplished observance and communal acceptance generated. Pride is communally contagious and contributes to the powerful bond between members who share the affirming mutual assessment of one another.[152] Paul would be seen as he would see others: as superlative members of a righteous (*dikaios*) community among an entire people chosen by the God of Israel.

Paul's dependency upon ideal imagos that would become internalized and shape the evaluations of his worth and relatedness was not achieved without cost. The failure of empathic mirroring causes painful fragmentation of the sensations of global body coherence. Paul's defensive response to primal disintegration is the attenuation of affect, which will later result in empathic numbness and rage. The nascent self's movement toward idealization and away from the nuclear wounded core of vulnerability is the splitting that results in the creation of a false self, which now mirrors the ideal expectations of the parents: "The infant lives, but falsely." "False" as used by Winnicott and Miller is the mask of authentic vulnerability, rather than a term of moral inadequacy.

Let us place this configuration of the archaic movements of Paul's self into a phenomenological interpretation of his experience of shame within the shame and honor cultural environment of the Mediterranean. If Paul is understood in terms of dyadic personality (self) rather than subjective individuality, shame is necessary to the formation of boundaries that protect the authentic self, as well as relating one to the communal environment upon whose relationships and responsivity one both depends and defends for its survival. The split between the false self and the wounded self is that boundary or mask that protects the bodily felt integrity of the self from further injury. This protected realm, however, can become partly fused with the ideal self.[153] One dimension of shame is the powerful fear based on the prior experience of rupture in the relationships of trust, acceptance, and inclusion.

The mask of the false self protects this vulnerable realm by conforming one's behavior to the expectations of others, within the relational matrix of one's *Mitvelt*. Unacceptable behavior causes the sudden and unexpected break in the relational suspension of global soothing coherence or *eirēnē*.

The coherent experience of the self is not confined or isolated to the individual but is inseparable from its shared diffusion in the fellowship of community. As I stated in chapter 2, this relational matrix of communal acceptance of one's self, which is maintained by conforming to the internalized perceptions of others, is also the creation and suspension of the symbol: the communal confirmation of the internalized imago of the self as demonstrated and enacted through the interaction with others. This understanding of "symbol" owes its ontological existence not to iconographic representations in material form, although these may serve as expressive reminders of a desired ideal, but to the existence of bonded interactive relationships within the context of community, the relational creation, and suspension of the symbol.

Shame—that sudden or anticipated rupture of this relational matrix—fragments this imago by severing the relational suspensions that uphold the self. The rupture in relationship is experienced as exposure or uncovering of one's most vulnerable core and the global, inextricable sense that the painfully overwhelming detestable core of oneself is unacceptable and indelibly stained. The self becomes individualized.

The words that describe this condition are suggestive of the experience. The Indo-European root *kâm/kêm*, "to cover, to veil to hide," forms the direct cognate through the addition of the reflexive prefix *s*: *skâm*, "to cover oneself." The Germanic root of the word is *scama*, "to cover oneself," from which *sceme* derives, a "cover or mask." The modern German term is *Schemen*, "shadow, ghost, or shadow soul." *Skâm* or *skêm* is the root of "skin" and means "hide."[154] The anticipation of exposure curtails one's behavior as it approaches the limits of the acceptable, while the experience of being exposed moves one suddenly to withdraw and hide, to no longer be seen. Shame is the claim upon the archaic self, penetrating to the core of one's lived memory, which resides in one's body memory, and is therefore powerfully regressive. One is caught in the present moment of exposure and simultaneously claimed by the painful past. The experience is one of "being gripped." In Classical Greek the word is *theasthai*, "to see, to watch, to be gripped and fascinated, to wonder and admire, to be amazed and impressed." Both "theater" and "theory" (see chapter 2) derive from this term.[155] Within the system of affect theory the term describes the affect fear-terror.[156]

An additional dimension of the experience of shame is revealed by the German term *Scheu*, meaning "reverence, awe, respect as in front of something sacred."[157] Wermser adds that the Greek term *aidōs* means the "shame parts" of one's body," or sexual organs and the disgrace that followed their public exposure. Wermser emphasizes that *aidōs* also conveys the same sense as the German term *Scheu*.[158]

Each of the terms is multivalent, conveying or implying multiple shifts in both experience and one's conscious awareness of others' assessment of one's self-worth and standing in the sight of others. Sight, vision, and value are inseparable elements in the phenomenological complex of shame. The Latin word *ideal* derives from the Greek *idea* or *eidōs*, the form or appearance of something, from *idein*, "to see, to look, to recognize."[159]

Paul's perfectionism, demonstrated by his consistent pursuit of ideal behavior as both a Pharisee and an apostle, would have origins in the experience of his nascent self (what I call formation) as well as in his membership in the community of Pharisees. Ideals have their origins in not only being seen but in being seen by ideal others.[160] Paul's location in the Jewish Diaspora of the Greco-Roman world adds a crucial dimension to the role of shame and honor in his experience.

In the Greco-Roman culture, honor would directly depend upon one's status, gender, and power.[161] One's birth, intelligence, virtue, physical appearance, oratorical skills, virility, and other expressions of status located one within a hierarchy of values based upon the manifestation of various forms of power.[162] Weakness, physical deformity, poverty, sickness, illegitimacy, subordination, and foolishness would be consigned to the realm of shame. While honor could be acquired, conferred, and inherited, and one could perform shameful acts, a certain class or type of persons were permanently identified without honor: slaves, while women were identified with shame.[163] This is not to suggest that others could not act dishonorably or shamefully, but that women and slaves embodied the culture's understanding of the dynamics of honor and shame. Both slaves and women, therefore, could be seen, from this Mediterranean cultural perspective, as people who were identified with the condition of vulnerability, which is the condition of shame.

As a Pharisee, Paul would bring another dimension to the Greco-Roman complex of honor and shame, the dimension of holiness. As a Pharisee, Paul's understanding of holiness would rest upon the sense of separation from that which is unclean or prescribed by Torah. But if we place this conception of ritual practice within the context of his community as described by Neusner, then "purity" becomes the communal mediation of God's holiness (*agnos*). Within the Pharisaical community the honor-shame axes would revolve around separation from polluting fellowship with pagan Greeks at table fellowship concerning dietary restrictions, sexual contact, and corpse pollution—all issues of the body's relationship to boundaries of social intercourse.[164] The successful maintenance of these boundaries and the approval these actions garnered from his ideal others provided Paul with a cohesive sense of self within the context of his *Mitwelt*.

All of the elements in Paul's identity did not cohere. On a general level of explanation, Rosemary Ruether claims that Diaspora Judaism in the face of hellenizing hegemony reached a "psychic breaking point," at which it could no longer hold the varied elements of its creative response into a coherent pattern.[165] On the analytical level of object-relations theory, we can suggest that the absence of adequate empathic mirroring, which sets the stage for Paul's ambitious pursuit of ideals and the internalization of an ideal imago, also precipitates tremendous rage: the rage of being helpless in the face of both the psychic disintegration of the nascent self

(Kohut) and the unmet need for empathic bonding with the primary self-object (Winnicott). Paul, when faced with the explosive rage precipitated by the archaic memory of disintegration in his early life could have resorted to the mechanism of projection: "The first and the most fundamental of our insurances or safety-measures against feelings of pain, of being attacked, or of helplessness . . . is that device we call projection. All painful and unpleasant sensations or feelings in the mind are . . . automatically relegated outside oneself. . . . We disown and repudiate them as emanating from ourselves; in the ungrammatical but psychologically accurate phrase, we blame them *on* to someone else."[166]

Projection operates at both the infant and adult levels to preserve the internal boundaries of the self. By unconsciously identifying the disturbingly painful actions and dispositions of the one the child depends upon with another person or group, the self preserves its relationship with and the positive qualities of the self-object. Rage can then be visited upon the external devalued heads of legitimate targets of aggression. Shame can be a source of rage. "I believe that underlying many expressions of rage is a feeling of shame—a feeling that reflects a sense of failure or inadequacy so intolerable that it leads to a flaying out, an attempt to *rid the self* of the despised subjective experience."[167]

The mechanism associated with shame for relocating the pain of the experience is contempt.

> In essence, subjective shame, over failure, inferiority, or defect, is disavowed or repressed and is "placed" into another, who must then "accept" and "contain" the projection. Therefore the object of contempt must bear a certain similarity to the subject, at least with respect to the source of the projected shame, and must be willing to interact with the subject on the basis of the implicit contempt. From this perspective, then, contempt can be seen as an interactive externalization of the shame experience, and thus, ultimately, as a defense against [subjective shame].[168]

More precisely, contempt is a dual movement: one wherein the person looks upon the object of contempt with disgust, the other wherein the person completely dissociates from the object.

Paul's rage would indicate a fissure in the cohesion of his communally sanctioned and supported perfectionist self. Like almost every other detail of his activity, the issue of Paul's persecution remains contested.[169] My focus is not whether Paul actually inflicted violence upon others (Acts 7:58–8:3) but his affective state and the targets of his aggression. Paul uses the term *zēlos* (Phil. 3:6) to denote the same commitment to persecuting the *ecclesia* as his commitment to the Pharisees (Gal. 1:14). By his confession he persecuted (*diōkō*) the *ecclesia kath' hyperbolēn*, "to the utmost" or "in the extreme" (Gal. 1:13).[170] The term refers to the *makkot arbaim*, the thirty-nine lashes prescribed by Jewish law, and the *makkot mardut*, "a disciplinary lashing administered at the discretion of the local court."[171] Paul uses the term to describe the same punishment he received in 2 Cor. 11:24. He both gave and received the maximum number of lashes.[172]

The key question for our purpose is, what would have provoked and allowed Paul to inflict injury and suffering upon other Jews without being restrained by empathy or compassion? To answer the question, we must try to identify the targets of his aggression. They had to be fellow Jews since the behavior of pagan Greeks would not have warranted an official response.[173] The question then becomes what actions of theirs aroused Paul's hostility? Paula Fredricksen identifies them as a group of Damascus Jews who proclaimed the imminent return of a crucified messiah, who would "execute judgement on the wicked and establish the kingdom."[174] In light of his return Gentiles could be admitted into the bonded fellowship of the Jewish community, synagogue, and home, without being circumcised, that is, without becoming Jews. While Fredricksen dismisses the collapse of boundaries between Diaspora Jew and Gentile as irrelevant, I contend the issue is crucial.

> The Pharisees held with special intensity the position that purity laws should be observed in everyday life by the people as a whole and not play a role only as Torah for the priests. This made the sanctifiction of everyday life a program for the whole people of Israel. To the extent that this goal was realized in the Hellenic Diaspora, the separation from all non-Jews was marked with particular clarity. If ritual sanctification in particular, or preservation of their own identity as people of the covenant, was the engine of Pharisaic activity, then we can understand why Paul proceeded so aggressively against Jewish Christians in Damascus, if they regarded this particular boundary as porous.[175]

The legal sanctions against the messianic Jews of Damascus might have been issued by officials for ideological reasons, but operations of the legal structure would have also provided Paul with legitimate and culturally approved ventilation for his rage and aggression.

We must add a further element, perhaps the most crucial to understand the portrait of Paul as persecutor. Members of the Damascus community reached out and welcomed Greek pagans, including God-fearers, into the inner circle of Jewish fellowship by proclaiming a crucified Messiah. The image of a naked, disfigured, slain messianic leader stands in irreconcilable oppostion to the traditions of the Messiah in Judaism, traditions to which the Pharisees were direct heirs.[176] Messianic expectations arose during periods of oppression in Israel's history. The Messiah reverses the condition and status of a victimized people: "Instead of the Jews being the helpless and inferior victims of outside aggression and narcissistic devaluation, they became the powerful and aggressive masters and came to occupy a narcissistically superior position. He is formal in the imagery of the idealized King, all-powerful, all-wise, generous, kind, and loving to those who are his faithful followers and just to those he has conquered. His image is cloaked in grandiosity, even to the extent that he may even be divine."[177] Located in the Greco-Roman Diaspora, the Messiah, who lived in past narrative traditions and in future expectations, would be the embodiment of the personal and collective idealized imago or self-representation of Jews in a pagan culture that equated honor with status and power.

In Paul's psychic configuration, purity through separation from Gentiles would have offered one defense against the injuries of shame in a Greco-Roman culture of honor with whose values of status and strength he was thoroughly intimate. He would look upon them as unclean and therefore inferior by the standards of his community of Pharisees. But the vulnerable core of Paul's wounded self would have projected upon those Jews who were less than zealous and more than lax in their observance of the law. He would therefore be able to look upon his Diaspora brother through the eyes of Greek onlookers and see in them the unidentified recepticle of his projected, narcissistically wounded self. In a double movement of intersubjectivity, Paul would unconsciously reconfigure the composite elements of his bicultural formation into the discrete and unrelated elements of both cultic purity (Hebrew) and honor/shame (Greek). The fundamental mechanisms of projection and dissociation would allow him to exist with stable boundaries of self within the socially complex demands of the Hellenic Diaspora. "In narcissistic terms related to the superior-introject, he would see himself as superior, special, privileged, perfect, entitled, and even grandiose. In terms of the inferior-introject, he would see himself as inferior, worthless, valueless, shameful, and humiliated."[178]

Messianic Jews who had adopted a version of the teaching the slain Yeshuah and adopted Damascus would have compromised both Paul's systems of value and self. Toward those Jews who proclaimed a humiliated Messiah, Paul could assure the posture of aggression and inflict the injuries upon that part of his wounded vulnerability now dissociated from his narcissistic core projected upon those Jews who blurred the boundaries of purity. They became to him both polluted and shameful, the convergent devalued elements of himself upon which he visited violence in order to restore the boundaries of a fragile self.

The Pharisees would serve as a form of communal mediation, a collective mitigation against the devaluative standards of Diaspora Greeks, who evaluated Jews by their system of honor and shame and found them wanting. Paul, intimate with and inextricably tied to this culture, could ventilate his aggressive energies through legitimate religious channels of violence against the ritualistically impure proclaimers of a humiliated and powerless Messiah. His archaic self, fragmented by inadequate empathic mirroring, would lead to attenuated affect and atrophied empathy toward the displaced, projected, and unrecognized elements of his self that he persecuted with zeal and to the extreme.

Chapter 5

Transformation

The Incorporation of Vulnerability and the Emergence of Heterogeneous Selfhood

Narcissism is a term that must be reserved for that part of our self-image that would be relinquished were we to accept shame.

—Donald Nathanson

If I am correct in concluding that Paul's formation enabled him to stabilize and maintain the boundaries of his narcissistically wounded self by ritualistically treating the Greeks as impure, therefore separated from holiness or purity—the source of his identity and value—while looking upon Jews of relatively less exacting Torah observance as the embodiment of his wounded, displaced vulnerability, then I may proceed to describe the transformation that took place in him through his mystical experience.

I have already described the collective mediation of the sacred in the setting of the table fellowship of Pharisees or "normal mysticism." Pharisees were also adept at ecstatic mystical disciplines.[1] Jewish mysticism developed from prophetic movements characterized by apocalyptic proclamations and visions of the world's destruction and judgment.[2] *Merkabah* mysticism's image is taken from Isaiah 6 and Ezekiel 1, wherein the prophet encounters a divine figure seated on a chariot/throne. The notion of "chariot" (*merkabah*) mysticism seems to come from Mishnah *Ḥagiga* 2:1.[3] *Merkabah* mysticism is characterized by heavenly ascents and out-of-body encounters with the creator of the universe.[4] Alan Segal identifies Ezekiel's vision of God's *kabod* (translated as "Glory") in the form of a seated figure as "the central image in Jewish mysticism."[5]

Merkabah mysticism differs from the classic descriptions of Christian mysticism as divine-human mystical union.[6] The heavenly traveler enters into the presence of the *eikōn* (image) or *eidōs* (form) of a man or angel ("the appearance of the likeness of the glory of the Lord" in Ezekiel 1) who is filled with *kabod* (heaviness) or *doxa* (glory) of the Lord. The encounter is a moment of ecstatic intensity and revelation of divine knowledge.[7]

While Jewish mystical visions are based upon prophetic texts, the prophetic texts do not portray mystical experience as the fulfillment of intentional expectancy. "Ezekiel's vision (like Isaiah's) is not, however, a mystic vision. It is nothing that the prophet has sought. It is nothing he has built up to by intellectual preparation and spiritual discipline. Rather, it is God who has seized the prophet and overwhelmed him with His majesty. The prophet has felt humbled, and the communication he has received is an ethical message for the people, a preachment."[8] As described by the prophetic narrator, the experience is both irruptive and eruptive. The prophetic tradition of being seized or arrested is placed within the apocalyptic context of eschatological revelation. Both the defining image of the *Merkabah* and the traditions of Jewish apocalytic inform the first-century apocalypse, *1 Enoch*.[9]

Paul's mystical experience belongs to this tradition of Jewish *Merkabah* mysticism.[10]

> I must boast; there is nothing to be gained by it, but I will go on to visions and revelations of the Lord. I know a man in Christ who fourteen years ago was caught up to the third heaven—whether in the body or out of the body I do not know, God knows. And I know that this man was caught up into Paradise—whether in the body or out of the body I do not know, God knows—and he heard things that cannot be told, which man may not utter. On behalf of this man I will boast, but on my own behalf I will not boast, except of my own weaknesses. Though I wish to boast, I shall be a fool, for I shall be speaking the truth. But I refrain from it, so that no one may think more of me than he sees in me or hears from me. And to keep me from being too elated by the abundance of revelations, a thorn was given me in the flesh, a messenger of Satan, to harass me, to keep me from being too elated. Three times I besought the Lord about this, that it should leave me; but he said to me, "My grace is sufficient for you, for my power is made perfect in weakness." (2 Cor. 12:1–9)

Segal finds material in *1 Enoch* that directly shaped Paul's mystical experience.

> Whatever the intention of the author of 1 Enoch, the relationship to Paul's experience is important. Like Enoch, Paul claims to have gazed on the Glory, whom Paul identifies as Christ; Paul understands that he has been transformed into a divine state, which will be fully realized after his death; Paul claims that his vision and transformation is somehow a mystical identification; and Paul claims to have received a calling, his special status as intermediary. Paul specifies the meaning of this calling for all believers, a concept absent in the Enochic texts, although it may have been assumed within the original community.[11]

In Gal. 1:12 Paul refers to his mystical encounter with the enthroned Christ as an *apokalypsis* (revelation), which relates his experience to the Jewish tradition. While Segal, James Tabor, and Ithamar Gruenwald clearly indicate that the prophetic, apocalyptic, and mystical elements inform Jewish mystical experiences of this era, the prophetic dimension plays a crucial role in Paul's mission to include the Gentiles within the sacred cultus of Israel.

Although scholars have stressed the importance of Jewish eschatology in the shaping of Paul's attitude toward Gentiles,[12] neither Jewish messianic traditions nor apocalyptic traditions envision an elimination of the law at the eschaton.[13] Yet "the gospel" Paul received is the gospel of Gentile inclusion:[14] "For I would have you know, brethren, that the gospel which was preached by me is not man's gospel. For I did not receive it from man, nor was I taught it, but it came through a revelation [*apokalypsis*] of Jesus Christ" (Gal. 1:11–12). Paul contrasts the gospel he has received (*paralabon*) in v. 12 with the (*paradoseōn*) of his ancestors or Pharisees in v. 14. He contrasts what he received from his fathers in the practices of exclusion, and what he received in revelation from Christ for the mission of Gentile inclusion. Contemporary scholars see the essential core of Paul's gospel as defined here to be at the heart of his apostolic mission and proclamation. Although scholars recognize the core of Paul's radical social revisioning, their efforts to account for the transformation are not as successful.[15] Segal's attempt to explore the movement from Paul's mystical experience to his inclusive mission focuses upon contemporary analysis of the psychodynamics of conversion and the role of community in providing a structure of meaning for the convert.[16]

The key to Paul's radical reversal toward the apostate Jews he persecuted, toward Gentiles he excluded, and toward the entire system of Pharisaical purity codes resides with the structure of his mystical experience and its resemblance to its prophetic portrayals. Paul's own portrayal of his transcendent experience relies upon prophetic tropes. "But when he who had set me apart before I was born, and had called me through his grace, was pleased to reveal his Son to me, in order that I might preach him among the Gentiles, I did not confer with flesh and blood, nor did I go up to Jerusalem to those who were apostles before me, but I returned to Damascus" (Gal. 1:15–17). Both Isaiah (49:1) and Jeremiah (1:5) describe themselves as being set apart or consecrated for a holy purpose, then being sent (Hebrew *shalaḥ*, Greek *apostellō*) by the Holy One:[17] in Jeremiah's call, "a prophet to the nations" (Jer. 1:5). Paul interpreted his call in light of Hebrew prophecy and alludes consistently to this in his lettters (1 Cor. 9:1; 15:8–10; Phil. 3:4–11), quoting frequently from Isaiah, twice as often as from Jeremiah.[18]

The evidence convincingly supportive of the prophetic character of Paul's mystical encounter with God comes from the *merkabah* and prophetic traditions themselves. *First Enoch* reports the ascent of Enoch through seven heavens to the throne of God. The journey both confirms his desire to dwell in heaven, and transforms him in the process. In *2 Enoch* he is transformed into the likeness of God, radiant and glorious, and receives his new garments similar to the transformed body Paul describes in 2 Cor. 5:1–10.[19] "In the concluding section to the vision Enoch describes the angels and the doxologies which they recite. These are two doxological formulae mentioned here. The one, 'Holy, holy, holy, is the Lord of Spirits: He filleth the earth with spirits' takes as its model the Sanctus of Isaiah 6:3; and the other one, 'Blessed be thou, and blessed be the name of the Lord for ever and ever,' is reminiscent of the Benedictus of Ezekiel 3:12."[20]

Paul's familiarity with *1 Enoch* is evident from the imagery that he takes from the literature and his experience that is, in turn, shared by the traditions of prophets and apocalypses.

Isaiah's ascent to the throne is both theophany and call.

> In the year that King Uzziah died, I saw the Lord of all sitting upon a throne, high and lifted up; and his train filled the temple. Above him stood the seraphim, each had six wings: with two he covered his feet, and with two he flew. And one called to another and said:
>
> "Holy, holy, holy is the Lord of hosts;
> the whole earth is full of his glory."
>
> And the foundations of the thresholds shook at the voice of him who called, and the house was filled with smoke. And I said: "Woe is me! For I am lost; for I am a man of unclean lips, and I dwell in the midst of a people of unclean lips; for my eyes have seen the King, the Lord of hosts!" (Isa. 6:1–5)

Paul, as a Pharisee, would have been familiar with apocalyptic and *merkabah* texts from the LXX including Isa. 6:1–11, since he participated in the 'explosion' of interest in the unseen world among Jews in Second Temple times. "The main features of his apocalyptic vision are known to us from texts of the period, though as a prophet himself, he adds his own detailed revelations (such as 1 Thess. 4:16–17). So we can safely assume, that if entering Paradise meant being taken before God's throne, given Paul's beliefs and expectations, this would have been an absolutely extraordinary experience."[21] And it would have had extraordinary results and implications. In order to understand some of the dimensions of Paul's experience, we must carefully observe the following about Isaiah's.

The theophany's site is the Jerusalem temple.[22] This setting would be the corresponding configuration of Paul's understanding of holiness: both the temple priests and the Pharisees possessed a cultic order of purity.[23] While Paul was communal-centered and the priests were temple-centered, the boundaries were analogous.[24] Yahweh's throne at the center of the temple is the seat of the holy, *qadosh* (set apart, separated), furthest removed from impurity and that which defiles. The theophany reveals the essence of sacral alterity: in its ultimate dissociation from that which is different from its being, the holy becomes the ultimate transcendent Other. But Paul also saw the enthroned figure as an ideal Other, for his mystogogical imagination would have been shaped by messianic expectations and informed by the language of the LXX.

The enthroned figure who appears in Ezekiel's vision (1:26) is described in the LXX as the *eidōs* (idea) or form of a man. "The figure [or *eidōs*] of man on the divine throne described in Genesis, Exodus, Ezekiel, Daniel, and the Psalms (forming the basis of the son of man speculation) was also understood as the ideal and immortal man. His immortality and glorious appearance were things Adam possessed in the Garden of Eden and lost when he sinned. In this form, the traditions concerning the son of man are centuries older than Christianity, and Paul uses them to good advantage."[25] Paul would eventually identify the *eidōs* as the *Christos*, the anointed (messiah) of Israel.

Paul's entry, like Isaiah's, into the cultic center of the temple and enthroned presence of Yahweh would also be the profane intrusion of defilement into the presence of sacred purity. The transgressive juxtaposition provokes a trisagionic outcry that signals and protects the boundary between the pure and the unclean: "Holy, Holy, Holy." The LXX uses *haginos*, "pure." Paul also uses the term *hagna* in Phil. 4:8. The entire earth is filled with Yahweh's *kabod* or *doxa*, except for the intrusive agent who suddenly becomes overwhelmed by the consciousness and pain of his impurity. Theophany becomes ecstasy, for the witness to the Divine becomes a spectacle to himself ("ecstasy" means literally to stand outside) or *theathai*.

Harpazō, the term identifying the prophet's call,[26] is also an accurate description of the experience of shame: to be gripped by the sudden, inexplicable self-conscious awareness of one's self as woefully inadequate. This sudden awareness is accompanied by the inextricable seizure of overwhelming pain that enters the core of one's self and manifests itself in a particular part of the body. "Near the upper range of terror will appear additional somatic experiences, such as a gripping sensation in the chest."[27] The sensation is global, but expressions of shame and its accompanying dimensions of fear and terror take the form of metonymy in honor/shame cultures. "The social map is usually condensed and expressed in somewhat compact symbolic form in one's physical person. Honor is displayed especially in certain body parts, head, face, and arms. Dishonor is associated with other bodily parts, such as 'lick the dirt off my feet' or 'kiss my ass.'"[28]

The face would be the site of archaic wounding in Paul, the source of the failed empathic mirroring, and therefore the place both sacred and vulnerable in the symbolic estimation of one's worth. In Isaiah the mouth is a trope for his prophetic vocation that must be purified by fire in order to become the oracle of a holy God. But the mouth would also be the expression of his impurity, the place where the collective impurity of Israel speaks blasphemously to Yahweh, therefore a site of collective/personal divine/human convergence. The pain of shame is described as a severe burning by its victims, the sensation of being caught in the devaluing gaze of another that fragments the eirenic coherency of the self, and forces one to stand outside oneself and join the company of one's objectifying onlookers who observe the spectacle of one's humiliation. What appears in the LXX and not in the RSV in v. 5 is "woe is me, for I am pricked to the heart"; the word translated as "pricked" is more accurately rendered as "stabbed," the effect of being caught by the penetrating pain of shame entering one's own inner sanctum.[29] *Akathartos*, "unclean," is "not just a lack of cleanness. It is a power which positively defiles. In particular, anything associated with a foreign cult, or hostile to Yahweh is unclean." The primary determination of purity is the law.[30]

If Paul's mystical experience and prophetic call resembled even aspects of Isaiah's, then the following interpretation is possible. Ecstatic experiences are moments of affective intensity and heightened self-awareness. Paul's presence before the source and in the center of holiness would also be a moment of shame, or the exposure of his hidden vulnerability, masked by his perfectionist idealizations as a Pharisee. The exposure of that which had been hidden from his fellowship and himself would be experienced as overwhelming pain in the presence of holiness. Shame would be experienced as self-revulsion at the exposure of his hidden vulnerable core, and symbolized as impurity or stain, while experiencing fear in the presence of the Divine. Yet shame has another simultaneous movement upon which the previous one depends. Shame begins in attention, the gravity of attraction, of being drawn toward another, which then turns into withdrawal in the face of relational rupture, the result of being exposed and devalued.

If the hidden core of Paul's authentic, hence vulnerable, self had become displaced through the mechanism of projection wherein the negative painful internalizations of disturbing self-objects are cast out of the psychic onto unrecognized embodiments of one's injured, devalued self, then Paul's rage at and persecution of Gentile-accepting Jews would be the embodiment of his own wounded core, which he would inflict injury upon with attenuated empathy as a defensive boundary against further narcissistic injury.

This double movement in shame—away from while desiring to return to the person who is both the object of one's interest and the source of one's shame—is the identical movement in structure of the holy described in Otto's phenomenology of the sacred:[31] the *mysterium tremendum* forces one to turn away in fear, while the *mysterium fascinans* compels one irresistibly toward the sacred source. In Paul's traditional understanding of Jewish purity, the boundaries between the sacred and profane would also be the boundaries between clean and unclean. If within Paul's experience the most objectionable part of himself, that which was dissociated and removed from conscious awareness and acceptance, became manifest and exposed—or in the configuration of Isaiah's experience—seen or looked upon with the hierarchical yet empathic gaze of the enthroned *kabod* of God, this movement would have been internalized as the boundary-crossing intensity of incorporating injured, displaced, and alien part(s) of himself, divested of vulnerability, and the derisive value or negative valance it carried into his self. Translated as "purge off," the LXX *perikathariei* is from the Hebrew כָּפַר, which is part of a complex of terms associated with cultic rituals of atonement, or *kipper* acts, performed by priests in the temple. Yahweh demanded that the forces of impurity, unleashed by the offenses committed, be kept away from his immediate environment.[32] The Greek term for this condition is *miasma* or pollution, the global condition for impurity, symbolized as stain.[33]

Ricoeur's discussion of the symbol of evil is a hermeneutical phenomenology of the representations of shame. The condition is brought to consciousness *before* the holy. The healing indicated by *kipper*, the burning sensation is both the pain of the affect shame, and the moment of healing, which I contend is the integration of split-off aspects of the narcissistic wounds to the self. The term *kipper* here is more accurately rendered as "covered," which describes both the desire and the relief to exposure as expressed in the etymology of "shame": *skam*, "to cover"; *sceme*, "mask"; and *scheu*, "awe and reverence for something sacred." Paul experienced healing in the moment of transformation before the throne of Yahweh.

Shame is understood psychoanalytically as a form of regression, a return to the wounded core of one's self whenever the expectations and needs of the self are unmet. "Kohut made it clear that our need and search for satisfying self-objects continues throughout life. If our needs have been severely thwarted and defects in the self have occurred, we will attempt to sustain ourselves through various regressive retreats. The depth of the regression depends upon the overall severity of the trauma, at what developmental level the trauma occurred, and the extent of the damage of the self."[34]

Mystical experiences are considered examples of regression in which one searches for lost experiences of trust or lost self-objects.[35] The basic mechanism is incorporation. If Paul, during the moments of mystical, heightened intensity reclaimed his despised vulnerability that he projected onto less strict Torah-observing Jews while allocating the elements of his identity intimately bound to Greek culture as impure, then he would emerge from his heavenly ascent a transformed man: a new self. The purifying gaze of the ideal spectral Other, which Paul terms "glory," would be experienced as compassion that would enable him to accept his hidden vulnerability and shame—that part of himself threatened by annihilation at an early age, by accepting the Holy One who had gazed upon his shame with empathy. The embrace of this vulnerability and devalued realm of the self would require an identification with weakness, suffering, shame, *and* his previously profane parts under his former system of purity. Although Paul's mystical experience was firmly in the tradition of Jewish *merkabah* mysticism and his understanding of the holy as sacral alterity, the results of this experience would not only be personally but divinely transformative. The sacred for Paul had changed from the homogeneous sacral alterity to the heterogeneous relational alterity. This new deity would be Lord of Paul's profane parts: suffering, vulnerability, weakness, and humiliation. Most important for the emerging cultus of messianic Jews, Paul's God was a mixed God, an *anakratheos*: a creolian Messiah.

REFORMATION: RECONCILIATION AS CREOLIZATION

Heterogeneous Communities and Relational Sacrality

If we have accurately rendered the essence of Paul's transformative ascent to the third heaven and encounter with the enthroned *eidos* of glory, then the result of that encounter would be experienced as the rupture of the lifelong boundary between his authentic vulnerable core self (nuclear self—Kohut) and the false self that mirrored communally sanctioned ideals, maintained by the affects shame-humiliation and pride-purity. The former description befits Paul's intersubjective consciousness of Hellenic diasporic values of stature and power; the latter emphasizes Pharisaical practices of purity. Purity would be maintained by idealized ritual practice; while his defense against shame-humiliation would be through the mechanism of projection wherein the negative introjects of his own archaic experience of empathic failure would be displaced upon Torah-lax, therefore impure, Jews and impure Gentile Greeks, while his positive idealizations would be identified with the traditions of his ancestors and the messianic ideal of the returning ruler of Israel who would vindicate culturally embedded diasporic Jews with a display of triumphal power and purity. Paul's ecstatic moment of intense exposure of himself in the presence of the ultimate "ideal spectator" (William James), wherein both his "shame parts" and his experience of the Deity is pervasive glory would enable him to incorporate the despised, devalued, and painfully intolerable realms of himself in the presence of divine empathy whose penetrating acceptance of the unacceptable in Paul results in the experience of wholeness as the heterogeneous self.

Cultically, the lines of purity had become inverted, wherein the profane (Latin *pro*, "outside"; *fano*, "temple": in front of or outside the temple) has now entered into the realm of the sacred—along with Paul's unacceptable, fragmented, and culturally intertangled aspects of his self—and found acceptance.[36] If the boundaries of the self have been reconfigured, along with cultic boundaries of purity and impurity, then the boundaries of community would also be reconfigured.

As already noted, the self is inherently unstable and requires both interactive, bonded relationships with an adequate degree of nurture and the various expressions of secondary processes: doctrines, constitutions, founding genealogies, cosmogonies, and creedal formulations.[37] Given Paul's formation in the diasporic *Mitwelt* which formed consciousness in terms of a relational understanding of the self rather than the isolation of subjectivity,[38] Paul's experience would leave him in a state of social liminality without the traditional processes of transition to recognizably familiar structures. Paul would have entered an extended period of disorientation as he attempted both to make sense of his transformative transport to heaven and to relocate himself in a community that would confirm and conform to his experience. Returning to the *haburot* or table fellowship of the Pharisees would have been deformative given their discrete and homogeneous construction of purity, sacrality, and community. "If the suppression of Christianity had been a correlative obligation of Paul's Pharisaism, then his conversion would have alienated him from his social base, and group embeddedness, within his particular strand of Judaism."[39]

Yet entering into pagan Greek society would have been unthinkable; Paul continued to think of himself as a Jew. "The consequence of Paul's conversion would therefore have been isolation and lack of social identity, until such time as he joined a Christian [*sic*] community."[40] Paul's testimony points to Damascus (Gal. 1:17);

he says he returned there. Given the variety of Judaism(s) in the Diaspora, varying degrees of cultural exchange and mutual social interest between Jews and Greeks who share a common language took place. One group of Gentiles took an active part in synagogue worship. Known as "God-fearers" (*phoboumenos*, fear of worship; *sebomenos*, worshiper; *theosebēs*, worshiper of God Most High), they did not enter the fold of the circumcised. "The God-fearers and sympathizers may not have been a well-defined class, but they are important because they illustrate the gray area where the boundary between Jew and Gentile becomes unclear and loses much of its importance."[41] This realm of social indeterminacy, where members of two different societies met yet did not relinquish their identity as Jew or Gentile, would perhaps provide a temporary holding group for Paul during the period between his formation and reformation.[42]

The God-fearers, in intimate association and proximity to the Diaspora Jews and synagogues, would have become anomalous boundary markers in Paul's emergent self and served as transitional self-objects. In the synagogue, God-fearers would be impure Gentiles in proximity to the circumcised Jews. As Greek Gentiles, they would have embodied vulnerability, while Jews who accepted them would have been seen by Paul as impure. Together they created the chiasmic liminal configuration Paul would internalize, proclaim, and enact repeatedly in rhetoric and ritual, as the kenotic meta-trope and narrative of relinquished power, suffering, and covenental vulnerability to Jews, Greeks, slaves and masters, male and female: the incarnate presence of intrapsychic, intercommunal, and cosmogonically transfigured valences of powerlessness and impurity.

While we cannot determine Paul's location, we can sketch his condition. Given the central role of ideality in the expectations for conditional approval, expectations that Paul fulfilled fueled by the intensity of his zeal and his need to distance himself from impurity, shame, and the accompanying and necessary attenuation of empathy, Paul's irruptive transformation would have brought him to reflective reexamination of his life in light of his recent experience of affective inundation. While this project does not examine the methodological questions concerning cross-cultural psychology,[43] the following description suggests an analogue portrait of Paul's post-transformative condition:

> It is one of the turning points in analysis when the narcissistically disturbed patient comes to the emotional insight that all the love he has captured with so much effort and self-denial was not meant for him as he really was, that the admiration for his beauty and achievements was aimed at this beauty and these achievements, and not at the child himself. In analysis, the small and lonely child that is hidden behind his achievements wakes up and asks: "What would have happened if I had appeared before you bad, ugly, angry, jealous, lazy, dirty, smelly? Where would your love have been then? And I was all these things as well. Does this mean that it was not really me whom you loved, but only what I pretended to be?"[44]

Caution is in order at this point, for with the invocation of the twentieth-century religion of psychoanalysis and the cult of the therapeutic wherein two individuals, one of superior status, knowledge, and power, the other possessing more pain than knowledge, enter into a set-apart space during a preappointed hour that the guilt and shame of one may be expiated and healed by the other, also evokes a linear model of first-century CE recovery from the abuse-sanctioning Judaism to become a fully recovered Christian. Paul's preprophetic condition is characterized by viability and functionality, not Augustinian or Lutheran neurosis. The transformation is particular to Paul. No one else—in spite of Augustinian and Lutheran archetypal exegesis—has an experience quite like Paul's in the context of Pauline narratives. The uniqueness of his experience is intensified when we relate his transformation to the unusual communities of social alterity he nurtured, a relationship I will examine below.

Paul's need for a post-transformational community that would conform to the reconfigured internal and interpersonal relationships would be as important to the stability and viability of his newly integrated self as it was to his former bipolar self, a self that had been "previously split off, repressed, and restricted to early archaic self-objects"[45]—now capable of developing an empathic relatedness with new and formerly alien self-objects. Paul would eventually belong to or attempt to establish eschatological communities of messianic expectation shaped by the values and dispositions of inclusive otherness, mutual vulnerability, and empathic bonding. The corpus of Pauline epistles are the documented traces, at times cryptic, of his results and failures at heterogeneous communal creation.

Although the situations or circumstances vary and Paul's purpose in responding gives different shape and strategy to the seven letters attributed to his authorship, a few things remain consistent. Part of that which Christians for close to two millennia have considered the sacred text of the New Testament is composed of letters written by Paul or written in his name. Since the Enlightenment, these have been subjected to prolonged, intensive, and ongoing examination by scholars, mainly European, using methods developed by confessional scholars, mostly Protestant, predominantly German, and almost always male. Paul has been the central literary subject of examination since he wrote (or dictated) letters that always include him as one of the principal subjects, while Jesus never wrote or dictated a single New Testament document, and what statements he purportedly made are increasingly suspect.[46]

Only of late, however, have scholars begun to see that these "sacred documents" by Paul, "called to be an apostle," are primarily concerned about the relationships between Jews and Gentiles sharing the same cultic space as bonded equals before the Divinity they have gathered to worship.[47] Given the documented preoccupations of Western theologians, whose systematic cataloguing of concerns, such as "soteriology," "eschatology," "pneumatology," "justification by faith," and "ecclesiology," rarely includes community as a primary subject of sustained intellectual examination or as a working category of analysis or epistemology, "community" is present only by virtue of its marginalization or absence.[48] What accounts for this millennial myopia demands another investigation. Creating, cultivating, and maintaining communities, however, is clearly

Paul's preoccupation. His efforts evinced several consistent and characteristic concerns.[49]

The composition of ethnically heterogeneous Pauline communities corresponds to the identity of Christ and the character of the sacred embodied by him, as experienced by Paul and interpreted through the post-transformative community. It is primarily this experience of the sacred and Paul's understanding of its claim upon him that informs and fuels his mission to the Gentiles and his insistent uncompromising commitment to their inclusion. In fulfillment of this mission, which grew out of the integrity of this experience of the sacred, Torah (Law) becomes an obstacle to be rhetorically redefined, misportrayed, distorted not in order to eliminate law or for law to be replaced by grace, but to avoid the creation of yet another community that mediates the holy or sacral alterity, the basis of homogeneous exclusiveness.

Mythos and Community

The reconfiguration of the community requires a sacred tradition of ancestral parentage, variously called ideology (critical theorists) or myth (history of religions), as well as a sacred narrative that embodies the beginning, middle, and end of the events of the Deity's life that becomes part of a new sapiential tradition, which portrays the problems of the community and prescribes their resolution in light of the new wisdom. This includes the application of those actions performed by the Deity as models of and for behavior. The controlling tropic movement in Paul is kenotic (because it replicates his movement from persecutor to apostle). Reconciliation, or what I have termed the process of creolization, is an attempt to cultivate the same transfigured understanding of integrity and sacrality to others who have not shared the same transformative experience as Paul.

Paul's communal labor is to create a new ethnos, one that reflects his experience of a new mode of sacral ontology. His letters contain elements of a larger narrative structure that he refers to in parts. A. D. Smith has shown that ethnic groups depend upon a shared collective history that both binds them together and distinguishes them from others.[50] Paul's narrative, however, attempts to create an equalizing order that levels boundaries between groups and creates a universal condition for all humanity, especially those whom he is trying to bring into bonded relatedness. The Adamic mythos creates a new commonality of sin among universalized humanity, while the Abrahamic genos creates an intergenerational lineage of Gentile kin.

Adam, whom Paul mentions in Rom. 5:14 and 1 Cor. 15:22, 45a–b, becomes the universal type in the myth of evil that situates and reconciles. "The first function of the myths of evil is to embrace mankind as a whole in one ideal history. . . . [E]xperience escapes its singularity, it is transmuted in its own 'archetype.'"[51] Paul's myth of evil's origins destroys all ethnic boundaries by assigning all of humanity the same origin and same condition. His method reverses the process found in Deuteronomy wherein categories of distinction are established based on

Israel's relationship to Yahweh. Holiness established Israel as Yahweh's ethnos; their first assignment was to purge the land of its profane inhabitants.[52] Paul uses one myth to dismantle the categories established by another. The Adamic myth, in Paul's method, reverses the creation by supplanting the prevailing order with another. In phenomenological terms, Paul is trying to create a shared or common horizon for both Jew and Gentile by locating the origins in primordial time, or *illo tempore*.[53] "*Pas/pasa/pan* occur at least twenty-five times in such weighty expressions as 'salvation to everyone who believes,' 'all have sinned,' and 'that he might have mercy on all,'—five times in conjunction with the phrase 'Jew(s) and Gentile(s)' ([Rom.] 1:16; 2:9, 10; 3:9; 10:12; cf. 4:11–12, 16)."[54]

Having established a common universal condition, Paul provides a common ancestor, Abraham, who acts as a mediating figure between Jew and Gentile, being both once himself. Abraham stands as the ordaining ancestor over the community at Rome rather than Moses, who is the prophet of a Gentile-excluding Torah. Paul suspends Abraham between his origin as a Gentile and his identity as a Jew by justifying Abraham through his faith rather than circumcision. Halvor Moxnes notes that "Paul reduces circumcision, the mark *par excellence* of their Jewishness, to a mere 'sign or seal of the righteousness he had by faith' (Rom. 4:11)."[55] By displacing the mark of Jewish inclusion (circumcision) and the mark of Gentile exclusion, Paul maintains the boundary-traversing character of Abraham, who is the father of a boundary-trespassing community.

Paul is drawing upon the resources from his former community of Pharisees and the tradition of Israel that constituted itself in terms of ancestral lineage. The Pharisees composed their own sources of ancestors in response to Greco-Roman philosophical schools present in Palestine and the Diaspora. (See E. P. Sanders and Rivkin in chapter 4 above.) But defining oneself intergenerationally through claiming direct descent from a primordial ancestor was also a familiar method of "world-making" for Jews as well as other primal peoples.[56] Paul's rhetoric has its origins in the "ancient Israelite-Jewish tradition, namely the narration of the events of *Heilsgeschichte* such as is found in the Song of Moses (Deut. 32) and Psalm 78 and 106."[57] As noted in his use of Adam's mythology, Paul here again uses a tradition from Judaism to dismantle and reassemble the tradition from whence it derived. The new community is based upon an inclusive "fictive kinship system."[58]

Paul therefore provides new origins and new sources for defining the relationship between members of this heterogeneous community. The source for the community's new identity is the gospel, received by Paul from Christ. It is around the question of the contents of Paul's gospel that interpretive issues arise regarding the meaning of law (*Torah*), works (*ergon*), and justification. The history of these terms' interpretation has been one of transcendental metaphysical translation, rather than interpretations mediated by the communal embodiment of relationality (see chapter 3).

Each of these key terms has undergone reinterpretation based on the growing scholarly consensus that Paul's use of "law," which has become a hermeneutical and controlling symbol of interpretation and self-understanding in Western civilization and religion, refers to ritual practices—works—that demarcate and maintain the boundaries of identity and community between Jews and Gentiles—*not*, as the history of Western theological interpretation has insisted, a term to describe human-centered efforts to achieve eternal salvation and the hosts of neurotic afflictions that are the psychological inheritance of Westerners.[59] Greek *nomos* means "law" or "rule," from which we derive "norm, normal"; it translates "*torah*" in the LXX (see chapter 3). (*Nomos* also refers to mode in the musical theory of ancient Greece; see chapter 1.) Of the 116 times Paul uses *nomos*, 33 appear in Galatians, and 74 in Romans: both situations of impending crisis concerning the status of Gentiles and the relationship between Gentile and Jewish believers in Christ.[60] *Nomos* can be defined generally as any system of law, a rule governing one's actions, or norm; it can refer to the Mosaic law, the Pentateuch, and the "new law" for Christians.[61] The two most important senses are in regard to ritual practice of identity and community construction.

Segal points out that although the term does not develop until the advent of Rabbinic Judaism, Paul uses one dimension of *nomos*, or Torah, as haggadah or the sacred story of Israel's salvation (Rom. 1–4, 9–11) or as Ulrich Wilckens indicates, *Heilsgeschichte*.[62] "What he [Paul] negates is the value of observing Torah [as halakah] for the purposes of defining who is part of the community of the saved."[63] Paul's vitriolic distortions of the meaning of Jewish law have less to do with the condemnation of boastful self-election and pride than with his attempt to decenter the controlling importance of Torah as the source of homogeneous community. Jews were not anti-Gentile. Gentiles could convert, and Jews actively sought Gentile converts during this century.[64] A Gentile could enter the community by undergoing circumcision, the ritual transformation that would mark him as a member and eliminate the sign of difference. Paul, however, is equally against forcing Jews to relinquish Torah in order to become "Christian" Jews. *Nomos* is the *entire* differential system of signs as a way of creating community and identity based upon sacral alterity. By redrawing the boundaries of community to include both Jews and Gentiles, Paul translates the law from its status as the constituting source of the social symbol, or controlling symbol, to a sign whose difference from other signs is necessary but not ultimate. Paul is using the singularity of the mark or sign, circumcision, which participates in the ritual system and legal system of Jewish self-definition, to dismantle an ultimate but homogeneous system, Torah.

In the new system created by Paul, faith and justification serve as the basis of the new relationship with God and other members of the community. What has been translated as "justification" and has obtained the status of theological symbol is the verb *dikaioun* (justify) and the noun *dikaiosynē* (justification). The use of these terms is a mistranslation, since English lacks the accurate terms. The cluster of "justify" terms used is borrowed from the French.[65] "Thus Abraham 'believed God, and it was reckoned to him as *righteousness*.' So you see that it is people of faith who are the sons of Abraham. And the scripture, foreseeing that God would *justify* the Gentiles by faith, preached the gospel beforehand to Abraham" (Gal.

3:6–7). Sanders points out that the only English verb that could accurately translate *dikaioun* is no longer in use, *rihtwisian*.[66] The term is relational and refers to the Gentiles' standing in right relationship to God, through faith (*pistis*), rather than the forensic implications of "justification" that have become institutionalized in Western theological imagination. Hendrikus Boers points out that the implication is that Abraham stood in right relationship as a heathen.[67] Baptism becomes the sign of membership in the new community. Faith in Christ becomes the new requirement.

The term *gospel* (Greek *euangelion*) refers to the source of this new community, for Paul uses the word as both a term of origin and content. As origin, "gospel" refers to "the gospel of God" (Rom. 1:1; 15:16; 2 Cor. 11:7) as content, "the gospel of Christ" (Rom. 15:19; 1 Cor. 9:12; 2 Cor. 2:12; 9:13; 10:14; Phil. 1:27; 1 Thess. 3:2), and "the gospel of his Son" (Rom. 1:9). Paul uses it to designate the divine sanction of radical inclusiveness of the Gentiles into the sacred community that all receive by faith.

Faith, therefore, operates as a means of embracing an identity of inclusive otherness in a community that includes previously profane pagan Greeks, but who bear no physical sign that resolves or erases their identity as "Other" in the perception of the Jews. While scholars have accurately described the experience of being faced with contradictions in the familiar established order as "cognitive dissonance," they incorrectly conclude that Paul attempts to resolve this condition through rhetorical redefinitions of familiar terms, and the creation of new social arrangements such as communities of converts.[68] The goal of such actions is the resolution of tensions in perception and understanding caused by transformative experiences. Gerd Theissen's application of Festinger's theory to Paul identifies righteousness, which would be Paul's culturally specific term, as the ideological resolution of the reduction of dissonance through the divinely approved and sanctioned relationships between God, Jew, and Gentile received by faith: "The doctrine of justification has primarily a social integrative function: it is intended to make it possible for Jews and Gentiles to live together in the Christian congregations."[69] If we examine "faith" in terms of the communal praxis Paul encourages, faith does not function according to Festinger's theory. Rather, faith describes the capacity and commitment to sustained irresolution of cognitive dissonance, through the embrace of others who bear the marks of exclusive otherness.

Mythos and Reconciliation

Paul's third primordial story, which forms the foundation of the other two, is the mythos of Jesus Christ. Although the story does not appear in a single unbroken narrative, Alexander J. M. Wedderburn has collected the fragments and placed them into narrative form. Paul

> tells us of God sending (out) his Son, born of woman, born under the Law (Gal 4:4), a Son who was at the same time the Lord "through whom are all things" (1 Cor 8:6). Being rich he beggared himself (2 Cor 8:9), and being

in the form of God he did not hold equality with God to be *arpagmos*, but rather "emptied" himself and took on a servile form, a human likeness; he humbled himself to the point of being subject to death, even crucifixion (Phil 2:6–8). He became a "servant of the circumcision for the sake of God"s truth" (Rom 15:8). Though he knew no sin he was made sin for our sakes, that we might become God's righteousness in him (2 Cor 5:21); he became a curse for us by being hanged on his cross that he might redeem us (Gal 3:13). He was betrayed and on that night held a last meal with his disciples (1 Cor 11:23–5). He was given up for our transgressions and raised for our justification (Rom 4:25). God's own Son was not spared by his Father, but was given up for us all (Rom 8:32). He died for our sins, was buried, was raised on the third day, and appeared to various disciples and Paul (1 Cor 15:3–8). He died, was raised, and was exalted to God's right hand (Rom 8:34). God greatly exalted him, to receive the homage of all things (Phil 2:9–11). He will descend from heaven to be reunited with the dead in Christ and those who are still alive (1 Thess 4:16–17).[70]

My concern here does not address the origins of the elements that compose Paul's story of Jesus, but the narrative trajectory, its movements in relationship to Paul and his communities.

The undergirding structure of the narrative is the movement of Jesus from a position of power, which he relinquishes, to the identification with those who were not equal to him in status or power, to the position of humiliation and powerlessness, to the restoration of power and the conferral of supreme status, or honor. The movement can be considered a homology, defined as "the depiction of an objective (mythical) event and a parallel description of inner processes."[71] This kenotic scenario of power to powerlessness expresses Paul's tranformation[72] and disposition and becomes both a model of and model for members of the community. Paul has been able to repossess the displaced and split-off vulnerable aspects of self through the acceptance of those thought to be defiled, and the identification with otherness. Both the reception of the other and identification with the other are actions that are initiated from a position of relative powerlessness and vulnerability.

In the context of the sensibilities and religious affections that Paul attempts to nurture among the members of the nascent *ecclesia*, Paul's term *katallassō* becomes paradigmatic, even though it appears, in various forms, in only two places in the authentic Pauline corpus: Rom. 5:10–11 and 2 Cor. 5:18ff. Technically, *katalassō*, *katallagē*, and *katellagēmēn* do not address the specific problem of Jews and Gentiles exclusively, but the transformed relationship between God and sinful humanity.

> All this is from God, who through Christ reconciled us to himself and gave us the ministry of reconciliation (*katallagēs*); for our sake he who was without sin became sin . . . in order that we might become the righteousness of God. (2 Cor. 5:18, 21)

> But God shows his love for us in that while we were yet sinners Christ died for us. . . . For if while we were enemies we were reconciled to God by the

death of his Son, much more, now that we reconciled, shall we be saved by his life. (Rom. 5:8, 10)

Sin, *hamartia*, is God's alterity, and by identifying and becoming one with that which is other to God and entering into suffering vulnerability with it, the relationship between self and other is mixed and transformed. In the Greek, *katallagē*, or reconciliation, is well suited to refer to and encompass both the relationship of divine human otherness and the conflict between members of the different ethnoi. Embedded in the terms for reconciliation, *katallagē, apokatallassō,* and *katallassō*, is the root term, *allo-*, Greek for "other." The term is from the Greek pagan culture with which Paul was familiar, and cannot be found as an equivalent in Hebrew or Aramaic.[73] The term was commonly used to describe the exchange of one currency's value for another, and the cessation of hostility between the gods and humans. Paul's usage does not fit any previous or familiar categories. In Paul, the victim of the transgression initiates the effort and assumes responsibility for the costs. I. Howard Marshall describes Paul's use in the following manner: X (God) removes the cause of his own anger against Y, namely Y's sin.[74] The "removal" is effected by suffering identification with that which is alien to one.

Paul embodies the attitudes and affects associated with the sensibilities of reconciliation in his disposition toward members during crises that threaten the unity of the community, such as in 1 and 2 Corinthians. Although the agents of division are considered to be different in each situation, Paul's response is similar.[75] Paul's opponents, by turning the community against him in a way that undermined the legitimacy of his apostolic office and the credibility of his gospel message, place him in a position of alienation wherein he embodies the only position and posture that makes reconciliation possible: vulnerability toward and acceptance of the agents of alienation.

In 1 Cor. 4:10–13 Paul makes an explicit identification with both powerlessness and impurity: "we have become and are now, as the refuse of the world, the offscouring of all things." The terms *perikatharmata* and *peripsēma* can be translated as "excrement" and "dirt," respectively.[76] The kenotic relinquishment of power and the accompanying identification and acceptance of anathema are possible in Paul through his experience of having his shame exposed and compassionately accepted. His experience of divine empathy provided him with empowered humility, the capacity for self-denigration in service to the creation of community divided and fragmented by patterns of status, humiliation, and intolerable otherness.

By virtue of his capacity to enact the sensibilities necessary for the maintenance of communities of inclusive otherness in the context of honor/shame purity/impurity codes, Paul becomes a somatic Torah for the embryonic communities. While the outlines of the exchange of power for humility and glory are evident in the Jesus narrative of Paul, and repeated in Gal. 3:13, 4:4, 2 Cor. 5:21, Phil. 2:5–11, and above, the mediating embodiment for communities in need of communal norms and sentiments unlike that of the surrounding societies would be provided by Paul in the presence of his letters and his person.[77]

CONCLUSION: THE CREATION OF THE CREOLE MESSIAH

"Empathy is not a mystical experience."[78]

Yet Paul in the moment of mystical rapture became exposed to the intensity of holy empathy before the *doxa* of Divinity. The enthroned Deity was the Holy Other of Israel, but looking upon Paul, Yahweh gazed upon a creature into the depths of his hidden deficiencies. If shame is the intersubjective movement from being seen to being seen wanting in an ideal other's eyes, then healing consists of the simultaneous shame of exposure and the compassion of acceptance. Shame's cure is not being forgiven but being exposed and empathically embraced in the depths of one's deepest desire to disappear. Being "caught up" or "seized" is necessary for both shame's hurting and healing.

Although the definitions proliferate and vary,[79] one theme begins to become recognizable: empathy is the boundary-traversing capacity of humans to think and feel their way into another human's being. "To be genuinely considerate implies that we can put ourselves in the place of other people: we identify ourselves with them. Now, this capacity for identification with another person is a most important element in human relations in general, and is also a condition for real and strong feelings of love."[80]

The power that fueled Paul's hunger for heterogeneous integrity and its material communal embodiments was a new-found capacity for empathic responsivity to the alien and his own alienated "shame parts."

> For though I am free from all men, I have made myself a slave to all, that I might win the more. To the Jews I became as a Jew, in order to win Jews; to those under the law, I became as one under the law—though not being myself under the law—that I might win those under the law. To those outside the law I became as one outside the law—not being without law toward God but under the law of Christ—that I might win those outside the law. To the weak I became weak, that I might win the weak. I have become all things to all men, that I might by all means save some. I do it all for the sake of the gospel, that I may share in its blessings. (1 Cor. 9:19–23)

The gospel Paul received was the prophetic message to include the Gentiles with the identical status and privileges as the Jews without first requiring removal of the mark of difference. To anyone who would offer a different or *heteron* gospel, Paul inveighs, "let such a one be cursed!" (Gal. 1:6, 9). Paul's uncompromising conviction to the sacrality of the relational bond with the other or *allo* is a measure of the seismic depth of the transformation of his personality, resulting in a radical reorientation of his understanding of the sacred. Paul has left the cultus of homogeneous sacral alterity to the community of heterogeneous relational sacrality. The realm between ethnic others becomes the site of divine visitation and presence, fraught with the power to stricken and afflict that surrounds *any* holy place.

> Whoever, therefore, eats the bread or drinks the cup of the Lord in an unworthy manner will be guilty of profaning the body and blood of the Lord. Let a man examine himself, and so eat of the bread and drink of the cup. . . . For anyone who eats and drinks without discerning the body eats and drinks judgment upon himself. That is why many of you are weak and ill, and some have died. . . . For just as the body is one and has many members, and all the members of the body, though many, are one body, so it is with Christ. For by one Spirit we were baptized into one body—Jews or Greeks, slaves or free—and all were made to drink of one Spirit. (1 Cor. 11:27–30; 12:12–13)

"In Christ," as used by Paul, is an ecclesial term that designates the collective, corporeal composition of the community, or body. "In Christ" there is neither Greek nor Jew, slave nor free, male or female. In this sense, "in Christ" operates to erase exclusionary differences. Yet Paul is unwilling to compromise on the inclusion of the Gentiles. They must be sought and brought into the same cultic space as the Jew—hence the mission to the Gentiles. Nor will he allow the Jew to drive out the Gentile by circumcision, or any qualifying homogeneous sign. The other must be included—hence the necessity of a heterogeneous, bi-ethnic body of difference. The corporate embodiment of heterogeneity, into which is situated the maxim "in Christ," creates a communal qualification of the term, a shared embodied mediation of Jesus Christ, a heterogeneous Christology.

Paul attempts to engender a common shared identity expressed in the dispositions and attitudes of the members toward one another. He is, by the definition I have outlined in chapter 2, creating a new *symbolon*. Not by the definition of creed or a representation, but defined as the mutual creative interaction among members of a community who create and enact within a liminal terrain: the shared and internalized experiences of belonging to one's self and another in the creative interplay in sacred space and time. "In Christ" therefore exists only in the bonded presence of the other, in the gathering composed of taxonomic transgressors. "In Christ" is both semantic and social rupture, which cannot be sustained by the return to or integration into structures. Paul has given his passion and his life to the cultivation of creolian consciousness among believers in order that the believers might worship and receive a creole Messiah by creating communities through the process of creolization that Paul calls reconciliation. Reconciliation, defined as the advent and commitment to those previously separated unknown parts of one's self, and the discovery of the inextricable character of one's interconnectedness within the competing and conflicting spheres of culture, is a diaspora phenomenon.[81] Reconciliation requires agents who embody the convergence of conflicting cultural elements and identities within themselves and have the mediating resources of empathy and viable vulnerablity (in contrast to helpless vulnerability).

The origins of empathic vitality, like the creation of the symbol, reside in the empathic mirroring of one's self in the face of another: "For now we see as through a glass darkly but then face to face. Now I know in part; then shall I understand fully, even as I have been fully understood" (1 Cor. 13:12).

During Paul's "mirroring stage" he gazed into a reflection of himself that was both known—"Now I know in part"—and unknown, an enigma (glass darkly). The full disclosure of his self-knowledge awaited the new eon. Paul, in other words, developed an eschatological personality capable of accepting a high degree of personal opacity in the face of promised divine disclosure. His consummate or ideal self awaited an anticipated transformation. Yet the first markings of that eschaton became manifest in the "other" of his day, the sinful pagan Gentile whom Paul passionately embraced while pathetically failing—with notable exceptions—to enkindle an equally passionate embrace among the Jews of his community.

To understand Paul, we must first emphasize that the symbol is as necessary to the constitution of the self as the sign is necessary to the construction of the subject; of equal importance is that the alienated "subject" is as redundant as the relational self. Whereas the subject as ego attempts to mask a fundamental heterogeneity born of alienation, the self is a fundamentally heterogeneous creation born of internalization. If we understand the self to be constituted symbolically, that is, in Winnicott's sense of that interactive realm wherein culture and self are created in the intersubjective suspension of the image ("illusion"), then both self and symbol are dependent upon the existence and maintenance of *community*. The self comes about through the experience of the other, who becomes an inherent part of the psychic economy of the self through its internalizations. The existence of the self depends upon heterogeneity and is inherently unstable and contingent upon the presence and power of its community to create the "connections . . . that enlarge the reference of the self throughout the world of experience."[82]

Culture and community defined in reference to the sacred as described by Otto are the collective effort to transform the inevitable and inherent heteronomy of culture and self into the homogeneous consistency of world and identity. The material studied by phenomenologists of religion are the various technologies of homogeneity: ritual initiations and sacred markings that identify and initiate and integrate members into the social structure and knowledge of the sacred; sacred texts that create verbal interpretations of the unpredicatble departures from the order of things and prescribe their return; the testimonies of pilgrims, saints, and mystics transformed by their journeys and encounters with the holy.

With the person of Paul, however, we have an intensified degree of heterogeneity in the realm of *Lebenswelt* understood as that preconscious awareness of the world that precludes other possible modalities, while in the realm of *Mitwelt* Paul exists within a primary community wholly committed to an understanding of the sacred that depends upon exclusive otherness. Paul's unique location and consciousness as a Jew *in* the Diaspora, but a Pharisee (a Hebrew of Hebrews), amplifies the multiple tensions between the culturally heterogeneous *Lebenswelt* and the valences of the sacred in the presence of which the Pharisees constituted themselves as a homogeneously holy community.

If we are to understand Paul, his tranformations, and the communities he attempted to nurture into existence, we must attend with care these intersections and their resistance to resolution, for within the space of their temporary suspended irresolution, the phenomena only later to be called "Christianity" emerged: its energy, like its primary holiness, residing in the trespass of boundaries.

Endnotes

Preface

1. Walter J. Ong, S.J. *Hopkins, the Self, and God* (Toronto: University of Toronto Press, 1986), 16. See also J. Hillis Miller, *The Disappearance of God: Five Nineteenth-Century Writers* (Cambridge, Mass.: Belknap Press of Harvard University Press, 1963), 293.

2. Joseph Meleze Modrzejewski notes that "Diaspora" as historically used by Jews refers to ancient Jews living among and freely associating with Greeks prior to the fall of the second temple, a definition which accurately describes the condition of Paul the Pharisee. See Modrzejewski, "How to Be a Jew in Hellenistic Egypt?" in J. D. C. Shaye and E. S. Frerichs, eds., *Disaporas in Antiquity* (Atlanta: Scholars Press), 65–91. Richard Marienstras stresses that exile has always been contained in the Jewish sense of Diaspora which also suggests diaspora consciousness, i.e., consciousness of one's diasporic condition of belonging to an alien environment. See Richard Marienstras, "On the Notion of Diaspora," in Gérard Chaliand, ed., *Minority Peoples in the Age of Nation-States* (London: Pluto, 1989), 119–25.

   Within the last thirty years, diaspora has become a conceptual tool to identify the proliferating experience and awareness of exile and displacement among increasingly diverse populations. See Edward Said, *Orientalism* (London: Routledge, 1979); Gérard Chaliand and Jean-Pierre Rageau, *The Penguin Atlas of Diasporas* (New York: Viking, 1995); and Richard Cohen, *Global Diaspora: An Introduction* (London: UCL Press, 1997). Creolian identity is, by definition, heterogeneous and marks a unique development in the diasporic consciousness. See chapters 4 and 5 of this book. I explore the phenomenon of creolization, diaspora, and Christian reconciliation in the modern context in my forthcoming work titled *Trauma and Reconciliation* to be published by Westminster John Knox Press.

3. Gerald Falk, *The Jew in Christian Theology* (Jefferson, N.C., & London: McFarland & Company, Inc., 1992), and James Carroll, *Constantine's Sword: The Church and the Jews: A History* (Boston: Houghton Mifflin, 2001).

4. See John Howard Yoder, *For the Nations: Essays Evangelical and Public* (Grand Rapids: Eerdmans, 1997).

117

Chapter 1

1. William James, *The Principles of Psychology*, 2 vols. (New York: Holt, 1905); idem, *The Varieties of Religious Experience: A Study in Human Nature* (New York: Longmans, Green, 1912).
2. See Wayne Proudfoot, *Religious Experience* (Berkeley: University of California Press, 1988).
3. James, *Varieties*, 31.
4. In *Religious Experience* Proudfoot indicates how difficult refining "pure" experience is from the interpretive language and symbols within which it is presented.
5. James, *Principles*, 1:291.
6. The first and third terms represent the two poles encompassed by the symbol in the hermeneutic phenomenology of Paul Ricoeur, *The Symbolism of Evil*, trans. Emerson Buchanan (Boston: Beacon, 1967), 13.
7. René Descartes, *Discourse on Method and Meditations on First Philosophy*, trans. Donald A. Cress (Indianapolis: Hackett, 1980).
8. Dalia Judovitz, *Subjectivity and Presentation in Descartes: The Origins of Modernity* (Cambridge and New York: Cambridge University Press, 1988), 94.
9. Saint Augustine, *Confessions*, trans. R. S. Pine-Coffin (New York: Viking Penguin, 1986), 3.9.
10. Paul Ricoeur, *The Conflict of Interpretations: Essays in Hermeneutics*, ed. Don Ihde, trans. Kathleen McLaughlin (Evanston: Northwestern University Press, 1974), 236.
11. Francis Barker, *The Tremulous Private Body* (London: Methuen, 1984), 99.
12. Judovitz, *Subjectivity*, 102.
13. Lucien Goldmann, *The Hidden God*, trans. Philip Thody (London: Routledge and Kegan Paul, 1964), 27.
14. René Descartes, *Descartes: Philosophical Letters*, letter to Gibieuf, 19 (January 1647), trans. Anthony Kenny (Oxford: Oxford University Press, 1970), 123.
15. Seppo Sajama and Matti Pamppinene, *A Historical Introduction to Phenomenology* (New York: Croom Helm with Methuen, 1987), 1.
16. William Kneale and Martha Kneale, *The Development of Logic* (Oxford: Clarendon, 1966), 229.
17. Edmund Husserl, *Ideas: General Introduction to Pure Phenomenology*, trans. W. R. Boyce Gibson (London and New York: Macmillan, 1952), 120–21.
18. Ricoeur, *Conflict of Interpretations*, 6. Descartes attempts to create the cogito solely dependent upon mathematic definitions. See Judovitz, *Subjectivity*, 25.
19. Second- and third-generation phenomenologists have redefined subjectivity through the reinclusion of the body in their interpretations of experience. See Michael Polanyi, *The Tacit Dimension* (Garden City, NY: Doubleday, 1966); Maurice Merleau-Ponty, *Phenomenology of Perception*, trans. Colin Smith (London: Routledge & Kegan Paul, 1962).
20. James, *Principles of Psychology*, vol. 1.
21. Ibid., vi, 224.
22. Ibid., 278.
23. Ibid., 275.
24. Husserl, *Ideas*, 249.
25. Ibid., 265.
26. Ibid., 266.
27. Thousands of pages of Husserl's manuscripts remain unpublished and untranslated. His thinking expressed in *Ideas* is neither exhaustive nor comprehensive.
28. Edmund Husserl, *Cartesian Meditations: An Introduction to Phenomenology*, trans. Dorian Cairus (The Hague: Nijhoff, 1973).

29. James, *Principles*, 1:229–300.
30. Ibid., 341.
31. Richard Rorty, *Philosophy and the Mirror of Nature* (Princeton: Princeton University Press, 1979), 50. Wilshire slips into the interchangeable use of "subject" and "self." See Bruce Wilshire, *William James and Phenomenology: A Study of the "Principles of Psychology"* (Bloomington: Indiana University Press, 1968), 125. Evan M. Zuesse notes that Husserl, in *Cartesian Meditations*, located the ego, before which the world is perceived, within the human body, which connects through its patterns of thought to the influences of the world. Husserl continues to emphasize essences in the transcendental reduction that turns toward idealism. See Evan M. Zuesse, "The Role of Intentionality in the Phenomenology of Religion," *Journal of the American Academy of Religion* 53, no. 1 (1985): 51–73.
32. Judovitz, *Subjectivity*, 112.
33. Martin Heidegger, *What is a Thing?* trans. W. B. Barton and V. Deutsch (New York: Harper & Row, 1977), 105.
34. Judovitz, *Subjectivity*, 113.
35. Heralds Biezals, "Typology of Religion and the Phenomenological Method," in *Science of Religion: Studies in Methodology*, ed. Lauri Honko (The Hague: Mouton, 1979), 153.
36. Rudolf Otto, *The Idea of the Holy: An Inquiry into the Non-Rational Factor in the Idea of the Divine and Its Relation to the Rations*, trans. John W. Harvey (London and New York: Oxford University Press, 1923); G. van der Leeuw, *Religion in Essence and Manifestation: A Study in Phenomenology*, trans. John Evan Turner (London: Allen & Unwin, 1938); Joaquim Wach, *The Comparative Study of Religion* (New York: Columbia University Press, 1958).
37. Charles Long, *Significations: Signs, Symbols, and Images in the Interpretation of Religion* (Philadelphia: Fortress Press, 1986), 29–30.
38. Jonathan Z. Smith denies the participation of humans in the holy since that realm exists only as a result of human construction. Smith shifts the methodology and the material of his inquiries from symbols, which characterized the work of Eliade and Ricoeur, to rituals. Smith has adopted the assumptions and methods that inform French modern linguistics and postmodern theories of literary criticism. In Smith's appropriation, ritual, like language, is a system of differences, used to generate mutually dependent distinctions between "sacred" and "profane." Therefore, humans do not participate in the sacred, they create it. From the perspective of empirical positivism, whose stance toward religion he has also adopted, he is correct; from the perspective of experiential subjectivity Smith removes both academic interpreter *and* indigenous participant further away from their subject. See Jonathan Z. Smith, *Map Is Not Territory: Studies in the History of Religions* (Leiden: Brill, 1978).
39. Edmund Husserl, *The Crisis of European Sciences and Transcendental Phenomenology*, trans. David Carr (Evanston, IL: Northwestern University Press, 1970), 122.
40. Ibid., 144.
41. Hans Blumenberg, "The Life World and the Concept of Reality," in *Life-World and Consciousness: Essays for Aron Gurwitsch*, ed. Lester E. Embrer (Evanston, IL: Northwestern University Press, 1972), 431.
42. Ibid.
43. Alfred Schutz and Thomas Luckmann, *The Structures of the Life-World*, trans. Richard M. Zaner and H. Tristan Engelhardt Jr. (Evanston, IL: Northwestern University Press, 1973), 27. Schutz and Luckmann err in the logic of their description of the epoche since those subjects who exist within the structures

of their *Lebenswelt* do not intentionally bracket doubt as to the existence of alternate world possibilities. The results are similar, but the intentionalities are not the same.

44. Paul Ricoeur, *Essays in Hermeneutics*, vol. 2: *From Text to Action*, trans. Kathleen Blamey and John B. Thompson (Evanston, IL: Northwestern University Press, 1991), 13–14.

45. David Carr, "Husserl's Problematic Concept of the Life-World," in *Husserl: Expositions and Appraisals*, ed. Frederick A. Elliston and Peter McCormick (Notre Dame: University of Notre Dame Press, 1977), 206–7.

46. Husserl, *Cartesian Meditations*, 70.

47. Carr, "Husserl's Problematic," 209.

48. Max Scheler, quoted in Manfred S. Grings, "Max Scheler: Focusing on Rarely Seen Complexities of Phenomenology," in *Phenomenology in Perspective*, ed. Fred Smith (The Hague: Nijhoff, 1970), 48–49.

49. Contemporary scholarship accepts Romans, 1 and 2 Corinthians, Galatians, Philippians, Philemon, and 1 Thessalonians as authored by Paul. See Calvin J. Roetzell, *The Letters of Paul: Conversations in Context* (Louisville: Westminster/John Knox Press, 1991); Alan F. Segal, *Paul the Convert: The Apostolate and Apostasy of Saul the Pharisee* (New Haven: Yale University Press, 1990); and W. G. Kümmel, *Introduction to the New Testament* (Nashville: Abingdon, 1975).

50. J. Christiaan Beker, *The Triumph of God: The Essence of Paul's Thought*, trans. Loren T. Stuckenbruck (Minneapolis: Augsburg Fortress Press, 1991), 5; Gustav Adolf Deissmann, *Light from the Ancient East: The New Testament Illustrated by Recently Discovered Texts of the Graeco-Roman World* (London: Hodder & Stoughton, 1910); Morna D. Hooker, *A Preface to Paul* (New York: Oxford University Press, 1980), 10, 17; Thomas R. Schreiner, *Interpreting the Pauline Epistles* (Grand Rapids: Baker, 1990), 18.

51. George Lyons, *Pauline Autobiography: Toward A New Understanding* (Atlanta: Scholars Press, 1985), 124.

52. Jacob Jarvell, *The Unknown Paul: Essays on Luke-Acts and Early Christian History* (Minneapolis: Augsburg, 1984), 55.

53. Günther Bornkamm, *Paul*, trans. D. M. G. Stalker (New York: Harper & Row, 1971); L. Cerfaux, *The Spiritual Journey of Saint Paul*, trans. John C. Guiness (New York: Sheed & Ward, 1968); F. F. Bruce, *Paul: Apostle of the Heart Set Free* (Grand Rapids: Eerdmans, 1977); E. W. Hunt, *Portrait of Paul* (London: Mowbray, 1968); E. P. Sanders, *Paul* (Oxford and New York: Oxford University Press, 1991).

54. Isobel Henderson, "Ancient Greek Music," in *Ancient and Oriental Music*, ed. Egon Wellesz, vol. 1 of *New Oxford History of Music* (London and New York: Oxford University Press, 1957), 345.

55. Eric Werner, "The Oldest Sources of Octave and Octoechos," *Acta Musicologica* 20 (1948): 1–9.

56. Athenaeus, *Deipnosophistae* 14.624d, in Andrew Barker, *Greek Musical Writings*, vol. 2: *Harmonic and Acoustic Theory* (Cambridge and New York: Cambridge University Press, 1989), 282. See also Plato, *Republic* 399 a-c, for a description of the Dorian.

57. Plutarch, *On Music* 1136 c-d, in Barker, *Harmonic and Acoustic Theory*, 221; see also Solon Michaelides, *The Music of Ancient Greece: An Encyclopedia* (London: Faber & Faber, 1978), 89.

58. Barker, *Harmonic and Acoustic Theory*, 360.

59. Thomas McLaughlin, "Figurative Language," in *Critical Terms for Literary Study*, ed. Frank Lentricci and Thomas McLaughlin (Chicago: University of Chicago Press, 1990), 81.

60. The LXX uses the term in Ps. 42:4: "how I went with the throng, and led them in procession to the house of God, with glad shouts and songs of thanksgiving a multitude keeping festival."

61. Donald J. Grout, *A History of Western Music* (New York: Norton, 1973), cited in David Reck, *Music of the Whole Earth* (New York: Scribner's, 1977), 203.

62. Clifford Geertz, *The Interpretation of Cultures* (New York: Basic Books, 1973), 209.

63. Stephen A. Erickson, *Language and Being: An Analytic Phenomenology* (New Haven: Yale University Press, 1970), 91.

64. Ricoeur, *Conflict of Interpretations*, 6.

65. Ricoeur, *From Text to Action*, 19.

66. Sigmund Freud, *Introductory Lectures on Psycho-Analysis*, trans. James Strachey, 4 vols. (London: Hogarth, 1961).

67. Heinz Kohut, *The Analysis of the Self* (New York: International Universities Press, 1971).

68. Geertz, *Interpretation of Cultures*.

69. Aidan Kavanagh, *On Liturgical Theology* (New York: Pueblo, 1984).

70. Don Ihde, *Listening and Voice: A Phenomenology of Sound* (Athens, OH: Ohio University Press, 1976).

71. Proudfoot, *Religious Experience*.

Chapter 2

1. See Don Ihde, *Listening and Voice: A Phenomenology of Sound* (Athens, OH: Ohio University Press, 1976); Walter Ong, *Interfaces of the Word: Studies in the Evolution of Consciousness and Culture* (Ithaca, NY: Cornell University Press, 1977), 136.

2. Theodor Thass-Thienemann, *Symbolic Behavior* (New York: Washington Square Press, 1968), 17.

3. C. M. Bowra, *The Greek Experience* (London: Weidenfield & Nicolson, 1957), 12.

4. Richard Rorty, *Philosophy and the Mirror of Nature* (Princeton: Princeton University Press, 1980), 49–50.

5. My ontological formulation differs from that of George Herbert Mead, who understood the self as social and developmental. The self has a character that differs from that of the physiological organism proper. "The self is something which has a development: it is not initially there at birth but arises in the process of social experience and activity, that is, develops in the given individual as a result of his relations to that process as a whole and to other individuals within that process." George Herbert Mead, "The Genesis of the Self," in *The Self in Social Interaction*, ed. Chad Gordon and Kenneth J. Gergen (New York: John Wiley and Sons, 1968), 57. I contend that the human being, not just the self, is ontologically constituted in relationship with other humans. Further, Mead distinguishes between the body and the self, a distinction I do not uphold. See the discussion below.

6. "Then, what does *I* refer to? To something very peculiar which is exclusively linguistic. *I* refers to the act of individual discourse in which it is pronounced, and by this it designates the speaker. . . . The reality to which it refers is the reality of the discourse. . . . And so it is literally true that the basis of subjectivity is the exercise of language." Emile Benveniste, *Problems in General Linguistics*, trans. Mary Elizabeth Meek (Coral Gables: University of Miami Press, 1971), 226.

7. This conclusion concerning the irreducible reality of human existence is common to Prasangika Madyamaka Buddhism, which denies the inherent exis-

tence of anything, including sentient beings, and affirms the dependent orig-
ination of all things. See Jeffrey Hopkins, "Meditation on Emptiness" (Ph.D.
diss., University of Wisconsin, 1973). See also Tsong Khapa, *Speech of Gold
in the Essence of True Eloquence: Reason and Enlightenment in the Central Philosophy of Tibet*, trans. Robert A. F. Thurman (Princeton: Princeton University Press, 1984). In the West, object-relations theory, built upon the theories
of Freudian clinical psychoanalysts such as Melanie Klein, Margaret Mahler,
and D. W. Winnicott, reach a similar but not identical conclusion. Mahler
insisted that the infant be considered a symbiotic unit: "The human being . . .
is at first absolutely, and remains later on even 'unto the grave' relatively
dependent on a mother." Margaret Mahler, "On the First Three Subphases of
the Separation-Individuation Process," *International Journal of Psycho-Analysis* 53 (1972): 333.

8. Donald W. Winnicott, "The Theory of the Parent-Infant Relationship," in
Essential Papers on Object Relations, ed. Peter Buckley (New York: New York
University Press, 1986), 255. See also Melanie Klein, *The Psycho-Analysis of
Children* (London: Hogarth, 1949). Prasangika Madyamaka Buddhism, how-
ever, would find all objects empty of inherent existence.

9. Jacques Lacan, *Ecrits: A Selection*, trans. Alan Sheridan (New York: Norton,
1977). Although postmodern critics, such as Lacan and Foucault, are skepti-
cal concerning the existential certainty of categories that include the "subject,"
"author," as well as the "self," the criticism exhibits thematic consistency. See
Michel Foucault, "What Is an Author?" in *Language, Counter-Memory, Practice*, trans. Sherry Simon, ed. Donald F. Bouchard (Ithaca, NY: Cornell University Press, 1977); John Sturrock, *Structuralism and Since: From Lévi-Strauss
to Derrida* (Oxford: Oxford University Press, 1979).

10. See the above discussion on language and subjectivity.

11. Louis A. Sass, "The Self and Its Vicissitudes: An Archeological Study of the
Psychoanalytic Avant-Garde," in *Constructions of the Self*, ed. George Levine
(New Brunswick, NJ: Rutgers University Press, 1992), 22, 24–25.

12. See Margaret Mahler, "On Human Symbiosis and the Vicissitudes of Individu-
ation," in *Essential Papers on Object Relations*, ed. Peter Buckley (New York: New
York University Press, 1986), 200–202; W. W. Meissner, *The Paranoid Process*
(New York: Aronson, 1978), 687; and M. Balint, quoted in Robert D. Stolorow,
"Toward a Functional Definition of Narcissism," in *Essential Papers on Narcis-
sism*, ed. Andrew P. Morrison (New York: New York University Press, 1986), 203.

13. D. W. Winnicott, *Playing and Reality* (New York: Basic Books, 1971), 130;
Heinz Kohut and Ernest S. Wolf, "The Disorders of the Self and Their Treatment: An Outline," in *Essential Papers on Object Relations*, 177.

14. Meissner, *Paranoid Process*, 101.

15. Winnicott, *Playing and Reality*, 10–11.

16. W. W. Meissner, *Internalization in Psychoanalysis* (New York: International
Universities Press, 1981), 24.

17. Otto Kernberg, *Object-Relations Theory and Clinical Psychoanalysis* (Northvale, NJ: Aronson, 1984), 35.

18. Kernberg, *Object-Relations Theory*, 36; he refers to E. Jacobson, *The Self and
the Object World* (New York: International Universities Press, 1964).

19. Kernberg, *Object-Relations Theory*, 35.

20. Otto Kernberg, "Structural Derivations of Object Relationships," in *Essential
Papers on Object Relations*, 356.

21. "The self as an interpretive act" is from a graduate seminar with Dr. Charles
Gerkin.

22. This term is commonly used by members of the British school of object relations. See Melanie Klein, "Notes on Some Schizoid Mechanism," in *Developments in Psycho-Analysis*, ed. J. Riviere (London: Hogarth, 1952); Winnicott, "Parent-Infant Relations," in *Essential Papers on Object Relations*.
23. Kernberg, *Object-Relations Theory*, 41.
24. Winnicott, *Playing and Reality*, 2.
25. Ibid., 12 and 11.
26. Ibid., 3–5.
27. Ibid., 14.
28. Winnicott, "Communicating and Not Communicating Leading to a Study of Certain Opposites," in *The Maturational Process and the Facilitating Environment* (London: Hogarth, 1965), 181.
29. Klein describes this development as the "depressive position," which is the integration of aggression and libido. See Melanie Klein, "A Contribution to the Psycho-Genesis of Manic-Depressive States," in *Contributions to Psycho-Analysis* (London: Hogarth, 1939), 282–310.
30. Winnicott, *Playing and Reality*, 96–97.
31. Liddell and Scott, *A Greek-English Lexicon*, s.v.
32. Winnicott, *Playing and Reality*, 97–98, 103.
33. Victor Turner's use of the term *liminal* to describe the space and relationship between preestablished and enduring social structures created by rituals of initiation derives from anthropologist Arnold van Gennep's work, *The Rites of Passage*, trans. Monika B. Vizedom and Gabrielle L. Caffee (London: Routledge & Kegan Paul, 1960). See Victor Turner, *The Ritual Process: Structure and Anti-Structure* (Ithaca, NY: Cornell University Press, 1966), 95, 125–30; idem, *Dramas, Fields, and Metaphors: Symbolic Action in Human Society* (Ithaca, NY: Cornell University Press, 1974), 237, 255, 274.
34. Winnicott, *Playing and Reality*, 55.
35. Ibid., 5. Lying is the basis of fiction, and stealing is an act of the possessive imagination. Hermes, messenger of the gods, was also the deity devoted to and worshiped by thieves. See Norman O. Brown, *Hermes the Thief: The Evolution of a Myth* (Madison: University of Wisconsin Press, 1947).
36. Ricoeur's hermeneutic phenomenology evokes similar concerns in the disclosure of the relationship between language and being, and sense and self: "On the one hand, self-understanding passes through the detour of understanding the cultural signs in which the self documents and forms itself. On the other hand, understanding the text is not an end in itself; it mediates the relation to himself of a subject who, in the short circuit of immediate reflection, does not find the meaning of his own life. Thus it must be said, with equal force, that reflection is nothing without the mediation of signs and works, and that explanation is nothing if it is not incorporated as an intermediary stage in the process of self-understanding. In short, in hermeneutical reflection—or in reflective hermeneutics—the constitution of the *self* is contemporaneous with the constituting of *meaning*." Ricoeur, "What Is a Text? Explanation and Understanding," in *From Text to Action*, 119.
37. See Mircea Eliade, *The Two and the One*, trans. J. M. Cohen (New York: Harper & Row, 1965), 203; Paul Ricoeur, *The Symbolism of Evil*, trans. Emerson Bochasu (Boston: Beacon, 1967), 169; idem, *Interpretation Theory: Discourse and the Surplus of Meaning* (Fort Worth: Texas Christian University Press, 1976), 17, 58.
38. Paul Ricoeur, *The Conflict of Interpretations: Essays in Hermeneutics*, ed. Don Ihde (Evanston, IL: Northwestern University Press, 1974), 308–9.

39. Ibid., 58. See Mikhail Bakhtin, *Problems of Dostoevsky's Poetics*, ed. and trans. Caryl Emerson (Minneapolis: University of Minnesota Press, 1984), for an excellent description of language that behaves as a verbal riot, i.e., carnival.

40. Ricoeur, *Conflict of Interpretation*, 59.

41. Winnicott, *Playing and Reality*, 19.

42. In chemistry, valence is the power or capacity of certain elements to combine with or displace a greater or less number of atoms. Heinz Kohut contends that the breakup of the self (which he describes as the "nuclear self") leads to "the appearance of isolated drives, aggression or libido, just as the split in the integrity of the atom releases deadly radioactive energy." The disintegration of the self is precipitated by the break in empathic bonding, which we will discuss below. See Heinz Kohut, *The Restoration of the Self* (New York: International Universities Press, 1977), 122.

43. This is also the role of therapeutic communities.

44. *Diabolos* means to draw across or away that which is together, literally to separate.

45. James, *Principles of Psychology*, 1:292.

46. The spelling of these terms follows James's, ibid., 1:292.

47. Ibid., 1:292–93.

48. Here I am using *imago* in the sense of an ideal image of one's self that governs or determines behavior befitting and expected of the role. See E. T. Higgins, "Self-discrepancy: A Theory Relating Self and Affect," *Psychological Review* 94 (1987): 319–40.

49. James, *Principles of Psychology*, 1:294.

50. See Dan P. McAdams, *The Stories We Live By: Personal Myths and the Making of the Self* (New York: Morrow, 1993).

51. James, *Principles of Psychology*, 1:296.

52. Ibid., 297.

53. Ibid.

54. Ibid., 304.

55. Ibid., 297.

56. Ibid., 340–46.

57. Bruce Wilshire contends that James's use of the term *conception* is James's expression of intentionality, or what he calls "the phenomenological breakthrough." See Bruce Wilshire, *William James and Phenomenology: A Study of "The Principles of Psychology"* (Bloomington: Indiana University Press, 1968), 154–55.

58. Ibid., 133. See also Maurice Merleau-Ponty, *The Structure of Behavior* (Boston: Beacon, 1963), 68.

59. James, *Varieties*, 31. "Religious experience, according to James, then, is a dimension of human intentional life as a unified whole. It is, we might say, a way in which a man uses his moods, feelings, emotions, aims, all of which are given in biological and psychological nature with their own specific nonreligious teleologies, but which, together and in various mixtures and gradations, can embody religious intentions and attitudes. *Religious experience, then, is an expressive use of the human body.*" See James M. Edie, *William James and Phenomenology* (Bloomington: Indiana University Press, 1987), 58.

60. James, *Principles of Psychology*, 1:341.

61. See chapter 1 above for a fuller explanation of the theological assumptions.

62. James, *Varieties*, 501–2.

63. James, *Principles of Psychology*, 1:316, 315.

64. Ibid., 321–22.

65. Husserl, *Cartesian Meditations*, 89–150.

66. Winnicott, *Playing and Reality*, 111–12.

67. See Margaret Mahler, *On Human Symbiosis and the Vicissitudes of Individuation* (New York: International Universities Press, 1968).

68. Kohut, *Restoration of the Self*, 187.

69. Silvan S. Tomkins, *Affect/Imagery/Consciousness*, vol. 1: *The Positive Affects* (New York: Springer, 1962); idem, *Affect/Imagery/Consciousness*, vol. 2: *The Negative Affects* (New York: Springer, 1962); idem, *Affect/Imagery/Consciousness*, vol. 3: *The Negative Affects: Anger and Fear* (New York: Springer, 1991). Tomkins provides a summary of his theory in the article, "Shame," in *The Many Faces of Shame*, ed. Donald M. Nathanson (New York: Guilford, 1987), 133–61.

70. Nathanson, a leading interpreter of Tomkins's research and shame theory, provides *three* groups: two positive (interest-excitement and enjoyment-joy); one neutral: surprise-startle; and six negative (fear-terror, distress-anguish, anger-rage, dissmell, disgust, and shame-humiliation). See Donald L. Nathanson, *Shame and Pride: Affect, Sex and the Birth of the Self* (New York: Norton, 1992), 59.

71. Tomkins, "Shame," 139.

72. Ibid.

73. Ibid., 137.

74. See, respectively, ibid., 139, 137; Nathanson, *Shame and Pride*, 246.

75. Nathanson, *Shame and Pride*, 139.

76. Tomkins, "Shame," 144.

77. Nathanson, *Shame and Pride*, 49.

78. "Theory" and "theater" derive from the same root. See chapter 4, n. 155.

79. Nathanson, *Shame and Pride*, 66.

80. Ferdinand de Saussure, *Course in General Linguistics*, trans. Wade Baskin (New York: McGraw-Hill, 1966), 67.

81. Nathanson, *Shame and Pride*, 76.

82. Ibid., 50.

83. Ricoeur, *From Text to Action*, 73. This openness of experience to what Ricoeur terms "retrospective rearrangements" or multiple interpretations and reinterpretations of past experiences is the result of not only linguistic instability but also the variability of the self. See Paul Ricoeur, *Time and Narrative*, trans. Kathleen McLaughlin and David Pellauer (Chicago: University of Chicago Press, 1984), 2:21.

84. Morrison, in *Essential Papers on Narcissism*, 361–66.

85. Kohut, *Restoration of the Self*, 177.

86. Ibid., 185.

87. D. W. Winnicott, "The Theory of the Parent-Infant Relationship," in *The Maturation Process and the Facilitating Environment* (London: Hogarth, 1965), 37.

88. Winnicott, "True and False Self," in *Maturation Process*, 145.

89. James, *Principles of Psychology*, 1:297, 298.

90. Kohut, *Restoration of the Self*, 185.

91. Daniel Stern, *The Interpersonal World of the Infant* (New York: Basic Books, 1985), 301.

92. Winnicott, "True and False Self," 3.

93. Alice Miller, *The Drama of the Gifted Child*, trans. Ruth Ward (New York: Harper Collins, 1981), 8.

94. Kohut, *Restoration of Self*, 185.

95. Ibid., 3.

96. Heinz Kohut, *Self Psychology and the Humanities* (New York: Norton, 1985), 23.

97. Kohut, *Restoration of the Self*, 10.

98. Winnicott, "True and False Self," 42.

99. Ibid.
100. Ibid., 147.
101. Ibid., 146.
102. Nathanson, *Shame and Pride*, 55.
103. Silvan S. Tomkins, *Affect/Imagery/Consciousness*, vol. 1, quoted in Nathanson, "A Timetable for Shame," in *The Many Faces of Shame*, ed. Donald M. Nathanson (New York: Guilford, 1987), 9.
104. Nathanson, "Timetable for Shame," 9.
105. Winnicott, "True and False Self," 146.
106. Morrison, in *Essential Papers on Narcissism*, 362–63.
107. Ibid., 363.
108. Kohut, *Restoration of the Self*, 9.
109. Morrison, in *Essential Papers on Narcissism*, 364.
110. Winnicott, "The True and False Self," 143.
111. Miller, *Drama of the Gifted Child*, xx.
112. Kinston's discussion of the relationship between narcissistic injury and self-protection describes the same dynamic as Kohut, Winnicott, and Miller. His terminology differs: "self-narcissism" describes the maneuver of withdrawal from interrelatedness, while "object-narcissism" describes fusion with idealized object demands, "custom, politeness, manners, and social skills." His most important insight is that an individual may move back and forth between archaic states of woundedness and states of social conformity. Each movement has its affect: rage in the former, apathy in the latter. These are also the two faces of anomie. See Warren Kinston, "The Shame of Narcissism," in *Many Faces of Shame*, 220–33.
113. Francis J. Broucek, *Shame and the Self* (New York: Guilford, 1991), 58.
114. Ibid., 59.
115. Ruth Benedict, *The Chrysanthemum and the Sword* (Boston: Houghton Mifflin, 1946); Margaret Mead, ed., *Cooperation and Competition among Primitive Peoples* (New York: McGraw-Hill, 1937).
116. Gerhart Piers and Milton B. Singer, *Shame and Guilt: A Psychoanalytic and a Cultural Study* (Springfield, IL: Charles C. Thomas, 1953), 48.
117. Sigmund Freud, *The Ego and the Id*, trans. Joan Riviere (New York: Norton, 1929); idem, *Totem and Taboo: Resemblances between the Psychic Lives of Savages and Neurotic* (New York: Moffat, Yard, 1819).
118. Piers and Singer, *Shame and Guilt*, 11.
119. Eric R. Dodds, *The Greeks and the Irrational* (Berkeley: University of California Press, 1951). Dodds is one of the "most remarkable classical scholars of this century," and Bernard Williams names Dodds's book as inspiration for his work on the Greeks and the role of shame in their literature. See Bernard Williams, *Shame and Necessity* (Berkeley: University of California Press, 1993), x–xi.
120. David H. Hesla, "Greek and Christian Tragedy," in *Art/Literature/Religion: Life on the Borders*, ed. Robert Detweiler (Chico, CA: Scholars Press, 1983), 73, 86.
121. Ibid., 81, 86.
122. Ibid., 80.
123. Piers and Singer, *Shame and Guilt*, 79, 77. Individuals may also exhibit "cycles" of shame and guilt wherein the state of guilt triggers the condition of shame. See Kinston, "Shame of Narcissism," 230.
124. Robin M. Williams Jr., *American Society: A Sociological Interpretation* (New York: Knopf, 1970), 621; J. G. Peristiany, ed., *Honour and Shame: The Values of Mediterranean Society* (Chicago: University of Chicago Press, 1966);

Julian Pitt-Rivers, *The Fate of Shechem, or the Politics of Sex: Essays in the Anthropology of the Mediterranean* (Cambridge: Cambridge University Press, 1977). Pitt-Rivers views honor and shame as transcultural values found in numerous ethnic groups. See Julian Pitt-Rivers, "The Law of Hospitality," in *Fate of Shechem*, 94–112. See also John Campbell, *Honour, Family, and Patronage* (Oxford: Oxford University Press, 1964); and David D. Gilmore, ed., *Honor and Shame and the Unity of the Mediterranean* (Washington, D.C.: American Anthropological Association, 1987).

125. Pitt-Rivers, *Fate of Shechem*, 1.

126. Pitt-Rivers, "Honour and Social Status," in *Honour and Shame*, 38.

127. See chapter 3.

128. Pitt-Rivers, *Fate of Shechem*, 8.

129. "The gods of the *Iliad* are primarily concerned with their own honour (τιμή). To speak lightly of a god, to neglect his cult, to maltreat his priest, all these understandably make him angry; in a shame culture gods, like men, are quick to resent a slight." Dodds, *Greeks and the Irrational*, 32.

130. Bruce J. Malina and Jerome H. Neyrey, "Honor and Shame in Luke-Acts: Pivotal Values of the Mediterranean World," in *The Social World of Luke-Acts: Models for Interpretation*, ed. Jerome H. Neyrey (Peabody, MA: Hendrickson, 1991).

131. Pitt-Rivers, *Fate of Shechem*, 95.

132. Edward L. Scheiffelin, *The Sorrow of the Lonely and the Burning of the Dancers* (New York: St. Martin's Press, 1976), 3.

133. See Peter Berger and Thomas Luckmann, *The Social Construction of Reality: A Treatise in the Sociology of Knowledge* (Garden City, NY: Doubleday, 1967); Emile Durkheim, *The Elementary Forms of the Religious Life*, trans. J. Swain (London: Allen & Unwin, 1915).

134. See Sherry B. Ortner, "The Virgin and the State," *Feminist Studies* 4 (1978): 19–33, for an example of this explanation.

135. Mary Douglas, *Natural Symbols: Explorations in Cosmology* (New York: Pantheon, 1982), especially her chapter, "A Rule of Method," 54–64, on group and grid; Bruce J. Malina, *Christian Origins and Cultural Anthropology: Practical Models for Biblical Interpretation* (Atlanta: John Knox Press, 1986).

136. Malina, *Christian Origins*, 16.

137. Julian Pitt-Rivers, "Honour," in *Encyclopedia of the Social Sciences*, 2d ed. (New York: Macmillan, 1968), 503–11.

138. Pitt-Rivers, *Fate of Shechem*, 10.

139. Unni Wikan, "Shame and Honor: A Contestable Pain," *Man* 19 (1984): 635–52, 638.

140. Gilmore, *Honor and Shame*, 10.

141. Anton Block, "Rams and Billy-Goats: A Key to the Mediterranean Code of Honor," in *Religion, Power and Protest in Local Communities: The Northern Shore of the Mediterranean*, ed. Eric R. Wolf (Berlin and New York: Mouton, 1984), 51–70.

142. Gilmore, *Honor and Shame*, 10.

143. The term appears increasingly in the textual commentaries informed by sociological and anthropological perspectives. Bruce Malina and Jerome H. Neyrey are popularly associated with its usage in the Gospel of Luke. See Bruce Malina, "The Individual and the Community-Personality in the Social World of Early Christianity," *Biblical Theological Bulletin* 9, no. 3 (1979): 126–38; Malina and Neyrey, "Honor and Shame"; and Nicholas Taylor, *Paul, Antioch, and Jerusalem: A Study in Relationships and Authority in Earliest Christianity* (Sheffield: JSOT Press, 1992), 24, 37; Wayne A. Meeks uses the term

"face to face" in *The First Urban Christians: The Social World of the Apostle Paul* (New Haven: Yale University Press, 1983), 78. "Dyadic personality" appears as a descriptive term in anthropology. See George M. Foster, "The Dyadic Contact: A Model for the Social Structure of a Mexican Peasant Village," *American Anthropologist* 63 (1961): 1173–92.

144. Peristiany, *Honor and Shame*, 11; Bertram Wyatt-Brown, *Southern Honor* (New York: Oxford University Press, 1982). The term finds early usage in Charles H. Cooley, *Social Organization: A Study of the Larger Mind* (New York: Scribner's Sons, 1921).

145. Bernard M. Loomer, "The Free and Relational Self," in *Belief and Ethnics*, ed. Gibson Winter and W. W. Schroeder (Chicago: University of Chicago Press, 1979); Archie Smith Jr., *The Relational Self: Ethics and Therapy from a Black Church Perspective* (Nashville: Abingdon, 1982).

146. Mead, *Mind, Self, and Society*; James, *Principles of Psychology*.

147. Melanie Klein, *The Psychoanalysis of Children* (New York: Free Press, 1984); Heinz Kohut, *The Analysis of the Self: A Systematic Approach to the Psychoanalytic Treatment of Narcissistic Personality Disorders* (New York: International Universities Press, 1971).

148. R. N. Emde, "The Prerepresentational Self and Its Affective Core," *Psychoanalytic Study of the Child* 38 (1983): 165–92; Michael Lewis, *Shame: The Exposed Self* (New York: Free Press, 1992), 200–204.

149. Maurice Natanson, *The Journeying Self: A Study in Philosophy and Social Role* (Reading, MA: Addison-Wesley, 1970), 47–51. Natanson's term is the "we-relationship"; "We are, therefore, I am," 47.

150. Peristiany, *Honour and Shame*, 11.

151. Nathanson, *Pride and Shame*, 83, 84. See Francis J. Broucek, "Efficacy in Infancy: A Review of Some Experimental Studies and Their Possible Implications for Clinical Theory," *International Journal of Psychoanalysis* 60 (1979): 311–16, quoted in Nathanson, *Pride and Shame*, 83.

152. Nathanson, *Shame and Pride*, 86.

153. See Andrew Morrison, *Shame, the Underside of Narcissism* (Hillsdale, NJ: Analytic Press, 1989), 78; Kohut, *Restoration of the Self*, xvi–xvii.

154. Morrison, *Shame, the Underside of Narcissism*, 79.

155. Wikan, "Shame and Honour," 637. The two terms enter anthropology by way of Clifford Geertz, who recognizes Kohut as his source. See Clifford Geertz, "From the Native's Point of View: On the Nature of Anthropological Understanding," in *Symbolic Anthropology*, ed. Janet L. Dulgin, David S. Kemnitzer, and David M. Schneider (New York: Columbia University Press, 1977), 781.

156. Nathanson, *Shame and Pride*, 210.

157. Ibid., 84.

158. S. Levin, "The Psychoanalysis of Shame," *International Journal of Psycho-Analysis* 52 (1971): 355–62.

159. Tomkins, "Shame," 143.

160. Nathanson, *Shame and Pride*, 139.

161. Kurt Riezler, *Man: Mutable and Immutable* (New York: Henry Regnery, 1951), 227, quoted in Carl D. Schneider, *Shame, Exposure, and Privacy* (Boston: Beacon, 1977), 18.

162. Schneider, *Shame, Exposure, and Privacy*, 18–19.

163. Ibid., 20.

164. James W. Fowler, "Bio-Cultural Roots of Shame, Conscience and Sin," *CTNS Bulletin* 13, no. 1 (1993): 5.

165. Schneider, *Shame, Exposure, and Privacy*, 22.

166. Fowler, "Bio-Cultural Roots of Shame," 6. See also Helen Merrell Lynd, *On Shame and the Search for Identity* (New York: Harcourt Brace & World, 1958), 20–26; Helen Block Lewis, *Shame and Guilt in Neurosis* (New York: International Universities Press, 1971); Hesla, "Greek and Christian Tragedy," 71–87, for literary interpretations of the distinction between guilt and shame.

167. See Riezler, *Man*, quoted in Schneider, *Shame, Exposure, and Privacy*, 23; Jean-Paul Sartre, *Being and Nothingness: An Essay on Phenomenological Ontology*, trans. Hazel E. Barnes (New York: Philosophical Library, 1956), 261.

168. Schneider, *Shame, Exposure, and Privacy*, 31.

169. Fowler, "Bio-Cultural Roots of Shame," 8.

170. This term is from the unpublished manuscript of Dr. Fowler's *Authority and the Broken Heart: Shame, Culture and the Self*, 20.

171. Fowler, *Authority and the Broken Heart*, 21.

172. Louis Wirth, "The Problem of Minority Groups," in *The Science of Man in the World Crisis*, ed. Ralph Linton (New York: Columbia University Press, 1945).

173. *The Analytical Lexicon to the Greek New Testament*, ed. William D. Mounce (Grand Rapids: Zondervan, 1993).

Chapter 3

1. For an excellent review of this theological perspective, see Paula Fredriksen, "Paul and Augustine: Conversion Narratives, Orthodox Traditions, and the Retrospective Self," *Journal of Theological Studies* 37 (1986): 3–34; E. P. Sanders, *Paul and Palestinian Judaism: A Comparison of Patterns of Religion* (Philadelphia: Fortress Press, 1977); Krister Stendahl, *Paul Among Jews and Gentiles and Other Essays* (Philadelphia: Fortress Press, 1989).

2. James, *Varieties*, 167.

3. Rudolf Otto, *The Idea of the Holy: An Inquiry into the Non-Rational Factor in the Idea of the Divine and Its Relation to the Rational*, trans. John W. Harvey (London and New York: Oxford University Press, 1923), 206.

4. Ibid., 168.

5. Ibid., 85–86.

6. Ninian Smart, *The Religious Experience* (New York: Macmillan, 1991), 346–55; Patrick L. Bourgeois, *The Religious Within Experience and Existence: A Phenomenological Investigation* (Pittsburgh: Duquesne University Press, 1990), 36–49. Both Smart and Bourgeois assume the reliability of Luke's account of Paul's Christianity, an assumption that New Testament scholars no longer share. See Alan F. Segal, *Paul the Convert: The Apostolate and Apostasy of Saul the Pharisee* (New Haven: Yale University Press, 1990).

7. See chapter 1.

8. Charles Taylor, *Sources of the Self: The Making of the Modern Identity* (Cambridge: Harvard University Press, 1989), 151.

9. Ibid., 131.

10. Ibid., 130.

11. Augustine, *Confessions*, trans. R. S. Pine-Coffin (New York: Viking Penguin, 1986), 7.7 (p. 143).

12. Taylor, *Sources*, 131.

13. Augustine, *Confessions*, 176.

14. Peter Brown, *Augustine of Hippo: A Biography* (Berkeley: University of California Press, 1969), 151.

15. Augustine, *Confessions*, 178.

16. Augustine, *Soliloquia* 1.13.22: 881, quoted in Peter Brown, *The Body and Society: Men, Women, and Sexual Renunciation in Early Christianity* (New York: Columbia University Press, 1988), 394.
17. Fredriksen, "Paul and Augustine," 27. Emphasis mine.
18. Taylor, *Sources*, 131.
19. Andrew Louth, *The Origins of the Christian Mystical Tradition: From Plato to Denys* (New York: Oxford University Press, 1981), 37–39.
20. Ibid., 40.
21. Brown, *Augustine*, 245.
22. Plotinus, *Enneads* 1.6.9.
23. Augustine, "Sermon on Romans 7:15," *The Works of Saint Augustine: A Translation for the 21st Century*, III/5, trans. Edmund Hill (New Rochelle, NY: New City Press, 1990), 79–80.
24. Plotinus, *Enneads*, 1.6.9.
25. Augustine, *Confessions* 10.17 in Brown, *Augustine*, 178.
26. Augustine, *Confessions* 29, 27, cited in Brown, *Augustine*, 179.
27. E. C. Blackman, "Justification, Justify," in *Interpreter's Dictionary of the Bible*, ed. G. Buttrick (New York: Abingdon, 1962), 2:1027.
28. Alister E. McGrath, "Justice and Justification: Semantic and Juristic Aspects of the Christian Doctrine of Justification," *Scottish Journal of Theology* 35 (1982): 406–7.
29. Ibid., 409–10.
30. Alister E. McGrath, *Iustitia Dei: A History of the Christian Doctrine of Justification*, vol. 1 (Cambridge: Cambridge University Press, 1986), 12–13.
31. Stendahl, *Paul*.
32. McGrath, *Iustitia Dei*, 19–20.
33. Ibid., 14–23.
34. Augustine, "On The Spirit and the Letter," in *Basic Writings of Saint Augustine*, vol. 1, ed. Whitney J. Oates (New York: Random House, 1948), 4.463.
35. Ibid., 15.472.
36. Martin Luther, *The Bondage of the Will* (Grand Rapids: Eerdmans, 1931), 40.
37. Brown, *Augustine*, 373–74.
38. Randall C. Zachman, *The Assurance of Faith: Conscience in the Theology of Martin Luther and John Calvin* (Minneapolis: Fortress Press, 1993), 2.
39. David C. Steinmetz, *Luther in Context* (Bloomington: Indiana University Press, 1986), 2–3. See also Gordon J. Spykman, *Attrition and Contrition at the Council of Trent* (Kampen: Kok, 1955); Thomas N. Teutler, *Sin and Confession on the Eve of the Reformation* (Princeton: Princeton University Press, 1977).
40. See Ian D. K. Siggins, *Luther and His Mother* (Philadelphia: Fortress Press, 1981), 48–52.
41. See Denis Jane, ed., *Three Reformation Catechisms: Catholic, Anabaptist, Lutheran* (New York and Toronto: Mellen, 1982), 82.
42. Steinmetz, *Luther in Context*, 5.
43. Regis A. Duffy, "Reconciliation," in *The New Dictionary of Theology*, ed. Joseph A. Komonchak, Mary Collins, and Dermot A. Lane (Wilmington, DE: Glazier, 1988), 835.
44. Ronald H. Bainton, *Here I Stand* (Nashville: Abingdon, 1950), 42.
45. Zachman, *Assurance of Faith*, 22.
46. *Luther's Works*, ed. Jaroslav Pelikan and Helmut T. Lehman (St. Louis: Concordia, 1957, 1963), 22:152; 26:406, cited in Zachman, *Assurance of Faith*, 34, 37.
47. Erik Erikson, *Young Man Luther* (New York: Norton, 1958).

48. See below.
49. Monika K. Hellwig, *Sign of Reconciliation and Conversion: The Sacrament of Penance for Our Times* (Collegeville, MN: Liturgical Press, 1991), 93.
50. Stendahl, *Paul*, 17.
51. Bainton, *Here I Stand*, 65.
52. Luther, *Preface to the Epistle to the Romans*; Stendahl, *Paul*, 26; Keith Clements, "*Sola fide*," in *Westminster Dictionary of Christian Theology*, ed. Alan Richardson and John Bowden (Philadelphia: Westminster Press, 1983), 545.
53. Rudolf Otto's phenomenology of the holy depends upon a Protestant understanding of religious experience, and on a Protestant anthropology of the individual encounter with divinity. Both William James (Calvinist) and Otto (Lutheran) conceived of religious experience as individual in both the event and the outcome.
54. John Dillenberger and Claude Welch, *Protestant Christianity, Interpreted Through Its Development* (New York: Scribner's Sons, 1954), 21.
55. Ibid., 33.
56. Alister E. McGrath, "'The Righteousness of God' from Augustine to Luther," *Studia Theologica* 36 (1982): 73.
57. Ibid., 64.
58. Ibid., 76.
59. *Luther's Works*, 10:404.
60. Martin Luther, *Lectures on Romans*, trans. and ed. Wilhelm Pauck (Philadelphia: Westminster Press, 1961), 71.
61. Zachman, *Assurance of Faith*, 39.
62. Gustaf Wingen, *Luther on Vocation* (Philadelphia: Muhlenberg, 1957).
63. Augustine, *Confessions* 8.9.176.
64. Ibid., 9.172.
65. Ibid., 12.177.
66. Luther, *Lectures on Romans*, 70–71.
67. Gustaf Aulen, *Christus Victor*, trans. A. G. Herbert (London: SPCK, 1931).
68. E. P. Sanders, *Jewish Law from Jesus to the Mishnah* (Philadelphia: Trinity Press International, 1990), 256.
69. Richard Batey, *Jesus and the Forgotten City: New Light on Sepphoris and the Urban World of Jesus* (Grand Rapids: Baker, 1991); John Dominic Crossan, *The Historical Jesus: The Life of a Mediterranean Jewish Peasant* (San Francisco: Harper & Row, 1991); F. Gerald Downing, *Jesus and the Threat of Freedom* (London: SCM, 1987); Burton Mack, *A Myth of Innocence* (Philadelphia: Fortress Press, 1988).
70. Albert Schweitzer, *Paul and His Interpreters: A Critical History* (London: Adam & Charles Black, 1948), 31, 45, 63.
71. John Collins, *Between Athens and Jerusalem: Jewish Identity in Hellenistic Diaspora* (New York: Crossroad, 1983), 80–81.
72. Jonathan A. Goldstein, *II Maccabees: A New Translation with Introduction and Commentary*, Anchor Bible (Garden City, NY: Doubleday, 1983), 79.
73. Martin Hengel, *Judaism and Hellenism: Studies in Their Encounter in Palestine During the Early Hellenistic Period*, trans. John Bowden (Philadelphia: Fortress Press, 1974), 7.
74. Goldstein, *II Maccabees*, 189.
75. Eugene B. Borowitz, "Judaism: An Overview," in *Encyclopedia of Religion*, ed. Mircea Eliade (New York: Macmillan, 1987), 8:127.
76. Henry George Liddell and Robert Scott, *A Greek-English Lexicon* (London: Oxford University Press, 1948), s.v.

77. Hengel, *Judaism and Hellenism*, 2; idem, *The 'Hellenization' of Judaea in the First Century after Christ* (Philadelphia: Trinity Press International, 1989), 7.
78. *Greek-English Lexicon*, s.v.
79. *Theological Dictionary of the New Testament*, ed. Gerhard Kritel and Gerhard Friedrich, trans. and ed. G. W. Bromiley, 10 vols. (Grand Rapids: Eerdmans, 1964–76), 2:507–8.
80. Goldstein, *II Maccabees*, 230.
81. Hengel, *Judaism and Hellenism*, 2.
82. Carsten Colpe, "Syncretism," in *Encyclopedia of Religion*, 14:221; Schweitzer, *Paul and His Interpreters*.
83. Hans Joachim Schoeps, *Paul: The Theology of the Apostle in the Light of Jewish Religious History*, trans. Harold Knight (Philadelphia: Westminster Press, 1961), 213; Hengel, *Judaism and Hellenism*, 309.
84. Joseph Klausner, *From Jesus to Paul*, trans. William F. Stinespring (New York: Macmillan, 1943), 463.
85. Schweitzer, *Paul and His Interpreters*, 176–77. Italics mine.
86. Schweitzer, *The Mysticism of Paul the Apostle*, trans. William Montgomery (New York: Holt, 1931). Italics mine.
87. *Mischerei* in German is a mongrelized or degenerate mixture. See Hermann Usener, *Gotternamen, Versuch einer Lehrevonder Reliogiösen Begriffsbildung* (Frankfurt am Main: G. Schulte-Bulmke, 1948), 337: "Das ist bereits synkretismus oder religionsmischerei."
88. The revisionist scholarship on this subject is extensive. Davies's work, however, is central. See *Paul and Rabbinic Judaism: Some Rabbinic Elements in Pauline Theology* (London: SPCK, 1948); "Paul and Judaism," in *The Bible in Modern Scholarship*, ed. J. Philip Hyatt (Nashville: Abingdon, 1965); "Reflections on Tradition: The Aboth Revisited," in *Christian History and Interpretation: Studies Presented to John Knox*, ed. W. R. Farmer, C. F. D. Moule, and R. R. Niebuhr (New York: Cambridge University Press, 1967), 138; "Reflections on Judaism and Christianity," in *L'Evangile hier et aujourd'hui: Mélanges offerts au Professeur Franz J. Leenhardt* (Geneva: Labor et Fides, 1968), 39–54. See also Helmut H. Koester, "Paul and Hellenism," and Johannes Monck, "Pauline Research Since Schweitzer," in *The Bible in Modern Scholarship*. Works that substantiate and extend Davies's insight are Hengel's *Judaism and Hellenism* and *'Hellenization' of Judaea*, as well as Sanders, *Paul and Palestinian Judaism*, 4–11; and Craig C. Hill, *Hellenists and Hebrews: Reappraising Division within the Earliest Church* (Minneapolis: Fortress Press, 1992), 1–3.
89. Davies, *Paul and Rabbinic Judaism*, 8.
90. Davies notes Hellenistic influences upon Jewish schools, apocalyptic and wisdom literature, funeral practices, and architecture in Davies, "Reflections on Tradition,"138–39, for a modest beginning.
91. Victor Tcherikover, *Hellenistic Civilization and the Jews*, trans. S. Applebaum (Philadelphia: Jewish Publication Society of America, 1959), 345.
92. Ibid., 349.
93. Hengel, *Judaism and Hellenism*, 7.
94. Martin Hengel, *Jews, Greeks, and Barbarians: Aspects of the Hellenization of Judaism in the Pre-Christian Period*, trans. John Bowden (Philadelphia: Fortress Press, 1980), 116.
95. Hengel, *Judaism and Hellenism*, 75.
96. E. P. Sanders, "Jesus in Historical Context," *Theology Today* 50 (1993): 429–48.
97. Sanders, *Paul and Palestinian Judaism*, 12.
98. Ibid., 17–18.

99. Ibid., 13.
100. Alister E. McGrath, *The Genesis of Doctrine: A Study in the Foundations of Doctrinal Criticism* (Cambridge, MA: Blackwell, 1990), 43–44.
101. David Tracy's categories are helpful in identifying this pattern. See *Blessed Rage for Order: The New Pluralism in Theology* (Minneapolis: Winston-Seabury, 1975), 24.
102. Sanders, *Paul and Palestinian Judaism*, 18.
103. Alexander Schmemann, *Introduction to Liturgical Theology*, trans. A. E. Moorhouse (New York: St. Vladimir's Seminary Press, 1975).
104. The term is borrowed from Peter Gay, who uses it to describe Enlightenment thinkers who redefined humanity and human nature without relying upon traditional Christian doctrines of original sin. I am employing the term in reference to an understanding of human behavior that focuses upon the role of reason as primary. See Peter Gay, *The Enlightenment: An Interpretation*, vol. 2: *The Science of Freedom* (New York: Knopf, 1969), 172.
105. Davies and Schweitzer represent notable departures. Davies's emphasis upon the identity of Jesus or Messiah, and Schweitzer's emphasis upon Paul's mysticism.
106. See chapter 4.

Chapter 4

1. See chapter 1.
2. Max Scheler, *Formalism in Ethics and Non-Formal Ethics of Value: A New Attempt Toward the Foundation of an Ethical Personalism*, trans. Manfred S. Frings and Riger L. Funk (Evanston, IL: Northwestern University Press, 1973), 529–31.
3. Abraham Leon Sachar, *A History of the Jews* (New York: Knopf, 1948), 108.
4. Abraham Schalit, ed. *The World History of the Jewish People: The Hellenistic Age* (New Brunswick, NJ: Rutgers University Press, 1972), 6:46.
5. Elias J. Bickerman, *The Jews in the Greek Age* (Cambridge: Harvard University Press, 1988), 93.
6. Ibid.
7. Sachar, *History of the Jews*, 109.
8. J. A. Fitzmyer, *Paul and His Theology: A Brief Sketch* (Englewood Cliffs, NJ: Prentice-Hall, 1989), 2.
9. Martin Hengel, "The Pre-Christian Paul," in *The Jews Among Pagans and Christians in the Roman Empire*, ed. Judith Lieu, John North, and Tessa Rajak (London: Routledge, 1992), 31.
10. Ibid., 9.
11. F. F. Bruce, *Paul: Apostle of the Heart Set Free* (Grand Rapids: Eerdmans, 1983), 42.
12. Philo, *On Dreams* 2.250; *Concerning Abraham* 28, cited in Bruce, *Paul*, 42–43.
13. Bruce, *Paul*, 42. See also Hengel, *'Hellenization' of Judaea*, 7, 113–14 (nn. 19–22); idem, *The Pre-Christian Paul*, 26.
14. E. W. Hunt, *Portrait of Paul* (London: Mowbray, 1968), 3.
15. On the unreliability of Acts, see Günther Bornkamm, *Paul*, trans. D. M. G. Stalker (New York: Harper & Row, 1971), xvff.; see Bent Noack, "Teste Paulo: Paul as the Principal Witness to Jesus and Primitive Christianity," in *Die paulinische Literature und Theologie*, ed. Sigfred Pedersen (Arhus: Forlaget Aros; Göttingen: Vandenhoeck & Ruprecht, 1980), 19; on the relationship beteen Acts and the historical Paul, see A. J. Mattill, "The Value of Acts as a Source for the Study of Paul," in *Perspectives on Luke-Acts*, ed. C. H. Talbert (Danville, VA: Association of Baptist Professors of Religion, 1978), 76–98.

16. Jürgen Becker, *Paul, Apostle to the Gentiles*, trans. O. C. Dean Jr. (Louisville: Westminster/John Knox Press, 1993), 34.

17. W. C. van Unnik, *Tarsus or Jerusalem: The City of Paul's Youth*, trans. Geroge Off (London: Epworth, 1962).

18. Ibid., 7.

19. Becker, *Paul, Apostle to the Gentiles*, 34.

20. U. von Wilamowitz-Moellendorf, "*Die griechische Literatur des Altermus*," in *Die Kultur der Gegenwart*, I, 8, 3d ed. (Leipzig and Berlin, 1912) 232. Quoted in Sherman E. Johnson, *Paul the Apostle and His Cities* (Wilmington, DE: Glazier, 1987), 33; see also Hengel, *Pre-Christian Paul*, 95, n. 31, for the same quotation.

21. R. H. Stein, "Jerusalem," in *Dictionary of Paul and His Letters*, ed. Gerald F. Hawthorn and Ralph P. Martin (Downers Grove, IL: InterVarsity Press, 1993), 464.

22. Bornkamm, *Paul*, 3; Bruce, *Paul*, 42; H. J. Cadbury, *The Book of Acts in History* (London: A. & C. Black, 1955), 80–81; Adolf Deissmann, *St. Paul: A Study in Social and Religious History*, trans. Lionel R. M. Strachan (New York: Hodder & Stoughton, 1912), 32; Hunt, *Portrait of Paul*, 6; Hengel, *Pre-Christian Paul*, 22–23; Richard N. Longenecker, *Paul, Apostle of Liberty* (New York: Harper & Row, 1964), 25, 27; E. P. Sanders, *Paul* (Oxford: Oxford University Press, 1991), 8; H. J. Schoeps, *Paul: The Theology of the Apostle in the Light of Jewish Religious History*, trans. Harold Knight (Philadelphia: Westminster Press, 1961), 24–25; A. N. Sherwin-White, *Roman Society and Roman Law in the New Testament* (Oxford: Clarendon, 1963), 178–79; C. B. Welles, "Hellenistic Tarsus," *Mélanges de l'université Saint-Joseph* 38 (1962): 61–62.

23. The evidence for Jews in Asia Minor is derived from Josephus, *Antiquities of the Jews* (in Greek) 14.10; 16.6. The second major source is found among inscriptions, at synagogues, gravesites, and the pagan cultic sites. See W. M. Ramsey, "The Jews in the Graeco-Asiatic Cities," *The Expositor* (July 1902): 32–47, for Jews in Tarsus: "Two inscriptions discovered in Western Cilicia, near the town of Elaeusa, represent resolutions of the Sabbatistae, a sect worshipping the god of the Sabbath. Dating from the period of Augustus, they testify to the influence of the Jews in Western Cilicia, and to the role of Judaism in the syncretist developments of the period" [Gaius Julius Caesar, c. 100–44 BCE]. See Michael Stern, "The Jewish Diaspora," in *The Jewish People in the First Century*, ed. Shemuel Safrai and Michael Stern, 2 vols. (Philadelphia: Fortress Press, 1974), 1:147; see also E. L. Hicks on inscriptions, "Inscriptions from Western Cilicia," *Journal of Hellenic Studies* 12 (1891): 233–36, nn. 16 and 17.

24. See chapter 2; also Leonhard Goppelt, *Theology of the New Testament*, vol. 2, trans. J. E. Alsup, ed. J. Roloff (Grand Rapids: Eerdmans, 1982), on the role of Hellenistic Judaism and syncretistic influences on Paul, 363–90. Paul does not explicitly state that he is a Pharisee in Galatians, but the term *patrikōn mou paradoseōn* (traditions of my fathers) suggests the written law and oral Torah of the Pharisees. See Frank J. Matera, *Galatians* (Collegeville, MN: Liturgical Press, 1992), 59.

25. Günther Bornkamm, "Paulus," in *Die Religion in Geschichte und Gegenwart*, 3d ed. (Tübingen: Mohr [Siebeck], 1961), 5:168, quoted by Hengel, *Pre-Christian Paul*, 30.

26. Becker, *Paul*, 40–51; Hengel, *Pre-Christian Paul*, 27, 30; Alan F. Segal, *Paul the Convert: The Apostolate and Apostasy of Saul the Pharisee* (New Haven: Yale University Press, 1990), 26; Bruce, *Paul*, 43; Bornkamm, *Paul*, 10–11; Davies, *Paul and Rabbinic Judaism*, 70; Deissmann, *St. Paul*, 95, 118–19; Hunt, *Portrait of Paul*, 20–21; Longenecker, *Paul*, 27; Sanders, *Paul*, 8–9,

101; Schoeps, *St. Paul*, 24; Hyam Maccoby has devoted a chapter of his book on Paul denying both affiliation with or influence of Pharisees: Hyam Maccoby, *Paul and Hellenism* (Philadelphia: Trinity Press International, 1991), 128–54.

27. Deissmann, *St. Paul*, 101.
28. Becker, *Paul*, 34: "Thus it is obvious that from childhood on he was accustomed to speaking as lingua franca the Greek vernacular of the diaspora Jews." See also J. A. L. Lee, *A Lexical Study of the Septuagint Version of the Pentateuch* (Chico, CA: Scholars Press, 1983), for the relationship between the LXX and everyday Greek diasporic usage.
29. Calvin J. Roetzel, *The Letters of Paul: Conversations in Context* (Louisville: Westminster/John Knox Press, 1991), 21. A similar relationship between Koine Greek and Hebraic religion appears in other semiotic forms among Jews in the Hellenic environment. Jews used the "symbolic 'vocabulary' of the gentile world of pagan symbols" to express biblical themes on the walls of synagogues at Dura and Sardis. [The term *synagoge*, "synagogue," is from the Greek dispersion. See J. A. Ziesler, *Pauline Christianity*, 18.] See A. T. Kraabel, "The Roman Diaspora: Six Questionable Assumptions," *Journal of Jewish Studies* 33 (1982): 459. Johannes Munck, far less confident in the cross-cultural transparency between language and religion, cautions that "we [contemporary readers] do not get the slight differences of meaning which are so important in the NT, showing us how the first Christian generation tried to express its Semitic religion in Greek words and thoughts." Johannes Munck, "Pauline Research Since Schweitzer," in *The Bible in Modern Scholarship*, ed. J. Philip Hyatt (Nashville: Abingdon, 1965), 175.
30. Roetzel, *Letters of Paul*, 21.
31. Ibid.
32. Hengel, *Pre-Christian Paul*, 35, 37.
33. Becker, *Paul*, 36; Roetzel, *Letters of Paul*, 29; Segal, *Paul the Convert*, 29.
34. James W. Aageson, "Scripture and Structure in the Development of the Argument in Romans 9–11," *Catholic Biblical Quarterly* 48 (1986): 265–89; James D. G. Dunn, "'Righteousness from the Law' and 'Righteousness from Faith': Paul's Interpretation of Scripture in Romans 10:1–10," in *Tradition and Interpretation in the New Testament*, ed. Gerald F. Hawthorn and Otto Betz (Grand Rapids: Eerdmans, 1957); C. A. Evans, "Paul and the Hermeneutics of 'True Prophecy:' A Study of Romans 9–11," *Biblica* 65 (1984): 560–70; E. Earle Ellis, *Paul's Use of the Old Testament* (Grand Rapids: Eerdmans, 1957); Anthony T. Hanson, *Studies in Paul's Technique and Theology* (London: SPCK, 1974), 136–278; Morna D. Hooker, "Beyond the Things That Are Written: St. Paul's Use of Scripture," *New Testament Studies* 27 (1981): 295–309.
35. Craig A. Evans, "'It is not as though the word of God had failed:' An Introduction to Paul and the Scriptures of Israel," in *Paul and the Scriptures of Israel*, ed. Craig A. Evans and James A. Sanders (Sheffield: JSOT Press, 1993), 14.
36. On Greek letter styles and influence see Gordon J. Bahr, "Paul and Letter Writing in the First Century," *Catholic Biblical Quarterly* 28 (1966): 465–77; idem, "The Subscription in the Pauline Letters," *Journal of Biblical Literature* 87 (1968): 27–41; Andrew J. Bandstra, "Paul, the Letter Writer," *Canadian Journal of Theology* 3 (1968): 176–88; William G. Doty, "The Classification of Epistolary Literature," *Catholic Biblical Quarterly* 31 (1969): 183–99; Helen Elsom, "The New Testament and Greco-Roman Writing," in *The Literary Guide to the Bible*, ed. Robert Alter and Frank Kermode (Cambridge: Harvard University Press, 1987); Chan-Hie Kim, *Form and Structure of the*

Familiar Greek Letter of Recommendation (Missoula, MT: Scholars Press, 1972); Martin Luther Stirewalt Jr., "The Form and Function of the Greek Letter-Essay, " in *The Romans Debate*, ed. K. P. Donfried (Minneapolis: Augsburg), 1977: 175–206; Jack T. Sanders, "The Transition from Opening Epistolary Thanksgiving to Body in the Letters of the Pauline Corpus," *Journal of Biblical Literature* 81 (1962): 348–62.

See also Clavin Roetzel's discussion of Hellenistic cultural and religious influences upon Paul in *Letters of Paul*, 25–28, 30–45.

For Paul's reliance upon methods of interpretation derived from the Pharisees see Ellis Rivkin, *A Hidden Revolution* (Nashville: Abingdon, 1978), 77–78, 273; Joachim Jeremias, "Paulus als Itilletit," in *Neotestamentica et Semitica: Studies in Honour of Principal Matthew Black*, ed. Edward Earle Ellis and Max Wilcox (Edinburgh: T. & T. Clark, 1969), 88–94; David Daube, *The New Testament and Rabbinic Judaism* (London: Athlone, 1956); Joseph Bonsirven, *Exégèse rabbinique et exégèse paulienne* (Paris: Beauchesne, 1939); Roetzel, *Letters of Paul*, 49–53; Segal, *Paul*.

37. William J. Doty, *Letters in Primitive Christianity* (Philadelphia: Fortress Press, 1973), 22. The first paragraph cited above appears, uncited, in Peter T. O'Brien, "Letters, Letter Forms," in *Dictionary of Paul and His Letters*, 553: "But the apostle, who had a sense of freedom in literary matters, was not tied to fixed models, and he often combined non-Jewish Hellenistic customs with Hellenistic ones." See also Doty, *Letters*, 23, 29–35, 38. Also Stirewalt, "The Form and Function of the Greek Letter-Essay."

38. Robin Scroggs, "Paul as Rhetorician: Two Homilies in Romans 1–11," in *Jews, Greeks and Christians: Religious Cultures in Late Antiquity*, ed. Robert Hamerton-Kelly and Robin Scroggs (Leiden: Brill, 1976), 271–98.

39. Translation modified from RSV. Psalm 32 is Psalm 31 in the LXX.

40. Scroggs, "Paul as Rhetorician," 279. See James D. G. Dunn, *Romans 1–8*, Word Biblical Commentary (Dallas: Word, 1988): "The Origin and Character of the Christian Community in Rome," xliv–liv. "Romans was a mixed [Jew and Gentile] church." See E. P. Sanders, *Paul, the Law, and the Jewish People* (Minneapolis: Fortress Press, 1983), 183. See also Rom. 2:17; 7:1, 16 for Paul's mention of Jewish members.

41. Stanley K. Stowers, *The Diatribe and Paul's Letters to the Romans* (Chico, CA: Scholars Press, 1981).

42. Otto Michel, *Der Brief au die Römer* (Göttingen: Vandenheock & Ruprecht, 1963), 113–15, cited in Scroggs, "Paul," 285.

43. Scroggs, "Paul as Rhetorician," 283–84.

44. Vernon K. Robbins, "Rhetoric and Culture: Exploring Types of Cultural Rhetoric in a Text," in *Rhetoric and the New Testament*, ed. Stanley E. Porter and Thomas H. Olbricht (Sheffield: JSOT Press, 1993), 456; the second quotation is from Wilhelm H. Wuellner, "Paul as Pastor: The Function of Rhetorical Questions in First Corinthians," in *L'Apôtre Paul: Personnalité, style et conception du ministère*, ed. Albert Vanhoye (Leuven: Leuven University Press, 1986), 73, quoted in Robbins, "Rhetoric and Culture," 455.

45. Edwin A. Judge, "St. Paul and Classical Society," *Jahrbuch für Antike und Christentum* 15 (1973): 30.

46. W. D. Davies, "Paul and Judaism," *The Bible in Modern Scholarship*, ed. J. Philip Hyatt (Nashville: Abingdon, 1965), 181.

47. Van Unnik, *Tarsus or Jerusalem*, 6, 7.

48. Hengel, *Pre-Christian Paul*, 34, 37.

49. Roetzel, *Letters of Paul*, 55, in reference to Paul's letter to the Philippians, in particular, the Jewish and Hellenistic elements that compose the hymnic section, Phil. 2:6–11.

50. Davies, "Paul and the Dead Sea Scrolls: Flesh and Spirit," in *The Dead Sea Scrolls and The New Testament*, ed. Krister Stendahl (New York: Harper & Brothers, 1957), 157.

51. Roetzel, *Letters of Paul*, 56.

52. See Schoeps, *Paul*, 149ff., 213ff., 259ff.; Klausner, *From Jesus to Paul*, 450ff., 496ff., 528ff., 600ff. Adolf Deissmann perhaps represents a third possible position: variegated parallelism: "Thus in St. Paul these run side by side with each other Eastern native Jewish, and Eastern, Hellenistic and cosmopolitan expressions of hope, and the great popular preacher feels no compulsion to harmonise them theoretically. [At this point he adopts a new metaphor:] The sacred stream which rolls its waters toward eternity shows for a long time the double colouring due to its two tributaries" (Deissmann, *St. Paul*, 190).

53. Rudolf Bultmann, *Theology of the New Testament*, trans. Kendrick Grobel, 2 vols. (New York: Scribner's, 1959).

54. Segal, *Paul the Convert*.

55. See Deissmann, *St. Paul*, 49, in which he distinguishes the neglected "social stratum in which he [Paul] moved" from the nineteenth-century traditions of exegesis that proceeded according to the "zeal for presenting the 'doctrine' of St. Paul in orderly paragraphs like so many anatomical preparations, lifeless and undated, [and] had no concern with the problem of St. Paul's social standing. . . . And I am convinced with many others that the problem of the social position of St. Paul is an important special aspect of our subject, 'the world of St. Paul.'" See also Ernst von Dobschütz, *Christian Life in the Primitive Church*, trans. William Douglas Morrison and George Bremner (London: Williams and Norgate; New York: Putnam's Sons, 1904).

56. John G. Gager, *Kingdom and Community: The Social World of Early Christianity* (Englewood Cliffs, NJ: Prentice-Hall, 1975), 10, 12. Peter Berger and Thomas Luckmann rely upon this concept and method, which derive from Alfred Schutz's social phenomenology. See Peter Berger and Thomas Luckmann, *The Social Construction of Reality: A Treatise in the Sociology of Knowledge* (Garden City, NY: Doubleday, 1966), 10; Alfred Schutz, *The Phenomenology of the Social World*, trans. George Walsh and Frederick Lehnert (Evanston, IL: Northwestern University Press, 1967). See also E. A. Judge, *The Social Pattern of Christian Groups in the First Century* (London: Tyndale, 1960); A. J. Malherbe, *Social Aspects of Early Christianity* (Baton Rouge: Louisiana State University Press, 1977); Wayne A. Meeks, *The First Urban Christians* (Philadelphia: Fortress Press, 1986); Gerd Theissen, *The Social Setting of Pauline Christianity: Essays on Corinth*, trans. John H. Schutz (Philadelphia: Fortress Press, 1982); idem, *Social Reality and the Early Christians: Theology, Ethics, and the World of the New Testament*, trans. Margaret Kohl (Minneapolis: Fortress Press, 1992).

57. Malina, *Christian Origins and Cultural Anthropology*, 4–5. See also idem, *The New Testament World: Insights from Cultural Anthropology* (Atlanta: John Knox, 1981). The anthropological approach draws heavily upon the corpus of Mary Douglas (in the order of citational frequency): *Purity and Danger: An Analysis of Concepts of Pollution and Taboo* (New York: Praeger, 1966); *Natural Symbols: Explorations in Cosmology* (New York: Random House, 1970); "Social Preconditions of Enthusiasm and Heterodoxy," in *Forms of Symbolic*

Action, Proceedings of the 1969 Annual Spring Meeting of the American Ethnological Society (Seattle: University of Washington Press, 1969), 69–80.

58. Vernon Robbins, *Jesus the Teacher: A Socio-Rhetorical Interpretation of Mark* (Minneapolis: Fortress Press, 1992), xxiii; idem, "The Social Location of the Implied Author of Luke-Acts," in *The Social World of Luke-Acts: Models for Interpretation,* ed. Jerome H. Neyrey (Peabody, MA: Hendrickson, 1991), 305–32; idem, "Rhetoric and Culture," in *Rhetoric and the New Testament*; Burton L. Mack, *A Myth of Innocence: Mark and Christian Origins* (Philadelphia: Fortress Press, 1988); Neyrey, ed., *Social World of Luke-Acts*; Burton L. Mack and Vernon K. Robbins, *Patterns of Persuasion in the Gospels* (Sonoma, CA: Polebridge, 1989); Richard Rohrbaugh, "Methodological Considerations in the Debate over the Social Class Status of Early Christians," *Journal of the American Academy of Religion* 52 (1984): 519–46; idem, "'Social Location of Thought' as a Heuristic Construct in New Testament Study," *Journal for the Study of the New Testament* 30 (1987): 103–19. See also Wilhelm H. Wuella, "Paul as Pastor," in *L'Apôtre Paul.*

59. Ricoeur, "Semantics and Ontology," 194.

60. This term is Robert Detweiler's, presented at Southeastern Humanities Consortium Seminar, Emory University, 1991–92.

61. Jacques Lacan, *Ecrits: A Selection,* trans. Alan Sheridan (New York: Norton, 1977).

62. Ferdinand de Saussure, *Course in General Linguistics.*

63. Jacques Derrida, *Writing and Difference,* trans. Alan Bass (Chicago: University of Chicago Press, 1978).

64. Derrida, *Of Grammatology,* trans. Gayatri Chakravorty Spivak (Baltimore: Johns Hopkins University Press, 1976), 11.

65. Lacan, *Ecrits,* 152.

66. Ibid., 153.

67. Ibid., 168.

68. Ricoeur, *Conflict of Interpretations,* 16.

69. St. John of the Cross, *The Ascent of Mount Carmel* (London: T. Baker, 1906); St. Gregory of Nyssa, *The Life of Moses* (New York: Paulist Press, 1978); *Meister Eckhart,* ed. Ramond Blackney (New York: Harper & Row, 1957); Jacob Boehme, *The Way to Christ: A New Translation,* trans. John Joseph Stoudt (New York: Harper, 1947).

70. John Lovell, *Black Song: The Forge and the Flame; The Story of How an Afro-American Spiritual Was Hammered Out* (New York: Macmillan, 1972).

71. Ricoeur, *Interpretation Theory,* 54.

72. Ibid., 55.

73. Ibid., 60–61.

74. I. M. Lewis, *Ecstatic Religion: An Anthropological Study of Spirit Possession and Shamanism* (Harmondsworth: Penguin, 1971).

75. Ricoeur, *From Text to Action,* 15.

76. Charles E. Winquist, *Homecoming: Interpretation, Transformation and Individualism* (Missoula, MT: Scholars Press, 1978), 33.

77. Ibid.

78. John Dominic Crossan, *The Dark Interval: Towards a Theology of Story* (Niles, IL: Argus Communications, 1975).

79. Lacan, "Fiction and Field of Speech and Language," *Ecrits,* 68.

80. See Lacan, "Agency of the Letter of the Unconscious," *Ecrits,* 168: "from where it was before the subject came into the world."

81. Gray Kochhar-Lindgren, *Narcissus Transformed: The Textual Subject in Psychoanalysis and Literature* (University Park: Pennsylvania State University

Press, 1993), 43. The quotation from Lacan is from *Four Fundamental Concepts of Psycho-Analysis*, ed. Jacques-Alian Miller, trans. Alan Sheridan (New York: Norton, 1978), 54.

82. The term *emic*, borrowed from linguistics, indicates its units of distinctiveness. The phonetic is that which embraces the entire range of sounds as heard by an observer, rather than governed by practical mundane usage. See Oswald Ducrot and Tzvetan Todorov, "Nonsignificative Units," *Encyclopedic Dictionary of the Sciences of Languages* (Baltimore: Johns Hopkins University Press, 1979), 169–76.

83. This is an application developed in the New World and is an apt description of a necessary adjustment to an unfamiliar environment for both agents of an old world civil order dislocated in the colonial wilderness, as well as the displaced Africans who repopulated the plantation settlements of the virtual extermination of its aboriginal environment. "There are creole whites, creole negroes, creole horses" (*OED*). See also Salikoko S. Mufwene, "On Recreolization: The Case of Gullah," in *Language and the Social Construction of Identity in Creole Situations*, eds. Marcyliena Morgan and Merryn C. Alleyne (Los Angeles: Centers for Afro-American Studies Special Publication Series) 10 (1994): 63–99, 70.

84. *OED* cites *D'Acosta's History of the West Indies*, IV, xxv (1604).

85. *OED* cites *Juan and Ulloa's Voyage* (3d ed.) I.I.iv.29 (1760–62).

86. Salikoko S. Mufwene, "On Decreolization," 71.

87. Roger Andersen, "A Language Acquisition Interpretation of Pidginization and Creolization," in idem, ed, *Pidginization and Creolization* (Rowley, MA: Newbury House, 1983), 8–9; Charles F. Hockett, *A Course in Modern Linguistics* (New York: Macmillan, 1958), 420–24.

88. Charles F. Hockett, *Modern Linguistics*, 423; J. Aitchison, "Pidgins, Creoles, and Change," *The Encyclopedia of Language and Linguistics* (Oxford: Pergamon, 1994), 3186.

89. John R. Rickford, "Pidgins and Creoles," in *International Encyclopedia of Linguistics*, ed. William Bright (New York: Oxford University Press, 1992), 1:225.

90. Derek Bickerton, "Pidginization and Creolization: Language Acquisition and Language Universals," in *Pidgin and Creole Linguistics*, ed. Albert Valdman (Bloomington: Indiana University Press, 1977), 49–50; Andersen, "Language Acquisition," 9.

91. Andersen, "Language Acquisition," 9.

92. David Decamp, "The Study of Pidgin and Creole Languages," in *Pidginization and Creolization of Languages*, ed. Dell Hymes (London: Cambridge University Press, 1971), 16.

93. Aitchison, "Pidgins, Creoles, and Change," 3182.

94. Bickerton, "Pidginization and Creolization," 49.

95. Hockett, *Modern Linguistics*, 423.

96. Virginia R. Domíngues, *White by Definition: Social Classification in Creole Louisiana* (New Brunswick, NJ: Rutgers University Press, 1986), 121–22.

97. Melville Herskovits's pioneering work on the African cultures of the New World identified the process that created new cultures and societies from elements of the old. See Melville Herskovits, *The Myth of the Negro Past* (New York: Harper & Brothers, 1941); idem, *The New World Negro* (New York: Minerva, 1966); idem, with Frances S. Herskovitz, *Suriname Folk-Lore* (New York: Columbia University Press, 1936). Sidney W. Mintz and Richard Price altered the conceptualization of New World African scholarship on the diaspora. See Sidney W. Mintz and Richard Price, *An Anthropological Approach to the Afro American Past: A Caribbean Perspective* (Philadelphia: Institute for the Study for Human Issues, 1973).

Daniel J. Crowley summarized the anthropological use of the term: "Creolization today describes more generally the process of adaptation Herskovitz synthesized as retention, reinterpretation and syncretism, and that the concept it represents is applicable in Latin America, . . . the Caribbean, southern Louisiana and the west coast of Africa, but also in any area where a culture neither aboriginal nor alien but a mixture of the two, with retentions on both sides and ample borrowing from the outside sources is in the process of becoming dominant—which is to say, most of the world." Quoted by Norman E. Whitten Jr. and John F. Szwed, eds., *Afro-American Anthropology: Contemporary Perspectives* (New York: Free Press, 1970), 38.

For "creole" as used by historians see Domínguez, *White by Definition*; Herbert G. Gutman, *The Black Family in Slavery and Freedom, 1750–1925* (New York: Vintage, 1976); T. H. Breen, "Creative Adaptations: Peoples and Cultures," in *Colonial British America: Essays in the New History of the Early Modern Era*, ed. Jack P. Green and J. P. Pole (Baltimore: Johns Hopkins University Press, 1984), 195–232; Gwendolyn Midlo Hall, "The Formation of Afro-Creole Culture," in *Creole New Orleans: Race and Americanization*, ed. Arnold R. Hirsch and Joseph Logsdon (Baton Rouge: Louisiana State University Press, 1992); William D. Piersen, *Black Yankees: The Development of an Afro-American Subculture in Eighteenth-Century New England* (Amherst: University of Massachusetts Press, 1988); Stephan Palmie, "Ethnogenetic Processes and Cultural Transfer in Afro-American Slave Populations," and "Slave Culture and Culture of Slavery in North America: A Few Recent Monographs," in *Slavery in the Americas*, ed. Wolfgang Binder (Würzburg: Könighausen & Neumann, 1993), 337–63, 22–55.

98. "Creole is intrinsically felt to be the code of the genuine. School teachers, even head teachers, may, or may be forced to, move into Creole to convince the children that they really mean what they are saying. Thus other forms of speech carry the aura of falseness." Karl Reisman, "Cultural and Linguistic Ambiguity in a West Indian Village," in *Afro-American Anthropology*, 40.

99. Breen, "Creative Adaptations," 206.

100. The term *emergent structure* describes the innovative theories of the chemist Ilya Prigogine, who describes the behavior of two biochemical systems: those which are stable, closed, and repetitive in states of equilibrium. "The remarkable feature [of the second kind] is that when we move from equilibrium to far-from-equilibrium conditions, we move among away from the repetitive and the universal to the specific and the unique." These new structures are not preexistent, emerge unpredictably, and are "self-organizing leading to nonhomogeneous structures to non-equilibrium crystals." Prigogine calls them "dissipative structures" in that they develop spontaneously, unpredictably, and far from the previous structures of order, hence they paradoxically resemble conditions of chaos. They are more complex than previous systems, self-organizing (in that the structures are not previously given), and can sustain themselves only with greater energy through interactive exchanges with the environment. They may also dissipate unpredictably and disappear. See Ilya Prigogine and Isabelle Stengers, *Order out of Chaos: Man's New Dialogue with Nature* (New York: Bantam, 1984), 12–13, 142–43, 162–63. See also Ilya Prigogine, *Chemical Thermodynamics* (London: Longmans, Green, 1954); idem, *Self-Organization in Nonequilibrium Systems: From Dissipative Structures to Order through Fluctuations* (New York: Wiley, 1977).

101. Breen, "Creative Adaptations," 218.

102. Berndt Ostendorf, "Urban Creole Slavery and Its Cultural Legacy: The Case of New Orleans," in *Slavery in the Americas*, ed. Wolfgang Binder (Würzburg: Könighausen & Neumann, 1993), 396–97.

103. William J. Samarin, "Salient and Substantive Pidginization," in *Pidginization and Creolization*, ed. Dell Hymes (London: Cambridge University Press, 1971), 133–34.

104. These terms are from the unpublished writings of, and personal conversation with, Professor Emerita Lauree Hersch-Meyer, Bethany Theological Seminary.

105. Bruce Lincoln, *Discourse and the Construction of Society: Comparative Studies of Myth, Ritual, and Classification* (New York: Oxford University Press, 1989).

106. Keith A. Roberts, "Toward a Generic Concept of Counter-Culture," *Sociological Focus* 11 (1978): 121; Steven E. Ozment, *Mysticism and Dissent: Religious Ideology and Social Protest in the Sixteenth Century* (New Haven: Yale University Press, 1973).

107. C. Eric Lincoln, *The Black Muslims in America* (Boston: Beacon, 1973); George Breitman, *The Last Year of Malcolm X: The Evolution of a Revolutionary* (New York: Schocken, 1967).

108. Thomas à Kempis, *Imitatio Christi* (Mount Vernon, NY: Peter Pauper, 1947); Clifton H. Johnson, *God Struck Me Dead: Religious Conversion Experiences and Autobiographies of Ex-Slaves* (Philadelphia: Pilgrim, 1969).

109. Mircea Eliade, *Rites and Symbols of Initiation*, trans. Willard R. Trask (New York: Harper & Row, 1965); Victor Turner, *The Forest of Symbols: Aspects of Ndembu Ritual* (Ithaca: Cornell University Press, 1967).

110. Ellis Rivkin, *A Hidden Revolution* (Nashville: Abingdon, 1978), 38, 68.

111. Morton Smith, "Palestinian Judaism in the First Century," in *Israel: Its Role in Civilization*, ed. Moshe Davis (New York: Jewish Theological Seminary of America, 1956), 70; Saul Lieberman, *Hellenism in Jewish Palestine* (New York: Jewish Theological Seminary of America, 1950).

112. Smith, "Palestinian Judaism," 70.

113. L. H. Silberman, "History of Judaism," *Encyclopedia Britannica*, 15th ed. (Chicago: University of Chicago Press), 22:402–79; E. Schürer, "Alexandrians in Jerusalem," *The Jewish Encyclopedia* (New York: KTAV, 1964), 11:351–72.

114. W. D. Davies, "Reflexions on Tradition: The Aboth Revisited," in *Christian History and Interpretation: Studies Presented to John Knox*, ed. W. R. Farmer, C. F. D. Moule, and R. R. Niebuhr (Cambridge: Cambridge University Press, 1967), 140; Hengel, *Judaism and Hellenism*, 68; Rivkin, *Hidden Revolution*, 242.

115. E. P. Sanders, *Judaism: Practice and Belief 63 BCE–66 CE* (Philadelphia: Trinity Press International, 1992), 422.

116. Davies, "Reflexions on Traditions," 141.

117. Ellis Rivkin, "Pharisees," in *Encyclopedia of Religion*, 8:272.

118. Rivkin, *Hidden Revolution*, 27.

119. Albert I. Baumgarten, "The Name of the Pharisees," *Journal of Biblical Literature* 102 (1983): 411–12.

120. Leo Baeck, *The Pharisees and Other Essays* (New York: Schocken, 1966), 5.

121. John W. Bowker, *The Religious Imagination and the Sense of God* (Oxford: Clarendon, 1978), 33.

122. Douglas, *Purity and Danger*, 7.

123. Jacob Neusner, "The Idea of Purity in Ancient Israel," *History of Religions* 18 (1975): 15–26, 16.

124. Jacob Neusner, "Mr. Maccoby's Red Cow, Mr. Sanders's Pharisees—and Mine," *Journal for the Study of Judaism* 23 (1992): 95.

125. Jacob Neusner, *The Idea of Purity in Ancient Judaism* (Leiden: Brill, 1973), 66.

126. John J. Collins, *Between Athens and Jerusalem: Jewish Identity in the Hellenistic Diaspora* (New York: Crossroad, 1986), 2–3.

127. John R. Bartlett, *Jews in the Hellenic World* (Cambridge: Cambridge University Press, 1985), 8–9.

128. E. P. Sanders, "Jewish Association with Gentiles and Galatians 2:11–14," in *The Conversation Continues*, ed. Robert T. Fortna and Beverly R. Gaventa (Nashville: Abingdon, 1990), 180. The extent of Gentile hostility toward diasporic Jews has recently been reexamined. Sevenster cites widespread evidence in support of the thesis: "Sharp criticism of the Jews because of their . . . non-mingling with the Gentiles, which was also well-known to Jewish writers (cf. 2 Macc. 14–38), resounds in a whole scale of tones in the literature of ancient writers. It is even present in writers who may certainly not be accounted violent anti-Semites and who, in many respects, comment favorably on Judaism." J. N. Sevenster, *The Roots of Pagan Anti-Semitism in the Ancient World* (Leiden: Brill, 1975), 89.

129. John G. Gager, *The Origins of Anti-Semitism: Attitudes Toward Judaism in Pagan and Christian Antiquity* (New York: Oxford University Press, 1983), 31. See also Hans Conzelmann, *Gentiles, Jews, Christians: Polemics and Apologetics in the Greco-Roman Era*, trans. M. Eugene Boring (Minneapolis: Fortress Press, 1992), 48–49, for a review of classical sources. Further, Paul Trebilco contends that classical authors critical of Jews are not representative of widespread attitudes of an entire region. The evidence is "tendentious and incomplete." Paul R. Trebilco, *Jewish Communities in Asia Minor* (Cambridge: Cambridge University Press, 1991), 188; Menahem Stern, *Greek and Latin Authors on Jews and Judaism*, 3 vols. (Jerusalem: Israel Academy of Sciences and Humanities, 1974–1984), 1:181–83.

130. Anthony J. Saldarini, *Pharisees, Scribes and Sadducees in Palestinian Society: A Sociological Approach* (Wilmington, DL: Glazier, 1988), 215.

131. Jacob Neusner, *Judaism: The Evidence of the Mishna* (Atlanta: Scholars Press, 1988), 75.

132. Sanders, *Judaism: Practice and Belief*, 428.

133. For the former see Mircea Eliade, *Rites and Symbols of Initiation: The Mysteries of Birth and Rebirth*, trans. Willard R. Trask (New York: Harper & Row, 1965); idem, *the Myth of the Eternal Return*, trans. Willard R. Trask (Princeton: Princeton University Press, 1971); idem, *The Sacred and the Profane: The Nature of Religion*, trans. Willard R. Trask (New York: Harper & Row, 1961). For the latter see Otto, *Idea of the Holy*; Mircea Eliade, *Shamanism: Archaic Techniques of Ecstasy* (New York: Pantheon, 1964).

134. James, *Varieties*, 28–29.

135. Meissner, *Psychoanalysis and Religious Experience*, 8.

136. Segal, *Paul*, 125.

137. Michael A. Fishbane, *Text and Texture: Close Readings of Selected Biblical Texts* (New York: Schocken, 1979), 7–11.

138. Douglas, *Purity and Danger*, 55.

139. Ibid., 53.

140. Ibid., 54.

141. Mary Douglas, "Critique and Commentary," in Jacob Neusner, *The Idea of Purity in Ancient Judaism* (Leiden: Brill, 1973), 140.

142. Clifford Geertz, *Interpretation of Cultures* (New York: Basic Books, 1973), 92–95.

143. Jacob Milgrom, "Sacrifices and Offerings in the Old Testament," in *Interpreter's Dictionary of the Bible, Supplement*, ed. Keith R. Crim (Nashville: Abingdon, 1976), 763–77.

144. Saldarini, *Pharisees*, 286.

145. Max Kadushin, *The Rabbinic Mind* (New York: Jewish Theological Seminary of America, 1952), 203.

146. Saldarini, *Pharisees*, 138. See also Jerome H. Neyrey, "Body Language in 1 Corinthians," *Semeia* 35 (1986): 147.
147. Sanders, *Judaism*, 120.
148. "It is thus apparent that whereas the components of the Pharisaic Revolution are incongruent with Scriptures, they are congruent with Greco-Roman models. It would therefore follow that the Pharisaic Revolution was seeking to incorporate within Judaism major structural components and major conceptual notions prevalent in the Greco-Roman world." Rivkin, *Hidden Revolution*, 243.
149. Halvor Moxnes, "Honour and Righteousness in Romans, " *Journal for the Study of the New Testament* 32 (1988): 61–77; idem, "Honor, Shame, and the Outside World in Paul's Letter to the Romans," in *The Social World of Formative Christianity and Judaism*, ed. Jacob Neusner et al. (Philadelphia: Fortress Press, 1988). Other terms within the letter are *doxazō*, 1:21; 8:30; 11:30; 15:6, 9; *epainos*, 2:29; 13:3; *epaineō*, 15:11; *kauchēma*, 4:2; *kauchēsis*, 3:27; 15:17; *kauchaomai*, 2:17, 23; 5:2, 3, 11; *aschēmosyne*, 1:27; *atimia*, 1:26; 9:21; *atimazō*, 1:24; 2:23; *epaischynomai*, 1:16; 6:21; *kataischynō*, 5:5; 9:33; 10:11. See Moxnes, "Honour and Righteousness," 77, n. 15.
150. For a discussion on the role of "zeal" in Judaism, see Terence L. Donaldson, "Zealot and Convert: The Origins of Paul's Christ-Torah Antithesis," *Catholic Biblical Quarterly* 51 (1989): 655–82.
151. See Kohut, *Self Psychology and the Humanities*, 23.
152. Nathanson, *Shame and Pride*, 84.
153. Wermser, *Mask of Shame*, 62.
154. Ibid., 29, 302.
155. Ibid., 158. Greek *theasthai* means "to gaze"; *theōros, theatron*, "contemplative," view as spectators, especially in a theater; *theōria*: the act of being a spectator at the theater or games, usually ambassadors sent to consult oracles, or attend games, from *thea*, "viewing," and *oros*, "seeing." See chapter 2, n. 77.
156. Nathanson, *Shame and Pride*, 92–93.
157. Wermser, *Mask of Shame*, 51–52.
158. See also Bernard Williams, *Shame and Necessity*, 78–79. See ibid., 194, for this discussion on "respect for power."
159. Wermser, *Mask of Shame*, 29.
160. James, *Principles*, 1:316.
161. See chapter 2; and Bruce J. Malina, *The New Testament World: Insights from Cultural Anthropology* (Atlanta: John Knox Press, 1981); A. W. Adkins, *Merit and Responsibility: A Study in Greek Values* (Oxford: Oxford University Press, 1960).
162. See Peter Marshall, *Enmity in Corinth: Social Conventions in Paul's Relations with the Corinthians* (Tübingen: Mohr [Siebeck], 1987); Bruce J. Malina and Jerome H. Neyrey, "Honor and Shame in Luke-Acts: Pivotal Values of the Mediterranean World," in *The Social World of Luke-Acts: Models for Interpretation*, ed. Jerome H. Neyrey (Peabody, MA: Hendrickson, 1991), 25–65.
163. Orlando Patterson, *Slavery and Social Death* (Cambridge: Harvard University Press, 1982), 90–91; Wikan, "Shame and Honour," 638.
164. See Jerome H. Neyrey, "Body Language in 1 Corinthians: The Use of Anthropological Models for Understanding Paul and His Opponents," *Semeia* 35 (1986): 129–70.
165. Rosemary Radford Ruether, *Faith and Fratricide: The Theological Roots of Anti-Semitism* (Minneapolis: Seabury, 1974), 48–49. Her argument is challenged by Gager, *Origins of Anti-Semitism*, 24–37.

166. Melanie Klein and Joan Riviere, *Love, Hate and Reparation* (New York: Norton, 1964), 11.
167. Morrison, *Shame*, 14. Shame is also considered a source of rage in shame/honor cultures. See Morrison in *Faces of Shame*, 281.
168. Morrison, *Shame*, 14.
169. See Kim, *Origin of Paul's Gospel*, 44–50; Lloyd W. Rodgers, "An Examination of Paul as Persecutor" (Ph.D. diss., Southern Baptist Theological Seminary, Louisville, 1989); Arland J. Hultgren, "Paul's Pre-Christian Persecutions of the Church: Their Purpose, Locale, and Nature," *Journal of Biblical Literature* 95 (1976): 97–111; Terence L. Donaldson, "Zealot and Convert: The Origin of Paul's Christ-Torah Antithesis," *Catholic Biblical Quarterly* 51 (1989): 655–82, 670–73.
170. Hultgren, "Paul's Pre-Christian Persecutions," 109.
171. Paula Fredriksen, *From Jesus to Christ: The Origins of the New Testament Images of Jesus* (New Haven: Yale University Press, 1988), 145.
172. Ibid., 145, 155, contra Hultgren.
173. Ibid., 155; Sanders, *Judaism*, 428.
174. Fredriksen, *From Jesus to Christ*, 153.
175. Becker, *Paul*, 42. Neyrey notes that Paul and the Pharisees demonstrate a preoccupation with maintaining strong boundaries against pollution, preserving purity of the body. See Neyrey, "Body Language."
176. Gershom G. Scholem, *The Messianic Idea in Judaism and Other Essays on Jewish Spirituality* (New York: Schocken, 1971); W. S. Green, "Introduction: Messianism in Judaism: Rethinking the Question," in *Judaism and Their Messiah at the Turn of the Christian Era*, ed. Jacob Neusner, W. S. Green, and E. S. Frerichs (Cambridge: Cambridge University Press, 1987), 1–13; Joseph Klausner, *The Messianic Idea in Israel* (New York: Macmillan, 1955).
177. W. W. Meissner, "Jewish Messianism and the Cultic Process," in *The Psychoanalytic Study of Society*, ed. L. Bryce Boyer and Simon A. Grolnick (Hillsdale, NJ: Analytic Press, 1990), 369.
178. W. W. Meissner, *Psychotherapy and the Paranoid Process* (Northvale, NJ: Aronson, 1986), 20.

Chapter 5

1. Gershom G. Scholem, *Jewish Gnosticism, Merkabah Mysticism and Talmudic Judaism* (New York: KTAV, 1960).
2. Alan F. Segal, "Paul and the Beginning of Christian Conversion," unpublished conference paper, Atlanta: Emory University, 1990.
3. David J. Halperin, *The Faces of the Chariot: Early Jewish Responses to Ezekiel's Vision* (Tübingen: Mohr [Siebeck], 1988).
4. Ithamar Gruenwald, *Apocalyptic and Merkabah Mysticism* (Leiden: Brill, 1979).
5. Segal, *Paul the Convert*, 39.
6. Evelyn Underhill, *Mysticism* (New York: Penguin, 1974).
7. Scholem, *Major Trends in Jewish Mysticism*.
8. David R. Blumenthal, *Understanding Jewish Mysticism: A Source Reader: The Merkabah Tradition and Zoharic Tradition* (New York: KTAV, 1978), 51.
9. Gruenwald, *Apocalyptic and Merkabah*, 46–47.
10. Ibid., 90–91; Segal, *Paul*, 46–47; Tabor, *Things Unutterable*, 113–25.
11. Segal, *Paul*, 47.
12. Schweitzer, *Mysticism of Paul*; Johan Christiaan Beker, *Paul's Apocalyptic Gospel: The Coming Triumph of God* (Philadelphia: Fortress Press, 1982).

13. Sanders, *Paul and Palestinian Judaism*, 496–97; Fredriksen, *From Jesus to Christ*, 108.
14. Terrance Callan, *Forgetting the Root: The Emergence of Christianity from Judaism* (New York: Paulist, 1986); Nilhs A. Dahl, *Studies in Paul: Theology of the Early Christian Mission* (Minneapolis: Augsburg, 1977); Davies, *Paul and Rabbinic Judaism*; Munck, *Paul and Salvation*; Heikki Räisänen, *Paul and the Law* (Tübingen: Mohr [Siebeck], 1987); Schoeps, *Paul*; Sanders, *Paul and Palestinian Judaism*; idem, *Paul, the Law*; Stendahl, *Paul*.
15. Kim, *Origin of Paul's Gospel*, 56–66, contends that the entire disclosure of Paul's mission and message took place during the mystical encounter. So much for the human structures of mediated experience.
16. Segal, *Paul*.
17. Stendahl, *Paul*, 8.
18. Roetzel, *Letters of Paul*, 185. See also Roetzel's discussion of Paul's use of prophetic material in *Judgement in the Community* (Leiden: Brill, 1972), 153ff. Paul's frequent use of Isaiah, especially chaps. 6 and 53, in Rom. 9–11, however, maybe due to Isaiah's polemical effectiveness in Paul's battles.
19. *1 Enoch* 37–71; *2 Enoch* 22:8–10 in Tabor, *Things Unutterable*, 82–85.
20. Gruenwald, *Apocalyptic and Merkavah*, 39.
21. Tabor, *Things Unutterable*, 123. See Gruenwald, *Apocalyptic and Merkavah*, 93.
22. Rolf Knierim, "The Vocation of Isaiah," *Vetus Testamentum* 18 (1968): 50; Gary Stansell, *Micah and Isaiah: A Form and Tradition Historical Comparison* (Atlanta: Scholars Press, 1988), 32.
23. On Isaiah's relationship to the temple cultus, see Knierim, "Vocation of Isaiah," 67.
24. See my previous discussion of Mary Douglas; Jonathan Z. Smith, *To Take Place: Toward Theory in Ritual* (Chicago: Jonathan Z. Smith, 1987), 47–73.
25. Segal, *Paul*, 42.
26. Blumenthal, *Understanding Jewish Mysticism*; Tabor, *Things Unutterable*, 115; Maccoby, *Paul and Hellenism*, 149, 200 n. 20.
27. Nathanson, *Shame and Pride*, 93.
28. Malina and Neyrey, "Honor an Shame in Luke-Acts," in *Social World of Luke-Acts*, 34, 25; Pitt-Rivers, *Fate of Schechem*, 4–5, on head and face; L. William Countryman, *Dirt, Greed, and Sex* (Philadelphia: Fortress Press, 1988), 24–25.
29. *The Septuagint Version of the Old Testament and Apocrypha*, trans. and ed. Sir Lancelot Charles Lee Brenton (Grand Rapids: Zondervan, 1972), 841 on Isa. 6:5. Max Scheler provides a phenomenological description of the sudden, unexpected moment of shame in "Shame and the Feelings of Modesty," in idem, *Person and Self-Value*, ed. Manfred S. Frings (Dordrecht: Nijhoff, 1987), 15–16.
30. "Καθαρος," in *Theological Dictionary of the New Testament*, ed. Gerhard Kittel and Gerhard Friedrich, trans. Geoffrey W. Bromiley, 10 vols. (Grand Rapids: Eerdmans, 1964–76), 3:416.
31. Otto, *Idea of the Holy*.
32. Baruch A. Levine, *In the Presence of the Lord* (Leiden: Brill, 1974), 77–78.
33. See Paul Ricoeur, *The Symbolism of Evil* (Boston: Beacon, 1967); Williams, *Shame and Necessity*, 59–60.
34. Crayton E. Rowe Jr. and David S. MacIsaac, *Empathic Attunement: The Technique of Psychoanalytic Self Psychology* (Northvale, NJ: Aronson, 1989).
35. Erikson, *Young Man Luther*, 264.
36. See Jonathan Z. Smith, *Imagining Religion: From Babylon to Jonestown* (Chicago: University of Chicago Press, 1988), 53–65.

37. Meissner, *Psychoanalysis and Religious Experience*, 18; Paul Ricoeur, "Ideology and Utopia," in *From Text to Action*, 308–24.
38. See James Thompson, *Between Self and World: The Novels of Jane Austin* (University Park: Pennsylvania State University Press, 1988), for a description of this process in fiction.
39. Nicholas Taylor, *Paul, Antioch, and Jerusalem: A Study in Relationships and Authority in Earliest Christianity* (Sheffield: JSOT Press, 1992), 72.
40. Ibid.
41. Collins, *Between Athens and Jerusalem*, 245.
42. Segal, *Paul*, 93. "Josephus reports that the Jews of Antioch 'were constantly attracting to their religious ceremonies multitudes of Greeks, and there they had in some measure incorporated with themselves.'" Collins points out that Josephus supports the stories in Acts in which the whole city came to the synagogue to hear Paul (Acts 13:16, 26, 43, 50, especially v. 44). Collins, *Athens and Jerusalem*, 163, 173, n. 101; Josephus, *Jewish Wars* 7.3.3. See also J. Andrew Overman, "The God-Fearers: Some Neglected Features," *Journal for the Study of the New Testament* 32 (1988): 22.
43. For questions concerning methodology, see Richard W. Brislin, *Applied Cross-Cultural Psychology* (Newbury Park, CA: Sage, 1990); Robert A. Paul, "The Question of Applied Psychoanalysis and the Interpretation of Cultural Symbolism," *Ethos* 15 (1987): 82–103; Stella Ting-Toomey, *The Challenge of Face Work: Cross-Cultural and International Issues* (Albany: State University of New York Press, 1984).
44. Miller, *Drama of the Gifted Child*, 15.
45. Crayton E. Rowe Jr. and David S. MacIssac, *Empathic Attunement: The "Technique" of Psychoanalytic Self Psychology* (Northvale, NJ: Aronson, 1989), 112.
46. The ongoing findings of the Jesus Seminar reveal the number of authors putting words in Yeshuah's mouth that as an Aramaic-, perhaps even Greek-speaking Palestinian peasant he could not have uttered. See Robert Walter Funk, Bernard Brandon Scott, and James R. Butts, eds., *The Parables of Jesus: Red Letter Edition: A Report of the Jesus Seminar* (Sonoma, CA: Polebridge, 1988).
47. Stendahl, *Paul*; Lucien Cerfaux, *The Christian in the Theology of St. Paul* (London: Chapman, 1967).
48. Important to note is that Plato, a foundational thinker in Western philosophy, was passionately preoccupied with the analysis of what provided the basis of the properly ordered community or *Republic*.
49. The following analysis is not presented as exhaustive, but a form of first phenomenology of Pauline community as the term is described by Ihde, *Listening and Voice*.
50. Anthony D. Smith, *The Ethnic Origins of Nations* (Oxford: Blackwell, 1986), 25–28.
51. Ricoeur, *Symbolism of Evil*, 162–63. See Marilyn McCord Adams, "Symbolic Value and the Problem of Evil: Honor and Shame," in *Interpretation in Religion*, ed. Shlomo Biderman and Ben-Ami Scharfstein (Leiden: Brill, 1992), 259–82.
52. E. Theodore Mullen Jr., "The Creation of Ethnic Distinctiveness," in *Narrative History and Ethnic Boundaries: The Deuteronomistic Historian and the Creation of Israelite National Identity* (Atlanta: Scholars Press, 1993), 63–76.
53. Eliade, *Sacred and Profane*, 70.
54. Sam K. Williams, "The 'Righteousness of God' in Romans," *Journal of Biblical Literature* 99 (1980): 247.
55. Halvor Moxnes, "Social Integration and the Problem of Gender in St. Paul's Letters," *Studia Theologica* 43 (1989): 103.

56. Mythological ancestry is also a foundational act of legitimation for moderns, but named as ideology by contemporary scholars and "American exceptionalism" by American historians. Ricoeur names three features of ideology's function to a group: (1) "Ideology is linked to the necessity for a social group to give itself an image of itself, to represent and to realize itself, in the theatrical sense of the word." (2) As a theory of social motivation, "it is to social praxis what a motive is to an individual project. For its mediating role is always more than a *reflection*, is always also a *justification and project*. This 'generative' character of ideology is expressed in the second-order foundational power that it exercises with respect to enterprises and institutions, which receive from it the belief in the just and necessary character of the instituted action." (3) "It is a grid or code for giving an overall view, not only of the group, but also of history and, ultimately, of the world." Ricoeur calls the third feature *doxic*, Greek for "opinion or belief." "Hence ideology is readily expressed in maxims ['dictatorship of the proletariate'], in slogans ['if you're not part of the solution you're part of the problem'], in lapidary formulas ['justification by faith, not works']. Hence also nothing is closer to rhetoric—the art of the probable and the persuasive—than ideology." Ricoeur is outlining the function and operation of what eventually becomes known as "theology." See Paul Ricoeur, "Science and Ideology," in *Hermeneutics and the Human Sciences*, ed. and trans. John B. Thompson (Cambridge: Cambridge University Press, 1981), 225–26.
57. Scroggs, "Paul as Rhetoritician," 290.
58. Moxnes, "Social Integration and the Problem of Gender," 102; idem, *Theology in Conflict* (Leiden: Brill, 1980), 108ff.
59. See E. P. Sanders's detailed summary of the history of this misunderstanding in *Paul and Palestinian Judaism*; also *Paul, the Law*. See also George Foot Moore, *Judaism in the First Centuries of the Christian Era: The Age of the Tannaim,* 3 vols. (Cambridge: Harvard University Press, 1927–30); James D. G. Dunn, "The New Perspective on Paul," *Bulletin of the John Rylands University Library of Manchester* 65 (1983): 95–122; idem, "Works of the Law and the Curse of the Law (Galatians 3:10–14)," *New Testament Studies* 31 (1985): 523–42; Gaston, *Paul and the Torah.*
60. Brice L. Martin, *Christ and the Law in Paul*, Novum Testamentum Supplement 62 (Leiden: Brill, 1989), 3–20.
61. Michael Winger, *By What Law: The Meaning of* Νόμος *in the Letters of Paul* (Atlanta: Scholars Press, 1992), 22; see In-Gyu Hong, *The Law in Galatians* (Sheffield: JSOT Press, 1993); Heikki Räisänen, "Paul's Word Play on νόμος," in *Jesus, Paul, and Torah: Collected Essays*, trans. David E. Orton (Sheffield: JSOT Press, 1992), 69–111.
62. Segal, *Paul*, 139; Ulrich Wilckens, *Die Missionsreden der Apostelgeschichte* (Neukirchen: Neukirchener Verlag, 1963), 50.
63. Segal, *Paul*, 139.
64. Scott McKnight, *A Light Among the Gentiles: Jewish Missionary Activity in the Second Temple Period* (Minneapolis: Fortress Press, 1991).
65. Sanders, *Paul*, 45–48.
66. Ibid., 45.
67. Hendrikus Boers, "We Who Are by Inheritance Jews; Not from the Gentiles, Sinners," *Journal of Biblical Literature* 111 (1992): 278.
68. For the source of the theory of cognitive dissonance, see Leo Festinger, *A Theory of Cognitive Dissonance* (Stanford: Stanford University Press, 1957); idem, *Conflict, Decision, and Dissonance* (London: Tavistock, 1964). For its applications in biblical studies, see John Gager, "Some Notes on Paul's Conversion,"

New Testament Studies 27 (1981): 697–704; Segal, *Paul*, 205–6; Taylor, *Paul, Antioch, and Jerusalem*, 43, 44, 69, 70, 72.

69. Gerd Theissen, *Social Reality and the Early Christians: Theology, Ethics, and the World of the New Testament*, trans. Margaret Kohl (Minneapolis: Fortress Press, 1992), 222.

70. Wedderburn, *Paul and Jesus*, 162–63; Morton Smith, contrary to most commentators, originally held the position that Jesus was believed to have ascended to heaven, then returned transformed (Morton Smith, "Ascent to the Heavens: and the Beginning of Christianity," in *Eranos Jahrbuch* 50 [1981]: 403–29; cf. Tabor, *Things Unutterable*). The passage's beginning contains the Philippian hymn 2:5–11. For scholarship on this disputed fragment, see L. D. Hurst, "Re-Enter the Pre-Existent Christ in Philippians 2:5–11?" *New Testament Studies* 32 (1986): 449–57; and Ralph P. Martin, *Carmen Christi* (Cambridge: Cambridge University Press, 1967).

71. Gerd Theissen, *Psychological Aspects of Pauline Theology*, trans. John P. Galvin (Philadelphia: Fortress Press, 1987), 47.

72. Morna D. Hooker, "Once More ΠΙΣΤΙΣ ΧΡΙΣΤΟΥ," *Society of Biblical Literature Seminar Papers* (Atlanta: Scholars Press, 1991), 743.

73. Joseph A. Fitzmyer, *Paul and His Theology: A Brief Sketch* (Englewood Cliffs, NJ: Prentice-Hall, 1989), 63.

74. I. Howard Marshall, "The Meaning of Reconciliation," in *Unity and Diversity in New Testament Theology*, ed. Robert Guelich (Grand Rapids: Eerdmans, 1978).

75. John J. Gunther, *St. Paul's Opponents and Their Background* (Leiden: Brill, 1973).

76. Anthony Tyrrell Hanson, *The Paradox of the Cross in the Thought of the Past* (Sheffield: JSOT Press, 1987), 35.

77. Doty, *Letters in Primitive Christianity*, 27, 36, on Paul's letters as a form of presence; Morna D. Hooker, *From Adam to Christ* (Cambridge: Cambridge University Press, 1990), 92; and George Lyons, *Pauline Autobiography: Toward a New Understanding* (Atlanta: Scholars Press, 1985), 136–76, on imitation of Paul.

78. D. Beres, "The Role of Empathy in Psychotherapy and Psychoanalysis," *Journal of Hillside Hospital* 17 (1968): 368.

79. See Max Scheler, *The Nature of Sympathy*, trans. P. Heath (Hamden, CT: Archon, 1970), for a phenomenological interpretation of empathy; Heinz Kohut, *The Analysis of the Self* (New York: International Universities Press, 1971), 300, for an object-relations definition.

80. Melanie Klein and Joan Riviere, *Love, Hate and Reparation* (New York: Norton, 1964), 66.

81. See Edouard Glissant, *Caribbean Discourse*, trans. J. Michael Dash (Charlottesville: University Press of Virginia, 1992), on "Caribbean consciousness," 65ff.

82. Winquist, *Homecoming*, 34.

Bibliography

Aageson, James W. "Scripture and Structure in the Development of the Argument in Romans 9–11," *Catholic Biblical Quarterly* 48 (1986): 265–89.

Adams, Marilyn McCord. "Symbolic Value and the Problem of Evil: Honor and Shame," in *Interpretation in Religion*, ed. Shlomo Biderman and Ben-Ami Scharfstein (Leiden: Brill, 1992).

Adkins, A. W. *Merit and Responsibility: A Study in Greek Values* (Oxford: Oxford University Press, 1960).

Aitchison, J. "Pidgins, Creoles, and Change," *The Encyclopedia of Language and Linguistics* (Oxford: Pergamon, 1994).

Andersen, Roger. "A Language Acquisition Interpretation of Pidginization and Creolization," in idem, ed., *Pidginization and Creolization as Language Acquisition* (Rowley, Mass.: Newbury House, 1983).

Augustine. "On the Spirit and the Letter, " in *Basic Writings of Saint Augustine*, ed. Whitney J. Oates (New York: Random House, 1948), vol. 1.

———. *Confessions*, trans. R. S. Pine-Coffin (New York: Viking Penguin, 1986).

———. "Sermon on Romans 7:15," *The Works of Saint Augustine: A Translation for the 21st Century*, III/5, trans. Edmund Hill (New Rochelle, NY: New City Press, 1990).

Aulen, Gustaf. *Christus Victor*, trans. A. G. Herbert (London: SPCK, 1931).

Baeck, Leo. *The Pharisees and Other Essays* (New York: Schocken, 1966).

Bahr, Gordon J. "Paul and Letter Writing in the First Century," *Catholic Biblical Quarterly* 28 (1966): 465–77.

———. "The Subscription in the Pauline Letters," *Journal of Biblical Literature* 87 (1968): 27–41.

Bainton, Ronald H. *Here I Stand* (Nashville: Abingdon-Cokesbury, 1950).

Bakhtin, Mikhail. *Problems of Dostoevsky's Poetics*, ed. and trans. Caryl Emerson (Minneapolis: University of Minnesota Press, 1984).

Bandstra, Andrew J. "Paul, the Letter Writer," *Canadian Journal of Theology* 3 (1968): 176–88.

Barker, Andrew. *Greek Musical Writings*, vol. 2: *Harmonic and Acoustic Theory* (Cambridge and New York: Cambridge University Press, 1989).

Barker, Francis. *The Tremulous Private Body* (London: Methuen, 1984).

Bartlett, John R. *Jews in the Hellenic World* (Cambridge: Cambridge University Press, 1985).

Batey, Richard. *Jesus and the Forgotten City: New Light on Sepphoris and the Urban World of Jesus* (Grand Rapids: Baker, 1991).

Baumgarten, Albert I. "The Name of the Pharisees," *Journal of Biblical Literature* 102 (1983): 411–28.

Becker, Jürgen. *Paul, Apostle to the Gentiles*, trans. O. C. Dean Jr. (Louisville: Westminster/John Knox Press, 1993).

Beker, Johan Christiaan. *Paul's Apocalyptic Gospel: The Coming Triumph of God* (Philadelphia: Fortress Press, 1982).

———. *The Triumph of God: The Essence of Paul's Thought*, trans. Loren T. Stuckenbruck (Minneapolis: Augsburg Fortress Press, 1991).

Benedict, Ruth. *The Chrysanthemum and the Sword* (Boston: Houghton Mifflin, 1946).

Benveniste, Emile. *Problems in General Linguistics*, trans. Mary Elizabeth Meek (Coral Gables: University of Miami Press, 1971).

Beres, D. "The Role of Empathy in Psychotherapy and Psychoanalysis," *Journal of Hillside Hospital* 17 (1968): 362–69.

Berger, Peter, and Thomas Luckmann. *The Social Construction of Reality: A Treatise in the Sociology of Knowledge* (Garden City, NY: Doubleday, 1966).

Bickerton, Derek. "Pidginization and Creolization: Language Acquisition and Language Universals," in *Pidgin and Creole Linguistics*, ed. Albert Valdman (Bloomington, IL: Indiana University Press, 1977).

Biezals, Heralds. "Typology of Religion and the Phenomenological Method," in *Science of Religion: Studies in Methodology*, ed. Lauri Honko (The Hague: Mouton, 1979).

Blackman, E. C. "Justification, Justify," in *The Interpreter's Dictionary of the Bible*, ed. G. Buttrick (New York: Abingdon, 1962), vol. 2.

Block, Anton. "Rams and Billy-Goats: A Key to the Mediterranean Code of Honour," in *Religion, Power and Protest in Local Communities: The Northern Shore of the Mediterranean*, ed. Eric R. Wolf (Berlin and New York: Mouton, 1984).

Blumenberg, Hans. "The Life World and the Concept of Reality," in *Life-World and Consciousness: Essays for Aron Gurwitsch*, ed. Lester E. Embrer (Evanston: Northwestern University Press, 1972).

Blumenthal, David R. *Understanding Jewish Mysticism: A Source Reader: The Merkabah Tradition and Zoharic Tradition* (New York: KTAV, 1978).

Boehme, Jacob. *Jacob Boehme's The Way to Christ; A New Translation*, trans. John Joseph Stoudt (New York: Harper, 1947).

Boers, Hendrikus. "We Who Are by Inheritance Jews; Not from the Gentiles, Sinners," *Journal of Biblical Literature* 111 (1992): 273–81.

Bonsirven, Joseph. *Exégèse rabbinique et exégèse paulienne* (Paris: Beauchesne, 1939).

Bornkamm, Günther. *Paul*, trans. D. M. G. Stalker (New York: Harper & Row, 1971).

Borowitz, Eugene B. "Judaism: An Overview," in *The Encyclopedia of Religion*, ed. Mircea Eliade (New York: Macmillan, 1987), vol. 8, pp. 127–49.

Bourgeouis, Patrick L. *The Religious Within Experience and Existence: A Phenomenological Investigation* (Pittsburgh: Duquesne University Press, 1990).

Bowker, John W. *The Religious Imagination and the Sense of God* (Oxford: Clarendon, 1978).

Bowra, C. M. *The Greek Experience* (London: Weidenfield & Nicolson, 1957).

Breen, T. H. "Creative Adaptations: Peoples and Cultures," in *Colonial British America: Essays in the New History of the Early Modern Era*, ed. Jack P. Green and J. R. Pole (Baltimore: Johns Hopkins University Press, 1984).

Breitman, George. *The Last Year of Malcolm X: The Evolution of a Revolutionary* (New York: Schocken, 1967).

Brenton, Lancelot Charles Lee, Sir, trans. and ed., *The Septuagint Version of the Old Testament and Apocrypha* (Grand Rapids: Zondervan, 1972).

Brislin, Richard W. *Applied Cross-Cultural Psychology* (Newbury Park, CA: Sage, 1990).

Broucek, Francis J. "Efficacy in Infancy: A Review of Some Experimental Studies and Their Possible Implications for Clinical Theory," *International Journal of Psychoanalysis* 60 (1979): 311–16.

———. *Shame and the Self* (New York: Guilford, 1991).

Brown, Norman O. *Hermes the Thief: The Evolution of a Myth* (Madison: University of Wisconsin Press, 1947).

Brown, Peter. *Augustine of Hippo: A Biography* (Berkeley: University of California Press, 1969).

———. *The Body and Society: Men, Women, and Sexual Renunciation in Early Christianity* (New York: Columbia University Press, 1988).

Bruce, F. F. *Paul: Apostle of the Heart Set Free* (Grand Rapids: Eerdmans, 1983).

Buckley, Peter, ed. *Essential Papers on Object Relations* (New York: New York University Press, 1986).

Bultmann, Rudolph. *Theology of the New Testament*, trans. Kendrick Grobel (New York: SCM, 1959), 2 vols.

Cadbury, H. J. *The Book of Acts in History* (London: A. & C. Black, 1955).

Callan, Terrance. *Forgetting the Root: The Emergence of Christianity from Judaism* (New York: Paulist Press, 1986).

Campbell, John. *Honour, Family, and Patronage* (Oxford: Oxford University Press, 1964).

Carr, David. "Husserl's Problematic Concept of the Life-World," in *Husserl: Expositions and Appraisals*, ed. Frederick A. Elliston and Peter McCormick (Notre Dame: University of Notre Dame Press, 1977).

Carroll, James. *Constantine's Sword: The Church and the Jews: A History* (Boston: Houghton Mifflin, 2001).

Cerfaux, Lucien. *The Christian in the Theology of St. Paul* (London: G. Chapman, 1967).

———. *The Spiritual Journey of Saint Paul*, trans. John C. Guiness (New York: Sheed & Ward, 1968).

Chaliand, Gérard, and Jean-Pierre Rageau, *The Penguin Atlas of Diasporas* (New York: Viking, 1995).

Clements, Keith. "*Sola fide,*" in *Westminster Dictionary of Christian Theology*, ed. Alan Richardson and John Bowden (Philadelphia: Westminster Press, 1983).

Cohen, Robin. *Global Diasporas: An Introduction* (London: UCL Press, 1997).

Collins, John J. *Between Athens and Jerusalem: Jewish Identity in the Hellenistic Diaspora* (New York: Crossroad, 1986).

Colpe, Carsten. "Syncretism," in *The Encyclopedia of Religion*, ed. Mircea Eliade (New York: Macmillan, 1987), 14:221.

Conzelmann, Hans. *Gentiles, Jews, Christians: Polemics and Apologetics in the Greco-Roman Era*, trans. M. Eugene Boring (Minneapolis: Fortress Press, 1992).

Cooley, Charles H. *Social Organization: A Study of the Larger Mind* (New York: Charles Scribner's Sons, 1921).

Countryman, L. William. *Dirt, Greed, and Sex* (Philadelphia: Fortress Press, 1988).

Crossan, John Dominic. *The Dark Interval: Towards a Theology of Story* (Niles, IL: Argus Communications, 1975).

———. *The Historical Jesus: The Life of a Mediterranean Jewish Peasant* (San Francisco: Harper & Row, 1991).

Dahl, Nilhs A. *Studies in Paul: Theology of the Early Christian Mission* (Minneapolis: Augsburg, 1977).

Daube, David. *The New Testament and Rabbinic Judaism* (London: Athlone, 1956).

Davies, W. D. *Paul and Rabbinic Judaism: Some Rabbinic Elements in Pauline Theology* (London: SPCK, 1948).

———. "Paul and the Dead Sea Scrolls: Flesh and Spirit," in *The Dead Sea Scrolls and the New Testament*, ed. Krister Stendahl (New York: Harper & Brothers, 1957).

———. "Paul and Judaism," in *The Bible in Modern Scholarship*, ed. J. Philip Hyatt (Nashville: Abingdon, 1965).

———. "Reflexions on Tradition: The Aboth Revisited," in *Christian History and Interpretation: Studies Presented to John Knox*, ed. W. R. Farmer, C. F. D. Moule, and R. R. Niebuhr (Cambridge: Cambridge University Press, 1967).

———. "Reflections on Judaism and Christianity," in *L'Evangile hier et aujourd'hui: Mélanges offerts au Professeur Franz J. Leenhardt* (Geneva: Labor et Fides, 1968).

Decamp, David. "The Study of Pidgin and Creole Languages," in *Pidginization and Creolization of Languages*, ed. Dell Hymes (London: Cambridge University Press, 1971).

Deissmann, Gustav Adolf. *Light from the Ancient East: The New Testament Illustrated by Recently Discovered Texts of the Graeco-Roman World* (London: Hodder & Stoughton, 1910).

———. *St. Paul: A Study in Social and Religious History*, trans. Lionel R. M. Strachan (New York: Hodder & Stoughton, 1912).

Derrida, Jacques. *Of Grammatology*, trans. Gayatri Chakravorty Spivak (Baltimore: Johns Hopkins University Press, 1976).

———. *Writing and Difference*, trans. Alan Bass (Chicago: University of Chicgao Press, 1978).

Descartes, René. *Discourse on Method and Meditations on First Philosophy*, trans. Donald A. Cress (Indianapolis: Hackett, 1980).

Dillenberger, John, and Claude Welch. *Protestant Christianity, Interpreted Through Its Development* (New York: Scribner's Sons, 1954).

Dobschütz, Ernst von. *Christian Life in the Primitive Church*, trans. William Douglas Morrison and George Bremner (London: Williams & Norgate; New York: Putnam's Sons, 1904).

Dodds, Eric R. *The Greeks and the Irrational* (Berkeley: University of California Press, 1951).

Domíngues, Virginia R. *White by Definition: Social Classification in Creole Louisiana* (New Brunswick, NJ: Rutgers University Press, 1986).

Donaldson, Terence L. "Zealot and Convert: The Origins of Paul's Christ-Torah Antithesis," *Catholic Biblical Quarterly* 51 (1989): 655–82.

Doty, William G. "The Classification of Epistolary Literature," *Catholic Biblical Quarterly* 31 (1969): 183–99.

———. *Letters in Primitive Christianity* (Philadelphia: Fortress Press, 1973).

Douglas, Mary. *Purity and Danger: An Analysis of Concepts of Pollution and Taboo* (New York: Praeger, 1966).

———. "Social Preconditions of Enthusiasm and Heterodoxy," in *Forms of Symbolic Action: Proceedings of the 1969 Annual Spring Meeting of the American Ethnological Society* (Seattle: University of Washington Press, 1969).

———. *Natural Symbols; Explorations in Cosmology* (New York: Random House, 1970).

———. "Critique and Commentary," in Jacob Neusner, *The Idea of Purity in Ancient Judaism* (Leiden: Brill, 1973).

Downing, F. Gerald. *Jesus and the Threat of Freedom* (London: SCM, 1987).

Ducrot, Oswald, and Tzvetan Todorov. *Encyclopedic Dictionary of the Sciences of Languages* (Baltimore: Johns Hopkins University Press, 1979).

Duffy, Regis A. "Reconciliation," in *The New Dictionary of Theology*, ed. Joseph A. Komonchak, Mary Collins, and Dermot A. Laue (Wilmington, DE: Glazier, 1988).

Dunn, James D. G. "The New Perspective on Paul," *Bulletin of the John Rylands University Library of Manchester* 65 (1983): 95–122.

————. "Works of the Law and the Curse of the Law (Galatians 3:10–14)," *New Testament Studies* 31 (1985): 523–42.

————. "'Righteousness from the Law' and 'Righteousness from Faith': Paul's Interpretation of Scripture in Romans 10:1–10," in Gerald F. Hawthorne and Otto Betz, eds. *Tradition and Interpretation in the New Testament* (Grand Rapids: Eerdmans, 1987).

————. *Romans 1–8* Word Biblical Commentary (Dallas: Word, 1988).

Durkheim, Emile. *The Elementary Forms of the Religious Life*, trans. J. Swain (London: Allen & Unwin, 1915).

Eckhart, Meister. *Meister Eckhart*, ed. Ramond Blackney (New York: Harper & Row, 1957).

Edie, James M. *William James and Phenomenology* (Bloomington: Indiana University Press, 1987).

Eliade, Mircea. *The Sacred and the Profane: The Nature of Religion*, trans. Willard R. Trask (New York: Harper & Row, 1961).

————. *Shamanism: Archaic Techniques of Ecstasy*, trans. Willard R. Trask (New York: Pantheon, 1964).

————. *Rites and Symbols of Initiation: The Mysteries of Birth and Rebirth*, trans. Willard R. Trask (New York: Harper & Row, 1965).

————. *The Two and the One*, trans. J. M. Cohen (New York: Harper & Row, 1965).

————. *The Myth of the Eternal Return*, trans. Willard R. Trask (Princeton: Princeton University Press, 1971).

Ellis, E. Earle. *Paul's Use of the Old Testament* (Grand Rapids: Eerdmans, 1957).

Elsom, Helen. "The New Testament and Greco-Roman Writing," in *The Literary Guide to the Bible*, ed. Robert Alter and Frank Kermode (Cambridge: Harvard University Press, 1987).

Emde, R. N. "The Prerepresentational Self and Its Affective Core," *Psychoanalytic Study of the Child* 38 (1983): 165–92.

Epp, Eldon Jay, and George W. MacRae. *The New Testament and Its Modern Interpretaters* (Philadelphia: Fortress Press; Atlanta: Scholars Press, 1989).

Erickson, Stephen A. *Language and Being: An Analytic Phenomenology* (New Haven: Yale University Press, 1970).

Erikson, Erik. *Young Man Luther* (New York: Norton, 1958).

Evans, Craig A. "Paul and the Hermeneutics of 'True Prophecy:' A Study of Romans 9–11," *Biblica* 65 (1984): 560–70.

————. "'It Is Not as Though the Word of God Had Failed': An Introduction to Paul and the Scriptures of Israel," in *Paul and the Scriptures of Israel*, ed. Craig A. Evans and James A. Sanders (Sheffield: JSOT Press, 1993).

Falk, Gerald. *The Jew in Christian Theology* (Jefferson, NC: McFarland & Company, 1992).

Festinger, Leo. *A Theory of Cognitive Dissonance* (Stanford: Stanford University Press, 1957).

————. *Conflict, Decision, and Dissonance* (London: Tavistock, 1964).

Fishbane, Michael A. *Text and Texture: Close Readings of Selected Biblical Texts* (New York: Schocken, 1979).

Fitzmyer, Joseph A. *Paul and His Theology: A Brief Sketch* (Englewood Cliffs, NJ: Prentice-Hall, 1989).

Foster, George M. "The Dyadic Contract: A Model for the Social Structure of a Mexican Peasant Village," *American Anthropologist* 63 (1961): 1173–92.

Foucault, Michel. "What Is an Author?" in *Language, Counter-Memory, Practice*, trans. Sherry Simon, ed. Donald F. Bouchard (Ithaca, NY: Cornell University Press, 1977).

Fowler, James W. "Bio-Cultural Roots of Shame, Conscience and Sin," *CTNS Bulletin* 13, no. 1 (1993): 1–11.

———. *Authority and the Broken Heart: Shame, Culture and the Self* (unpublished manuscript).

Fredriksen, Paula. "Paul and Augustine: Conversion Narratives, Orthodox Traditions, and the Retrospective Self," *Journal of Theological Studies* 37 (1986): 3–34.

———. *From Jesus to Christ: The Origins of the New Testament Images of Jesus* (New Haven: Yale University Press, 1988).

Freud, Sigmund. *Totem and Taboo: Resemblances between the Psychic Lives of Savages and Neurotics* (New York: Moffat, Yard, 1918).

———. *The Ego and the Id*, trans. Joan Riviere (New York: Norton: Hogarth, 1929).

———. *Introductory Lectures on Psycho-Analysis*, trans. James Strachey, 4 vols. (London: Hogarth, 1961).

Frings, Manfred S. "Max Scheler: Focusing on Rarely Seen Complexities of Phenomenology," in *Phenomenology in Perspective*, ed. Fred Smith (The Hague: Nijhoff, 1970).

Funk, Robert Walter, Bernard Brandon Scott, and James R. Butts, eds., *The Parables of Jesus: Red Letter Edition: A Report of the Jesus Seminar* (Sonoma, CA: Polebridge, 1988).

Gager, John G. *Kingdom and Community: The Social World of Early Christianity* (Englewood Cliffs, NJ: Prentice-Hall, 1975).

———. "Some Notes on Paul's Conversion," *New Testament Studies* 27 (1981): 697–704.

———. *The Origins of Anti-Semitism: Attitudes Toward Judaism in Pagan and Christian Antiquity* (New York: Oxford University Press, 1983).

Gaventa, Beverly Roberts. *From Darkness to Light: Aspects of Conversion in the New Testament* (Philadelphia: Fortress Press, 1986).

Gay, Peter. *The Enlightenment: An Interpretation*, vol. 2: *The Science of Freedom* (New York: Knopf, 1969).

Geertz, Clifford. *The Interpretation of Cultures* (New York: Basic Books, 1973).

———. "From the Native's Point of View: On the Nature of Anthropological Understanding," in *Symbolic Anthropology*, ed. Janet L. Dulgin, David S. Kemnitzer, and David M. Schneider (New York: Columbia University Press, 1977).

Gennep, Arnold van. *The Rites of Passage*, trans. Monika B. Vizedom and Gabrielle L. Caffee (London: Routledge & Kegan Paul, 1960).

Gilhus, Ingvild Sëlid. "The Phenomenology of Religion and Theories of Interpretation," in *Temenos: Studies in Comparative Religion*, ed. Lauri Honko (Helsinki: Finnish Society for the Study of Comparative Religion, 1984), vol. 20.

Gilmore, David D., ed. *Honor and Shame and the Unity of the Mediterranean*, A Special Publication of the American Anthropological Association, no. 22 (Washington, D.C.: American Anthropological Association, 1987).

Glissant, Edouard. *Caribbean Discourse*, trans. J. Michael Dash (Charlottesville: University Press of Virginia, 1992).

Goldmann, Lucien. *The Hidden God*, trans. Philip Thody (London: Routledge & Kegan Paul, 1964).

Goldstein, Jonathan A. *I Maccabes: A New Translation with Introduction and Commentary*, Anchor Bible (Garden City: NY: Doubleday, 1976).

———. *II Maccabees: A New Translation with Introduction and Commentary*, Anchor Bible (Garden City, NY: Doubleday, 1983).

Goppelt, Leonhard. *Theology of the New Testament*, trans. J. E. Alsup, ed. J. Roloff, 2 vols. (Grand Rapids: Eerdmans, 1981–82).

Gorman, Frank H., Jr. *The Ideology of Ritual: Space, Time and Status in the Priestly Theology* (Sheffield: JSOT Press, 1990).

Green, W. S. "Introduction: Messianism in Judaism: Rethinking the Question," in *Judaism and Their Messiah at the Turn of the Christian Era*, ed. Jacob Neusner, W. S. Green, and E. S. Frerichs (Cambridge: Cambridge University Press, 1987).

Gregory of Nyssa, *The Life of Moses* (New York: Paulist Press, 1978).

Grout, Donald J. *A History of Western Music* (New York: Norton, 1973).

Gruenwald, Ithamar. *Apocalyptic and Merkavah Mysticism* (Leiden: Brill, 1979).

Gunther, John J. *St. Paul's Opponents and Their Background* (Leiden: Brill, 1973).

Gutman, Herbert G. *The Black Family in Slavery and Freedom, 1750–1925* (New York: Vintage, 1976).

Hall, Gwendolyn Midlo. "The Formation of Afro-Creole Culture," in *Creole New Orleans: Race and Americanization*, ed. Arnold R. Hirsch and Joseph Logsdon (Baton Rouge: Louisiana State University Press, 1992).

Halperin, David J. *The Faces of the Chariot: Early Jewish Responses to Ezekiel's Vision* (Tübingen: Mohr (Siebeck), 1988).

Hanson, Anthony T. *Studies in Paul's Technique and Theology* (London: SPCK, 1974).

Heidegger, Martin. *What is a Thing?* trans. W. B. Barton and V. Deutsch (New York: Harper & Row, 1977).

Hellwig, Monika K. *Sign of Reconciliation and Conversion: The Sacrament of Penance for Our Times* (Collegeville, MN: Liturgical Press, 1991).

Henderson, Isobel. "Ancient Greek Music" in *Ancient and Oriental Music*, Egon Wellesz, ed., vol. 1 of *New Oxford History of Music* (London and New York: Oxford University Press, 1957).

Hengel, Martin. *Judaism and Hellenism: Studies in Their Encounter in Palestine During the Early Hellenistic Period*, trans. John Bowden (Philadelphia: Fortress Press, 1974).

———. *The Pre-Christian Paul* (Philadelphia: Trinity Press International, 1991).

———. "The Pre-Christian Paul," in *The Jews among Pagans and Christians in the Roman Empire*, ed. Judith Lieu, John North, and Tessa Rajak (London: Routledge, 1992).

Herskovits, Melville. *The Myth of the Negro Past* (New York: Harper & Brothers, 1941).

———. *The New World Negro* (New York: Minerva Press, 1966).

———, and Frances S. Herskovitz. *Suriname Folk-Lore* (New York: Columbia University Press, 1936).

Hesla, David H. "Greek and Christian Tragedy," in *Art/Literature/Religion: Life on the Borders*, ed. Robert Detweiler, Journal of the American Academy of Religion Thematic Studies 49, no. 2 (Chico, CA: Scholars Press, 1983).

Hicks, E. L. "Inscriptions from Western Cilicia, " *Journal of Hellenic Studies* 12 (1891): 225–73.

Higgins, E. T. "Self-discrepancy: A Theory Relating Self and Affect," *Psychological Review* 94 (1987): 319–40.

Hill, Craig C. *Hellenists and Hebrews: Reappraising Division within the Earliest Church* (Minneapolis: Fortress Press, 1992).

Hockett, Charles F. *A Course in Modern Linguistics* (New York: Macmillan, 1958).

Hong, In-Gyu. *The Law in Galatians* (Sheffield: JSOT Press, 1993).

Hooker, Morna D. *A Preface to Paul* (New York: Oxford University Press, 1980).

———. "Beyond the Things that are Written: St. Paul's Use of Scripture," *New Testament Studies*, 27 (1981): 295–309.

———. *From Adam to Christ* (Cambridge: Cambridge University Press, 1990).

———. "Once More ΠΙΣΤΙΣ ΧΡΙΣΤΟΥ," *Society of Biblical Literature Seminar Papers* (Atlanta: Scholars Press, 1991).

Hopkins, Jeffrey. "Meditation on Emptiness" (Ph.D. diss., University of Wisconsin, 1973).

Houston, Walter. *Purity and Monotheism: Clean and Unclean Animals in Biblical Law* (Sheffield: JSOT Press, 1993).

Howard, Marshall I. "The Meaning of Reconciliation," in *Unity and Diversity in New Testament Theology*, ed. Robert Guelich (Grand Rapids: Eerdmans, 1978).

Hultgren, Arland J. "Paul's Pre-Christian Persecutions of the Church: Their Purpose, Locale, and Nature," *Journal of Biblical Literature* 95 (1976): 97–111.

Hunt, E. W. *Portrait of Paul* (London: Mowbray, 1968).

Hurst, L. D. "Re-Enter the Pre-Existent Christ in Philippians 2:5–11?" *New Testament Studies* 32 (1986): 449–57.

Husserl, Edmund. *Ideas: General Introduction to Pure Phenomenology*, trans. W. R. Boyce Gibson (New York: Macmillan, 1952).

———. *The Crisis of European Sciences and Transcendental Phenomenology*, trans. David Carr (Evanston: Northwestern University Press, 1970).

———. *Cartesian Meditations; An Introduction to Phenomenology*, trans. Dorian Cairus (The Hague: Nijhoff, 1973).

Ihde, Don. *Listening and Voice: A Phenomenology of Sound* (Athens, OH: Ohio University Press, 1976).

Jacobson, E. *The Self and the Object World* (New York: International Universities Press, 1964).

James, William. *The Principles of Psychology*, 2 vols. (New York: Henry Holt, 1905).

———. *The Varieties of Religious Experience: A Study in Human Nature* (New York: Longmans, Green, 1912).

Jarvell, Jacob. *The Unknown Paul: Essays on Luke-Acts and Early Christian History* (Minneapolis: Augsburg, 1984).

Jeremias, Joachim. "Paulus als Itilletit," in *Neotestamentica et Semitica: Studies in Honour of Principal Matthew Black*, ed. Edward Earle Ellis and Max Wilcox (Edinburgh: T. & T. Clark, 1969).

John of the Cross, *The Ascent of Mount Carmel* (London: T. Baker, 1906).

Johnson, Clifton H. *God Struck Me Dead; Religious Conversion Experiences and Autobiographies of Ex-Slaves* (Philadelphia: Pilgrim, 1969).

Johnson, Sherman E. *Paul the Apostle and His Cities* (Wilmington, DE: Michael Glazier, 1987).

Judge, Edwin A. *The Social Pattern of Christian Groups in the First Century* (London: Tyndale, 1960).

———. "St. Paul and Classical Society," *Jahrbuch für Antike und Christentum* 15 (1973): 19–36.

Judovitz, Dalia. *Subjectivity and Presentation in Descartes: The Origins of Modernity* (Cambridge and New York: Cambridge University Press, 1988).

Kadushin, Max. *The Rabbinic Mind* (New York: Jewish Theological Seminary of America, 1952).

Kavanagh, Aidan. *On Liturgical Theology* (New York: Pueblo, 1984).

Kernberg, Otto. *Object Relations Theory and Clinical Psychoanalysis* (Northvale, NJ: Jason Aronson, 1984).

———. "Structural Derivations of Object Relationships," in *Essential Papers on Object Relations*, ed. Peter Buckley (New York: New York University Press, 1986).

Khapa, Tsong. *Speech of Gold in the Essence of True Eloquence: Reason and Enlightenment in the Central Philosophy of Tibet*, trans. Robert A. F. Thurman (Princeton: Princeton University Press, 1984).

Kim, Chan-Hie. *Form and Structure of the Familiar Greek Letter of Recommendation* (Missoula, MT: Scholars Press, 1972).

Kinston, Warren. "The Shame of Narcissism," in *Many Faces of Shame*, ed. Donald L. Nathanson (New York: Guilford, 1987).

Kittle, Gerhard, and Gerhard Friedrich, eds. *A Theological Dictionary of the New Testament*, trans. and ed. Geoffrey W. Bromiley 10 vols. (Grand Rapids: Eerdmans, 1964–76).

Klausner, Joseph. *From Jesus to Paul*, trans. William F. Stinespring (New York: Macmillan, 1943).

———. *The Messianic Idea in Israel* (New York: Macmillan, 1955.)

Klein, Melanie. "A Contribution to the Psycho-genesis of Manic-depressive States," in *Contributions to Psycho-Analysis* (London: Hogarth, 1939).

———. *The Psychoanalysis of Children* (London: Hogarth, 1949).

———. "Notes on Some Schizoid Mechanism," in *Developments in Psycho-Analysis*, ed. J. Riviere (London: Hogarth, 1952).

———. *The Psychoanalysis of Children* (New York: Free Press, 1984).

———, and Joan Riviere, *Love, Hate and Reparation* (New York: Norton, 1964).

Kneale, William, and Martha Kneale. *The Development of Logic* (Oxford: Clarendon, 1966).

Knierim, Rolf. "The Vocation of Isaiah," *Vetus Testamentum* 18 (1968): 47–68.

Kochhar-Lindgren, Gray. *Narcissus Transformed: The Textual Subject in Psychoanalysis and Literature* (University Park: Pennsylvania State University Press, 1993).

Koester, Helmut H. "Paul and Hellenism," in *The Bible in Modern Scholarship*, ed. J. Philip Hyatt (Nashville: Abingdon, 1965).

Kohut, Heinz. *The Analysis of the Self: A Systematic Approach to the Psychoanalytic Treatment of Narcissistic Personality Disorders* (New York: International Universities Press, 1971).

———. *The Restoration of the Self* (New York: International Universities Press, 1977).

———. *Self Psychology and the Humanities* (New York: Norton, 1985).

———, and Ernest S. Wolf. "The Disorders of the Self and Their Treatment: An Outline," in *Essential Papers on Narcissism*, ed. Andrew P. Morrison (New York: New York University Press, 1986).

Kraabel, A. T. "The Roman Diaspora: Six Questionable Assumptions," *Journal of Jewish Studies* 33 (1982): 445–64.

Kümmel, W. G. *Introduction to the New Testament* (Nashville: Abingdon, 1975).

Lacan, Jacques. *Ecrits: A Selection*, trans. Alan Sheridan (New York: Norton, 1977).

Lee, J. A. L. *A Lexical Study of the Septuagint Version of the Pentateuch* (Chico, CA: Scholars Press, 1983).

Leeuw, G. van der. *Religion in Essence and Manifestation: A Study in Phenomenology*, trans. John Evan Turner (London: Allen & Unwin, 1938).

Levin, S. "The Psychoanalysis of Shame," *International Journal of Psycho-Analysis* 52 (1971): 355–62.

Levine, Baruch A. *In the Presence of the Lord* (Leiden: Brill, 1974).

Lewis, Michael. *Shame: The Exposed Self* (New York: Free Press, 1992).

Lewis, I. M. *Ecstatic Religion: An Anthropological Study of Spirit Possession and Shamanism* (Harmondsworth: Penguin, 1971).

Lewis, Helen Block. *Shame and Guilt in Neurosis* (New York: International Universities Press, 1971).

Liddell, Henry George, and Robert Scott. *A Greek-English Lexicon* (London: Oxford University Press, 1948).

Lieberman, Saul. *Hellenism in Jewish Palestine* (New York: Jewish Theological Seminary of America, 1950).

Lincoln, Bruce. *Discourse and the Construction of Society: Comparative Studies of Myth, Ritual, and Classification* (New York: Oxford University Press, 1989).

Lincoln, C. Eric. *The Black Muslims in America* (Boston: Beacon, 1973).

Long, Charles. *Significations: Signs, Symbols, and Images in the Interpretation of Religion* (Philadelphia: Fortress Press, 1986).

Longenecker, Richard N. *Paul, Apostle of Liberty* (New York: Harper & Row, 1964).

Loomer, Bernard M. "The Free and Relational Self," *Belief and Ethnics*, ed. Gibson Winter and W. W. Schroeder (Chicago: University of Chicago Press, 1979).

Louth, Andrew. *The Origins of the Christian Mystical Tradition: From Plato to Denys* (New York: Oxford University Press, 1981).

Lovell, John. *Black Song: The Forge and the Flame; The Story of How an Afro-American Spiritual Was Hammered Out* (New York: Macmillan, 1972).

Luther, Martin. *The Bondage of the Will* (Grand Rapids: Eerdmans, 1931).

———. *Lectures on Romans*, trans. and ed. Wilhelm Pauck (Philadelphia: Westminster Press, 1961).

———. "Preface to the Epistle to the Romans," *Selections from His Writings*, ed. John Dillenberger (Garden City, NY: Doubleday, 1961).

Lynd, Helen Merrell. *On Shame and the Search for Identity* (New York: Harcourt Brace & World, 1958).

Lyons, George. *Pauline Autobiography: Toward a New Understanding* (Atlanta: Scholars Press, 1985).

Maccoby, Hyam. *Paul and Hellenism* (Philadelphia: Trinity Press International, 1991).

Mack, Burton L. *A Myth of Innocence: Mark and Christian Origins* (Philadelphia: Fortress Press, 1988).

———, and Vernon K. Robbins, *Patterns of Persuasion in the Gospels* (Sonoma, CA: Polebridge, 1989).

Mahler, Margaret, in collaboration with Manuel Furer. *On Human Symbiosis and the Vicissitudes of Individuation* (New York: International Universities Press, 1968).

———. "On the First Three Subphases of the Separation-Individuation Process," *International Journal of Psycho-Analysis* 53 (1972).

———. "On Human Symbiosis and the Vicissitudes of Individuation," in *Essential Papers on Object Relations*, ed. Peter Buckley (New York: New York University Press, 1986).

Malherbe, A. J. *Social Aspects of Early Christianity* (Baton Rouge: Louisiana State University Press, 1977).

Malina, Bruce J. "The Individual and the Community-Personality in the Social World of Early Christianity," *Biblical Theological Bulletin* 9, no. 3 (1979): 126–38.

———. *The New Testament World: Insights from Cultural Anthropology* (Atlanta: John Knox Press, 1981).

———. *Christian Origins and Cultural Anthropology: Practical Models for Biblical Interpretation* (Atlanta: John Knox Press, 1986).

———, and Jerome H. Neyrey, "Honor and Shame in Luke-Acts: Pivotal Values of the Mediterranean World," in *The Social World of Luke-Acts: Models for Interpretation*, ed. Jerome H. Neyrey (Peabody, MA: Hendrickson, 1991).

Marienstras, Richard. "On the Notion of Diaspora," in Gérard Chaliand, ed. *Minority Peoples in the Age of Nation-States* (London: Pluto, 1989).

Marshall, Peter. *Enmity in Corinth: Social Conventions in Paul's Relations with the Corinthians* (Tübingen: Mohr [Siebeck], 1987).

Martin, Brice L. *Christ and the Law in Paul*. Novum Testamentum Supplement 62 (Leiden: Brill, 1989).

Martin, Ralph P. *Carmen Christi* (Cambridge: Cambridge University Press, 1967).

———. *Reconciliation: A Study of Paul's Theology* (Atlanta: John Knox Press, 1981).

Matera, Frank J. *Galatians* (Collegeville, Minn.: Liturgical Press, 1992).

Mattill, A. J. "The Value of Acts as a Source for the Study of Paul" in *Perspectives on Luke-Acts*, ed. C. H. Talbert (Danville, VA: Association of Baptist Professors of Religion, 1978).

McAdams, Dan P. *The Stories We Live By: Personal Myths and the Making of the Self* (New York: William Morrow, 1993).

McGrath, Alister E. "Justice and Justification: Semantic and Juristic Aspects of the Christian Doctrine of Justification," *Scottish Journal of Theology* 35 (1982): 403–18.

———. "'The Righteousness of God' from Augustine to Luther," *Studia Theologica* 36 (1982): 63–78.

———. *Iustitia Dei: A History of the Christian Doctrine of Justification*, vol. 1 (Cambridge: Cambridge University Press, 1986).

———. *The Genesis of Doctrine: A Study in the Foundations of Doctrinal Criticism* (Cambridge, MA: Blackwell, 1990).

McKnight, Scott. *A Light Among the Gentiles: Jewish Missionary Activity in the Second Temple Period* (Minneapolis: Fortress Press, 1991).

McLaughlin, Thomas. "Figurative Language," in *Critical Terms for Literary Study*, ed. Frank Lentricci and Thomas McLaughlin (Chicago: University of Chicago Press, 1990).

Mead, George Herbert. "The Genesis of the Self," in *The Self in Social Interaction,* ed. Chad Gordon and Kenneth J. Gergen (New York: John Wiley & Sons, 1968).

Mead, Margaret, ed. *Cooperation and Competition among Primitive Peoples* (New York: McGraw Hill, 1937).

Meeks, Wayne A. *The First Urban Christians: The Social World of the Apostle Paul* (New Haven: Yale University Press, 1983).

Meissner, W. W. *The Paranoid Process* (New York: Aronson, 1978).

———. *Internalization in Psychoanalysis* (New York: International Universities Press, 1981).

———. *Psychotherapy and the Paranoid Process* (Northvale, NJ: Aronson, 1986).

———. "Jewish Messianism and the Cultic Process," in *The Psychoanalytic Study of Society*, ed. L. Bryce Boyer and Simon A. Grolnick (Hillsdale, NJ: Analytic Press, 1990).

Merleau-Ponty, Maurice. *Phenomenology of Perception*, trans. Colin Smith (London: Routledge & Kegan Paul, 1962).

———. *The Structure of Behavior* (Boston: Beacon, 1963).

———. *The Tacit Dimension* (Garden City, NY: Doubleday, 1966).

Michaelides, Solon. *The Music of Ancient Greece: An Encyclopedia* (London: Faber & Faber, 1978).

Michel, Otto. *Der Brief an die Römer* (Göttingen: Vandenheock & Ruprecht, 1963).

Milgrom, Jacob. "Sacrifices and Offerings in the Old Testament," in *Interpreter's Dictionary of the Bible, Supplement*, ed. Keith R. Crim (Nashville: Abingdon, 1976).

Miller, Alice. *The Drama of the Gifted Child*, trans. Ruth Ward (New York: HarperCollins, 1981).

Miller, J. Hillis. *The Disappearance of God: Five Nineteenth-Century Writers* (Cambridge: Belknap Press of Harvard University Press, 1963).

Miller, Jaques-Alian. *Four Fundamental Concepts of Psycho-Analysis*, trans. Alan Sheridan (New York: Norton, 1978).

Mintz, Sidney W., and Richard Price, *An Anthropological Approach to the Afro-American Past: A Caribbean Perspective* (Philadelphia: Institute for the Study for Human Issues, 1976).

Mitchell, Margaret M. *Paul and the Rhetoric of Reconciliation: An Exegetical Investigation of the Language and Composition of 1 Corinthians* (Louisville: Westminster/John Knox Press, 1992).

Modrzejewski, Joseph Meleze. "How to Be a Jew in Hellenistic Egypt?" in J. D. C. Shaye and E. S. Frerichs eds. *Diasporas in Antiquity* (Atlanta: Scholars Press).

Moore, George Foot. *Judaism in the First Centuries of the Christian Era: The Age of the Tannaim*, 3 vols. (Cambridge: Harvard University Press, 1927–30).

Morrison, Andrew P. *Shame, the Underside of Narcissism* (Hillsdale, NJ: Analytic Press, 1989).

Mounce, Willilam D., ed. *The Analytical Lexicon to the Greek New Testament* (Grand Rapids: Zondervan, 1993).

Moxnes, Halvor. *Theology in Conflict* (Leiden: Brill, 1980).

———. "Honor, Shame, and the Outside World in Paul's Letter to the Romans," in *The Social World of Formative Christianity and Judaism*, ed. Jacob Neusner et al. (Philadelphia: Fortress Press, 1988).

————. "Honour and Righteousness in Romans, " *Journal for the Study of the New Testament* 32 (1988): 61–77.

————. "Social Integration and the Problem of Gender in St. Paul's Letters," *Studia Theologica* 43 (1989): 99–113.

Mufwene, Salikoko S. "On Recreolization: The Case of Gullah," *Language and the Social Construction of Identity in Creole Situations,* ed. Marcyliena Morgan and Merryn C. Alleyne (Los Angeles: Centers for Afro-American Studies Special Publication Series 10, 1994): 63–99.

Mullen, E. Theodore Jr., "The Creation of Ethnic Distinctiveness," in *Narrative History and Ethnic Boundaries: The Deuteronomistic Historian and the Creation of Israelite National Identity* (Atlanta: Scholars Press, 1993).

Munck, Johannes. "Pauline Research Since Schweitzer," in *The Bible in Modern Scholarship*, ed. J. Philip Hyatt (Nashville: Abingdon, 1965).

Natanson, Maurice. *The Journeying Self: A Study in Philosophy and Social Role* (Reading, Mass.: Addison-Wesley, 1970).

Nathanson, Donald L. *Shame and Pride: Affect, Sex and the Birth of the Self* (New York: W. W. Norton, 1992).

Neusner, Jacob. *The Idea of Purity in Ancient Judaism* (Leiden: Brill, 1973).

————. "The Idea of Purity in Ancient Israel," *History of Religions* 18 (1975): 15–26.

————. *Judaism: The Evidence of the Mishna* (Atlanta: Scholars Press, 1988).

————. "Mr. Maccoby's Red Cow, Mr. Sanders's Pharisees—and Mine," *Journal for the Study of Judaism* 23 (1992): 81–98.

Neyrey, Jerome H. "Body Language in 1 Corinthians: The Use of Anthropological Models for Understanding Paul and His Opponents," *Semiea* 35 (1986): 129–70.

————, ed. *The Social World of Luke-Acts: Models for Interpretations* (Peabody, MA: Hendrickson, 1991).

Noack, Bent. "Teste Paulo: Paul as the Principle Witness to Jesus and Primitive Christianity," in *Die paulinische Literatur und Theologie*, ed. Sigfred Pedersen (Arhus: Forlaget Aros; Göttingen: Vandenhoeck & Ruprechet, 1980).

O'Brien, Peter T. "Letters, Letter Forms," in *Dictionary of Paul and His Letters*, ed. Gerald F. Hawthorne and Ralph P. Martin (Downers Grove, IL: InterVarsity Press, 1993).

Ong, Walter J. *Interfaces of the Word: Studies in the Evolution of Consciousness and Culture* (Ithaca, NY: Cornell University Press, 1977).

————. *Hopkins, the Self and God* (Toronto: University of Toronto Press, 1986).

Ortner, Sherry B. "The Virgin and the State," *Feminist Studies* 4 (1978): 19–33.

Ostendorf, Berndt. "Urban Creole Slavery and its Cultural Legacy: The Case of New Orleans," in *Slavery in the Americas*, ed. Wolfgang Binder (Würzburg: Könighausen & Neumann, 1993).

Otto, Rudolf. *The Idea of the Holy: An Inquiry into the Non-Rational Factor in the Idea of the Divine and Its Relation to the Rational*, trans. John W. Harvey (London and New York: Oxford University Press, 1923).

Overman, J. Andrew, "The God-Fearers: Some Neglected Features," *Journal for the Study of the New Testament* 32 (1988): 17–26.

Ozment, Steven E. *Mysticism and Dissent: Religious Ideology and Social Protest in the Sixteenth Century* (New Haven: Yale University Press, 1973).

Palmié, Stephan. "Ethnogenetic Processes and Cultural Transfer in Afro-American Slave Populations," in *Slavery in the Americas*, ed. Wolfgang Binder (Würzburg: Könighausen & Neumann, 1993), 337–63.

————. "Slave Culture and the Culture of Slavery in North America: A Few Recent Monographs," in *Slavery in the Americas*, ed. Wolfgang Binder (Würzburg: Könighausen & Neumann, 1993), 25–55.

Patterson, Orlando. *Slavery and Social Death* (Cambridge: Harvard University Press, 1982).

Paul, Robert A. "The Question of Applied Psychoanalysis and the Interpretation of Cultural Symbolism," *Ethos* 15 (1987): 82–103.

Peristiany, J. G., ed. *Honour and Shame: The Values of Mediterranean Society* (Chicago: University of Chicago Press, 1966).

Piers, Gerhart, and Milton B. Singer, *Shame and Guilt: A Psychoanalytic and a Cultural Study* (Springfield, IL: Charles C. Thomas, 1953).

Piersen, William D. *Black Yankees: The Development of an Afro-American Subculture in Eighteenth-Century New England* (Amherst: University of Massachusetts Press, 1988).

Pitt-Rivers, Julian. "Honour," in *Encyclopedia of the Social Sciences*, 2d ed. (New York: Macmillan, 1968), 503–11.

———. *The Fate of Shechem, or the Politics of Sex: Essays in the Anthropology of the Mediterranean* (Cambridge: Cambridge University Press, 1977).

Plato. *Plato's Republic*, ed. G. M. A. Grube (Indianapolis: Hackett, 1974).

Plotinus. *The Enneads*, trans. Stephen MacKenna (London: Faber, 1969).

Prigogine, Ilya. *Chemical Thermodynamics* (London: Longmans, Green, 1954).

———. *Self-Organization in Nonequilibrium Systems: From Dissipative Structures to Order through Fluctuations* (New York: Wiley, 1977).

———, and Isabelle Stengers. *Order out of Chaos: Man's New Dialogue with Nature* (New York: Bantam, 1984).

Proudfoot, Wayne. *Religious Experience* (Berkeley: University of California Press, 1988).

Räisänen, Heikki. *Paul and the Law* (Tübingen: Mohr [Siebeck], 1987).

———. "Paul's Word Play on νόμος," in *Jesus, Paul, and Torah: Collected Essays*, trans. David E. Orton (Sheffield: JSOT Press, 1992).

Ramsey, W. M. "The Jews in the Graeco-Asiatic Cities," *The Expositor* 6, no. 5 (1902): 19–33, 92–109.

Reck, David. *Music of the Whole Earth* (New York: Scribner's Sons, 1977).

Reisman, Karl. "Cultural and Linguistic Ambiguity in a West Indian Village," in *Afro-American Anthropology: Contemporary Perspectives*, ed. Norman E. Whitten Jr. and John F. Szwed (New York: Free Press, 1970).

Rickford, John R. "Pidgins and Creoles," in *International Encyclopedia of Linguistics*, ed. William Bright (New York: Oxford University Press, 1992).

Ricoeur, Paul. *The Symbolism of Evil*, trans. Emerson Buchanan (Boston: Beacon, 1967).

———. *The Conflict of Interpretations: Essays in Hermeneutics*, ed. Don Ihde (Evanston, IL: Northwestern University Press, 1974).

———. *Interpretation Theory: Discourse and the Surplus of Meaning* (Fort Worth: Texas Christian University Press, 1976).

———. "Science and Ideology," in *Hermeneutics and the Human Sciences*, ed. and trans. John B. Thompson (Cambridge: Cambridge University Press, 1981).

———. *Time and Narrative*, trans. Kathleen McLaughlin and David Pellauer (Chicago: University of Chicago Press, 1984).

———. *Essays in Hermentutics*, vol. 2: *From Text to Action*, trans. Kathleen Blamey and John B. Thompson (Evanston: Northwestern University Press, 1991).

Rivkin, Ellis. *A Hidden Revolution* (Nashville: Abingdon, 1978).

———. "Pharisees," in *The Encyclopedia of Religion*, ed. Mircea Eliade (New York: Macmillan, 1987), 8:272.

Robbins, Vernon K. "The Social Location of the Implied Author of Luke-Acts," in *The Social World of Luke-Acts: Models for Interpretations*, ed. Jerome H. Neyrey (Peabody, MA: Hendrickson, 1991).

———. *Jesus the Teacher: A Socio-Rhetorical Interpretation of Mark* (Minneapolis: Fortress Press, 1992).

———. "Rhetoric and Culture: Exploring Types of Cultural Rhetoric in a Text," in *Rhetoric and the New Testament*, ed. Stanley E. Porter and Thomas H. Olbricht (Sheffield: JSOT Press, 1993).

Robert, Keith A. "Toward a Generic Concept of Counter-Culture," *Sociological Focus* 11 (1978): 111–26.

Rodgers, Lloyd W. "An Examination of Paul as Persecutor" (Ph.D. diss., Southern Baptist Theological Seminary, Louisville, 1989).

Roetzel, Calvin J. *Judgement in the Community* (Leiden: Brill, 1972).

———. *The Letters of Paul: Conversations in Context* (Louisville: Westminster/John Knox Press, 1991).

Rohrbaugh, Richard. "Methodological Considerations in the Debate over the Social Class Status of Early Christian," *Journal of the American Academy of Religion* 52 (1984): 519–46.

———. " 'Social Location of Thought' as a Heuristic Construct in New Testament Study," *Journal for the Study of the New Testament* 30 (1987): 103–19.

Rorty, Richard. *Philosophy and the Mirror of Nature* (Princeton: Princeton University Press, 1979).

Rowe, Crayton E. Jr., and David S. MacIsaac. *The Technique of Psychoanalytic Self Psychology* (Northvale, NJ: Aronson, 1989).

Ruether, Rosemary Radford. *Faith and Fratricide: The Theological Roots of Anti-Semitism* (Minneapolis: Seabury Press, 1974).

Sachar, Abraham Leon. *A History of the Jews* (New York: Knopf, 1948).

Said, Edward. *Orientalism* (London: Routledge, 1979).

Sajama, Seppo, and Matti Pamppinene, *A Historical Introduction to Phenomenology* (New York: Croom Helm with Methuen, 1987).

Saldarini, Anthony J. *Pharisees, Scribes and Sadducees in Palestinian Society: A Sociological Approach* (Wilmington, DL: Glazier, 1988).

Samarin, William J. "Salient and Substantive Pidginization," in *Pidginization and Creolization of Languages*, ed. Dell Hymes (London: Cambridge University Press, 1971).

Sanders, E. P. *Paul and Palestinian Judaism: A Comparison of Patterns of Religion* (Philadelphia: Fortress Press, 1977).

———. *Paul, the Law, and the Jewish People* (Minneapolis: Fortress Press, 1983).

———. *Jewish Law from Jesus to the Mishnah* (Philadelphia: Trinity Press International, 1990).

———. "Jewish Association with Gentiles and Galatians 2:11–14," in *The Conversation Continues*, ed. Robert T. Fortna and Beverly R. Gaventa (Nashville: Abingdon, 1990).

———. *Paul* (Oxford: Oxford University Press, 1991).

———. *Judaism: Practice and Belief 63 BCE–66 CE* (Philadelphia: Trinity Press International, 1992).

———. "Jesus in Historical Context," *Theology Today* 50 (1993): 429–48.

Sanders, Jack T. "The Transition from Opening Epistolary Thanksgiving to Body in the Letters of the Pauline Corpus," *Journal of Biblical Literature* 81 (1962): 348–62.

Sartre, Jean-Paul. *Being and Nothingness: An Essay on Phenomenological Ontology*, trans. Hazel E. Barnes (New York: Philosophical Library, 1956).

Sass, Louis A. "The Self and Its Vicissitudes: An Archeological Study of the Psychanalytic Avant-Garde," in *Constructions of the Self*, ed. George Levine (New Brunswick, NJ: Rutgers University Press, 1992).

Saussure, Ferdinand de. *Course in General Linguistics*, trans. Wade Baskin (New York: McGraw-Hill, 1966).

Schalit, Abraham, ed. *The World History of the Jewish People* (New York: Knopf, 1948).

Scheiffelin, Edward L. *The Sorrow of the Lonely and the Burning of the Dancers* (New York: St. Martin's Press, 1976).

Scheler, Max. *The Nature of Sympathy*, trans. P. Heath (Hamden, CT: Archon, 1970).

———. *Formalism in Ethics and Non-Formal Ethics of Value: A New Attempt Toward the Foundation of an Ethical Personalism*, trans. Manfred S. Frings and Roger L. Funk (Evanston, IL: Northwestern University Press, 1973).

————. "Shame and the Feelings of Modesty," in *Person and Self-Value*, ed. Manfred S. Frings (Dordrecht: Nijhoff, 1987).

Schmemann, Alexander. *Introduction to Liturgical Theology*, trans. A. E. Moorhouse (New York: St. Vladimir's Seminary Press, 1975).

Schneider, Carl D. *Shame, Exposure, and Privacy* (New York: Norton, 1977).

Schoeps, Hans Joachim. *Paul: The Theology of the Apostle in the Light of Jewish Religious History*, trans. Harold Knight (Philadelphia: Westminster Press, 1961).

Scholem, Gershom G. *Jewish Gnosticism, Merkabah Mysticism and Talmudic Judaism* (New York: KTAV, 1960).

————. *The Messianic Idea in Judaism and Other Essays on Jewish Spirituality* (New York: Schocken, 1971).

Schreiner, Thomas R. *Interpreting the Pauline Epistles* (Grand Rapids: Baker, 1990).

Schürer, E. "Alexandrians in Jerusalem," *The Jewish Encyclopedia* (New York: KTAV, 1964), vol. 11, 351–72.

Schutz, Alfred. *The Phenomenology of the Social World*, trans. George Walsh and Frederick Lehnert (Evanston, IL: Northwestern University Press, 1967).

————, and Thomas Luckmann, *The Structures of the Life-World*, trans. Richard M. Zaner and H. Tristan Engelhardt Jr. (Evanston, IL: Northwestern University Press, 1973).

Schweitzer, Albert. *The Mysticism of Paul the Apostle*, trans. William Montgomery (New York: Henry Holt, 1931).

————. *Paul and His Interpreters: A Critical History* (London: Adam and Charles Black, 1948).

Scroggs, Robin. "Paul as Rhetorician: Two Homilies in Romans 1–11," in *Jews, Greeks and Christians: Religious Cultures in Late Antiquity*, ed. Robert Hammerton-Kelly and Robin Scroggs (Leiden: Brill, 1976).

Segal, Alan F. "Paul and the Beginning of Christian Conversion," unpublished conference paper (Atlanta: Emory University, 1990).

————. *Paul the Convert: The Apostolate and Apostasy of Saul the Pharisee* (New Haven: Yale University Press, 1990).

Sevenster, J. N. *The Roots of Pagan Anti-Semitism in the Ancient World* (Leiden: Brill, 1975).

Sherwin-White, A. N. *Roman Society and Roman Law in the New Testament* (Oxford: Clarendon, 1963).

Siggins, Ian D. K. *Luther and His Mother* (Philadelphia: Fortress Press, 1981).

Silberman, L. H. "History of Judaism," *Encyclopedia Britannica*, 15th ed. (Chicago: University of Chicago Press), vol. 22, 402–79.

Simpson, J. A., and E. S. C. Weiner, *Oxford English Dictionary* (Oxford: Clarendon, 1989).

Smart, Ninian. *The Religious Experience* (New York: Macmillan, 1991).

Smith, Anthony D. *The Ethnic Origins of Nations* (Oxford: Blackwell, 1986).

Smith, Archie Jr. *The Relational Self: Ethics and Therapy from a Black Church Perspective* (Nashville: Abingdon, 1982).

Smith, Jonathan Z. *Map Is Not Territory: Studies in the History of Religions* (Leiden: Brill, 1978).

————. *To Take Place: Toward Theory in Ritual* (Chicago: University of Chicago Press, 1987).

————. *Imagining Religion: From Babylon to Jonestown* (Chicago: University of Chicago Press, 1988).

Smith, Morton. "Palestinian Judaism in the First Century," in *Israel: Its Role in Civilization*, ed. Moshe Davis (New York: Jewish Theological Seminary of America, 1956).

————. "Ascent to the Heavens: and the Beginning of Christianity," in *Eranos Jahrbuch* (Switzerland: Eranos Foundations Association, 1981).

Stansell, Gary. *Micah and Isaiah: A Form and Tradition Historical Comparison* (Atlanta: Scholars Press, 1988).

Stein, R. H. "Jerusalem," in *Dictionary of Paul and His Letters*, ed. Gerald F. Hawthorn and Ralph P. Martin (Downers Grove, IL: InterVarsity Press, 1993).

Steinmetz, David C. *Luther in Context* (Bloomington: Indian University Press, 1986).

Stendahl, Krister. *Paul Among Jews and Gentiles and Other Essays* (Philadelphia: Fortress Press, 1989).

Stern, Daniel. *The Interpersonal World of the Infant* (New York: Basic Books, 1985).

Stern, Menahem. *Greek and Latin Authors on Jews and Judaism*, 3 vols. (Jerusalem: Israel Academy of Sciences and Humanities, 1974–1984).

Stern, Michael. "The Jewish Diaspora," in *The Jewish People in the First Century*, ed. Shemuel Safrai and Michael Stern, 2 vols. (Philadelphia: Fortress Press, 1974).

Stirewalt, Martin Luther, Jr. "The Form and Function of the Greek Letter-Essay," in *The Romans Debate*, ed. K. P. Donfried (Minneapolis: Augsburg, 1977).

Stolorow, Robert D. "Toward a Functional Definition of Narcissism," in *Essential Papers on Narcissism*, ed. Andrew P. Morrison (New York: New York University Press, 1986).

Stowers, Stanley K. *The Diatribe and Paul's Letters to the Romans* (Chico, CA: Scholars Press, 1981).

Sturrock, John. *Structuralism and Since: From Levi-Strauss to Derrida* (Oxford: Oxford University Press, 1979).

Taylor, Charles. *Sources of the Self: The Making of the Modern Identity* (Cambridge: Harvard University Press, 1989).

Taylor, Nicholas. *Paul, Antioch and Jerusalem: A Study in Relationships and Authority in Earliest Christianity* (Sheffield: JSOT Press, 1992).

Tcherikover, Victor. *Hellenistic Civilization and the Jews*, trans. S. Applebaum (Philadelphia: Jewish Publication Society of America, 1959).

Teutler, Thomas N. *Sin and Confession on the Eve of the Reformation* (Princeton: Princeton University Press, 1977).

Thass-Thienemann, Theodor. *Symbolic Behavior* (New York: Washington Square Press, 1968).

Theissen, Gerd. *The Social Setting of Pauline Christianity: Essays on Corinth*, trans. John H. Schutz (Philadelphia: Fortress Press, 1982).

———. *Psychological Aspects of Pauline Theology*, trans. John P. Galvin (Philadelphia: Fortress Press, 1987).

———. *Social Reality and the Early Christians: Theology, Ethics, and the World of the New Testament*, trans. Margaret Kohl (Minneapolis: Fortress Press, 1992).

Thomas à Kempis. *Imitatio Christi* (Mount Vernon, NY: Peter Pauper, 1947).

Thompson, James. *Between Self and World: The Novels of Jane Austen* (University Park: Pennsylvania State University Press, 1988).

Ting-Toomey, Stella. *The Challenge of Face Work: Cross-Cultural and International Issues* (Albany: State University of New York Press, 1984).

Tomkins, Silvan S. *Affect/Imagery/Consciousness*, vol 1: *The Positive Affects* (New York: Springer, 1962).

———. *Affect/Imagery/Consciousness*, vol. 2: *The Negative Affects* (New York: Springer, 1962).

———. "Shame," in *The Many Faces of Shame*, ed. Donald M. Nathanson (New York: Guilford, 1987).

———. *Affect/Imagery/Consciousness*, vol. 3: *The Negative Affects: Anger and Fear* (New York: Springer, 1991).

Tracy, David. *Blessed Rage for Order: The New Pluralism in Theology* (Minneapolis: Winston-Seabury, 1975).

Trebilco, Paul R. *Jewish Communities in Asia Minor* (Cambridge: Cambridge University Press, 1991).

Turner, Victor. *The Ritual Process: Structure and Anti-Structure* (Ithaca, NY: Cornell University Press, 1966).

———. *The Forest of Symbols: Aspects of Ndembu Ritual* (Ithaca, NY: Cornell University Press, 1967).

———. *Dramas, Fields, and Metaphors: Symbolic Action in Human Society* (Ithaca, NY: Cornell University Press, 1974).

Underhill, Evelyn. *Mysticism* (New York: Penguin, 1974).

Unnik, W. C. van. *Tarsus or Jerusalem: The City of Paul's Youth*, trans. George Ogg (London: Epworth, 1962).

Usener, Herman. *Gotternamen, Versuch einer Lehrevonder Religiosen Begriffsbildung* (Frankfurt am Main: Schulte-Bulmke, 1948).

Wach, Joaquim. *The Comparative Study of Religion* (New York: Columbia Universtiy Press, 1958).

Welles, C. B. "Hellenistic Tarsus," *Mélanges de l'université Saint-Joseph* 38 (1962): 43–75.

Werner, Eric. "The Oldest Sources of Octave and Octoechos," *Acta Musicologica* 20 (1948): 1–9.

Whitten, Norman E., Jr., and John F. Szwed, eds. *Afro-American Anthropology: Contemporary Perspectives* (New York: Free Press, 1970).

Wikan, Unni. "Shame and Honor: A Contestable Pain," *Man* 19 (1984): 635–52.

Wilamowitz-Moellendorf, U. von "Die griechische Literatur des Altertums," in *Die Kultur der Gegenwart*, I, 8 (Leipzig and Berlin, 1912).

Wilckens, Ulrich. *Die Missionsreden der Apostelgeschichte* (Neukirchen: Neukirchener Verlag, 1963).

Williams, Bernard. *Shame and Necessity* (Berkeley: University of California Press, 1993).

Williams, Robin M., Jr. *American Society: A Sociological Interpretation* (New York: Knopf, 1970).

Williams, Sam K. "The 'Righteousness of God' in Romans," *Journal of Biblical Literature* 99 (1980): 241–90.

Wilshire, Bruce. *William James and Phenomenology: A Study of the "Principles of Psychology"* (Bloomington: Indiana University Press, 1968).

Winger, Michael. *By What Law: The Meaning of* Νόμος *in the Letters of Paul* (Atlanta: Scholars Press, 1992).

Winnicott, D. W. "Communicating and Not Communicating Leading to a Study of Certain Opposites," in *The Maturational Process and the Facilitating Environment* (London: Hogarth, 1965).

———. "The Theory of the Parent-Infant Relationship," in *The Maturation Process and the Facilitating Environment* (London: Hogarth, 1965).

———. *Playing and Reality* (New York: Basic Books, 1971).

———. "The Theory of the Parent-Infant Relationship," in *Essential Papers on Object Relations*, ed. Peter Buckley (New York: New York University Press, 1986).

Winquist, Charles E. *Homecoming: Interpretation, Transformation and Individualism* (Missoula, MT: Scholars Press, 1978).

Wirth, Louis. "The Problem of Minority Groups," in *The Science of Man in the World Crisis*, ed. Ralph Linton (New York: Columbia University Press, 1945).

Wuellner, Wilhelm H. "Paul as Pastor: The Function of Rhetorical Questions in First Corinthians," in *L'Apôtre Paul: Personnalité, style et conception du ministère*, ed. Albert Vanhoye (Leuven: Leuven University Press, 1986).

Wyatt-Brown, Bertram. *Southern Honor* (New York: Oxford University Press, 1982).

Yoder, John Howard. *For the Nations: Essays Evangelical and Public* (Grand Rapids: Eerdmans, 1997).

Zachman, Randall C. *The Assurance of Faith: Conscience in the Theology of Martin Luther and John Calvin* (Minneapolis: Fortress Press, 1993).

Zuesse, Evan M. "The Role of Intentionality in the Phenomenology of Religion," *Journal of the American Academy of Religion* 53, no. 1 (1985): 51–73.

Index of Scripture

Index of Subjects and Names

New World variation of, 79–83, 140
    n.97
reconciliation experience as, 79, 103–12
Crossan, John Dominic, 56
cultic rituals. *See* rituals
Cyrus (ruler of the Medes), 58

Damascus
    legal sanctions against messianic Jews
        of, 95
    Paul's integration into community of, 12
Davies, W. D., 60, 85
deformation experiences, 84
Deissmann, Gustav Adolf, 72
Derrida, Jacques, 74, 76, 77
Descartes, René, 2, 3, 6, 14, 44
deus absconditus (God's absence), 53, 54
deus revelatus (God's presence), 52, 54
Dewey, John, 1
diabolic/demonic possession, 20–21
Diaspora. *See* Hellenistic Jewish Diaspora
Dikaiosynē (to justify), 47, 109–10
discretion-shame, 37
disillusionment, 17–18
"divided self," 41
Divine
    James's presentation of self as, 2
    theophany as witness to the, 101
    See also God; the sacred
Dobschütz, Ernst von, 72
Dodds, Eric R., 32
Doty, William G., 70
Douglas, Mary, 86, 88
Downing, F. Gerald, 56
Droysen, J. G., 58
DuBois, W.E.B., 1
dyadic personality, 35–36

ecstatic speech (or glossolalia), 76
ego
    child's formation of, 16–17
    Husserl's interpretation of, 119 n.31
    introjections as nuclei of, 16
    object-relations theory on self com-
        pared to, 11–12
    shame as distance between ego-ideal
        and, 31
eidomai (seeing/knowing), 14

eidos (notion or idea)
    described, 14
    of figure in Ezekiel's vision, 100–101
    Paul's identification of *Christos* with,
        101, 103
    Plato's search for clues in realm of, 43
The Elementary Structures of Kinship (Lévi-
        Strauss), 78
Eliade, Mircea, 7, 19, 76, 77
emergent structure, 140 n.100
emic, 12, 83
empathic failure
    described, 29, 30, 91
    rage produced from, 93–94
empathic mirroring, 93, 114, 115
empathic vitality, 114–15
empathy, 113
ethnic shame, 39
ethnos (otherness), 39
    See also Other
etic, 12, 83
experience
    Husserl's examination of consciousness
        and, 3–5
    James's examination of consciousness
        and, 4
    manifested through the self, 15
    modes of formational, 83–84
    mother's "miracle role" in child's expe-
        rience, 25
    noetic possibilities of, 5
    phenomenological task of identifying
        intentional, 8–9, 11
    phenomenology on relationship
        between language and, 73–74
    retrospective rearrangements of, 125
        n.83
    self formation in children through con-
        tinuum of, 15–16
    Winnicott's vs. Kernberg's interpreta-
        tions of, 15–19
    See also Paul's experiences
experience-distant, 37
"experience near," 36, 37, 83

faith
    justification by, 52
    Luther's reconstruction of, 53–54